The Institute of Chartered Accountants in England and Wales

MANAGEMENT INFORMATION

For exams in 2017

Question Bank

ICAEW

www.icaew.com

Management Information
The Institute of Chartered Accountants in England and Wales

ISBN: 978-1-78363-459-0

Previous ISBN: 978-1-78363-204-6

First edition 2007
Tenth edition 2016

The content of this publication is intended to prepare students for the ICAEW examinations, and should not be used as professional advice.

British Library Cataloguing-in-Publication Data
A catalogue record for this book has been applied for from the British Library

Originally printed in the United Kingdom by Wheatons on paper obtained from traceable, sustainable sources.

Wheatons
Hennock Road
Marsh Barton
Exeter
EX2 8RP

Contents

The following questions are exam standard. Unless told otherwise, these questions are the style, content and format that you can expect in your exam.

Management Information: Question Bank

Assessment Guide

This assessment consists of 33 questions in total. There will be 32 objective-test questions (80% of the marks) which will be of three types:

- Multiple choice – select 1 from 4 options A, B, C or D (see Chapter 1 Q1)

- Multi-part multiple choice - select 1 from 2 or 3 options, for two or more question parts (see Chapter 1 Q25)

- Multiple response – select 2 or 3 responses from 4 or more options (see Chapter 1 Q26)

There will be ONE scenario-based question (20% of the marks) which will be drawn from either syllabus area 1 (costing and pricing) or syllabus area 3 (performance management).

The specific topics that may be examined on syllabus area 1 are: allocation, apportionment and absorption of overheads; activity based costing; absorption v marginal profits/losses; mark-up and margin (learning outcomes 1b, c and e).

The specific topics that may be examined on syllabus area 3 are: calculation of variances; reconciling absorption and marginal costing profits/losses (learning outcomes 3 e and f)

The assessment is 1.5 hours long and at least 55 marks are required to pass this assessment.

Our website has the latest information, guidance and exclusive resources to help you prepare for this assessment. Find everything you need, from exam webinars, sample assessments, errata sheets and the syllabus to advice from the examiners at icaew.com/exams if you're studying the ACA and icaew.com/cfabstudents if you're studying ICAEW CFAB.

Chapter 1: The fundamentals of costing

1   A cost unit is

    A   a unit of product or service in relation to which costs are ascertained

    B   the cost per hour of operating a machine

    C   the cost per unit of electricity consumed

    D   a measure of output of work in a standard hour   LO 1a

2   Certain types of income and cost are of no interest to the cost accountant.

    An example of one such income or cost is

    A   indirect labour

    B   purchase of raw materials

    C   dividends received

    D   rent paid on a factory   LO 1a

3   Variable costs are conventionally deemed to

    A   be constant in total when production volume changes

    B   be constant per unit of output

    C   vary per unit of output as production volume changes

    D   vary, in total, from period to period when production is constant   LO 1b

4   Which of the following costs would **not** be the concern of the supervisor of a production department?

    A   Material costs

    B   Labour costs

    C   Maintenance costs for a machine

    D   Lease payments on a machine   LO 1a

5   A company makes one delivery per week to all of its customers.

    The cost of these deliveries is

    A   a selling and distribution cost

    B   a prime cost

    C   a production overhead

    D   a direct production expense   LO 1b

6   A hospital has total costs of £1m for 20X1. During 20X1, 200,000 patients were treated and doctors were paid £500,000.

What is the most appropriate cost per patient for the hospital to use?

A   £0.20

B   £2.50

C   £5.00

D   £7.50

LO 1b

---

7   A business has ascertained that its total costs (TC) can be estimated for any level of production (P) and sales (S) according to the following equation:

$$TC = (£5 \times P + £1,000) + (£2 \times S + £500)$$

If the production level was 500 units and sales were 400 units, what would be the company's fixed costs?

A   £1,500

B   £4,800

C   £3,500

D   £3,300

LO 1b

---

8   Bo Feeters Shoes Ltd manufactures two types of shoe in its factory.

A typical monthly budget is as follows:

	Shoe Type A	Shoe Type B
Monthly output	2,100 units	4,400 units
Time per unit	24 minutes	36 minutes

Unavoidable non-productive time is 20% of productive time, and is paid £4 per hour.

Operatives are paid £3.60 **per unit** of shoe Type A produced and £6 **per unit** of shoe Type B.

What is the monthly cost of operatives' wages in the factory?

A   £13,920

B   £33,960

C   £36,744

D   £50,664

LO 1b

---

9   If a sales representative is paid a basic salary plus commission for each sale made, this wage cost is best described as

A   a semi-variable cost

B   a fixed cost

C   a variable cost

D   a production cost

LO 1b

10 Prime cost is

    A   the total of all direct costs

    B   the total of all costs incurred in manufacturing a product

    C   the same as the fixed cost of a cost unit

    D   any cost which does not vary with changes in output levels   LO 1b

11 A cost which contains both fixed and variable components, and so is partly affected by changes in the level of activity is known as

    A   a direct cost

    B   a variable cost

    C   an indirect cost

    D   a semi-variable cost   LO 1b

12 Which of the following costs are fixed per unit, but change in total, as production levels change?

    A   Variable costs

    B   Direct costs

    C   Fixed costs

    D   Step costs   LO 1b

13 If an assembly line supervisor is paid a salary of £100 each week and an additional £0.10 for every unit of production made in the week, this wage could be described as

    A   a semi-variable cost

    B   a fixed cost

    C   a variable cost

    D   a step cost   LO 1b

14 A company has a photocopier for which a fixed rental is payable up to a certain number of copies each period. If the number of copies exceeds this amount, a constant charge per copy is made for all subsequent copies during that period.

Which of the following graphs depicts the cost described?

A

B

C

D

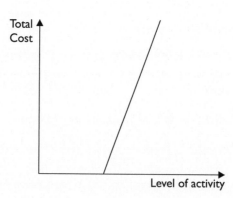

LO 1b

15 A factory making soft toys uses a particular machine on each production line. Each machine costs £1,000 per month to hire. Each production line can make up to 100 toys per month.

Which of the following best describes the cost of hiring the machines?

A A step cost

B A variable cost

C A fixed cost

D A semi-variable cost   LO 1b

16 The annual salary paid to a business's financial accountant would best be described as

A a variable administrative cost

B a fixed production cost

C part of prime cost

D a fixed administrative cost   LO 1b

17 The following is a graph of cost against level of activity:

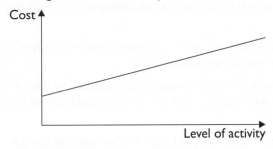

To which of the following costs does the graph correspond?

A Electricity bills made up of a standing charge and a variable charge

B Bonus payments to employees when production reaches a certain level

C Sales representatives' commissions payable per unit up to a maximum amount of commission

D Bulk discounts on purchases, the discount being given on all units purchased   LO 1b

18 A company's telephone bill consists of two parts:

(1) a charge of £40 per month for line rental

(2) a charge of £0.01 per minute of call time

Which of the following equations describes the total annual telephone cost, C if the company uses T minutes of call time in a year?

A C = 480 + 0.01T

B C = 40 + 0.01T

C C = 480 + 0.12T

D C = 40 + 0.01T/12   LO 1b

19

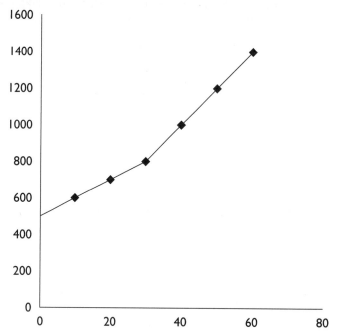

In the graph above, the x-axis represents volume of output, and the y-axis represents total costs. Which of the following could explain the shape of the graph?

A   Fixed costs = 500. Variable costs per unit are constant until output is 30, then additional costs per unit are higher.

B   Fixed costs = 500. Variable costs per unit are constant until output is 30, then all costs per unit (from the first unit onwards) are higher.

C   Fixed costs cannot be determined, because the two parts of the line will intersect the y-axis at different points. Variable costs per unit are constant until output is 30, then additional costs per unit are higher.

D   Fixed costs cannot be determined, because the two parts of the line will intersect the y-axis at different points. Variable costs per unit are constant until output is 30, then all costs per unit (from the first unit onwards) are higher.

LO 1b

20   Which of the following statements is correct?

A   The use of cost accounting is restricted to manufacturing operations.

B   The format of management accounts is regulated by Financial Reporting Standards.

C   Management accounts are usually prepared for internal use by an organisation's managers.

D   Financial accounts and management accounts are each prepared from completely different sets of basic data.

LO 1a

21   Which of the following would be most useful for monitoring and controlling the costs incurred by a freight transport organisation?

A   Cost per tonne carried

B   Cost per kilometre travelled

C   Cost per driver hour

D   Cost per tonne-kilometre

LO 1a

22 Which of the following items might be a suitable cost unit within the accounts payable department?

   (1) Postage cost

   (2) Invoice processed

   (3) Supplier account

   A   Item (1) only

   B   Item (2) only

   C   Item (3) only

   D   Items (2) and (3) only   LO 1a

23 What is the correct description of the following graph?

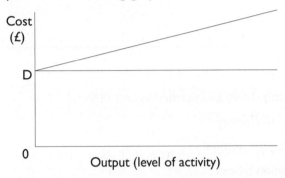

   A   The line with the constant upward slope represents fixed costs; D represents variable cost per unit

   B   The line with the constant upward slope represents variable costs; D represents fixed costs

   C   The line with the constant upward slope represents total costs; D represents fixed costs

   D   The line with the constant upward slope represents total costs; D represents variable cost per unit   LO 1b

24 What is the correct description of the following graph?

   A   Total fixed costs fall after production reaches Q, but variable costs per unit increase.

   B   Fixed costs are constant until production reaches Q after which fixed costs step up to a higher level.

   C   Variable costs per unit are constant until output reaches Q after which all production (from the first unit onwards) incurs higher variable costs per unit.

   D   Variable costs per unit are constant until output reaches Q after which further production incurs higher variable costs per unit.   LO 1b

25 Select the cost classification that best describes each of the following:

Labour paid per hour worked

A   Fixed

B   Variable

C   Semi-variable

Rent of a factory

D   Fixed

E   Variable

F   Semi-variable

Salary plus profit-related pay

G   Fixed

H   Variable

I   Semi-variable   LO 1b

26 Which **two** of the following would be regarded as cost objects?

A   Business rates paid on a factory

B   An operating theatre in a hospital

C   Labour used in cleaning offices

D   A branch of a high street bank

E   Glue used in making a chair   LO 1a

27 Which **two** of the following would be regarded as elements of cost?

A   A meal in a restaurant

B   An operation in a hospital

C   A branch of a high street building society

D   Labour used in assembling a car

E   Wood used in making a chair   LO 1a

28 Adam is responsible for preparing a monthly analysis of total department costs for the Managing
Director of XYZ. Adam's boss, the Department Manager, has asked Adam to exclude a number of
costs from the monthly analysis to 'give a better impression' of the department, and has threatened
to start disciplinary proceedings against Adam for poor work if he fails to do so.

Which threat does this represent?

A   Familiarity

B   Self-interest

C   Intimidation

D   Self-review   LO 5a

29 The ICAEW Code of Ethics exemplifies which of the following theoretical approaches to ethical codes?

    A   A rules-based approach

    B   A framework-based approach

    C   A compliance-based approach

    D   A tick box approach   LO 5a

Chapter 2: Calculating unit costs (Part 1)

1   Which of the following would normally be classified as a direct labour cost?

    A   The basic pay of production line staff

    B   Overtime premiums paid – if the overtime is not worked at the specific request of a customer

    C   The basic pay of production line supervisors

    D   Idle time payments to production line staff   LO 1c

2   A manufacturing firm is very busy and overtime is being worked.

    The amount of overtime premium paid to production line workers would normally be classed as

    A   factory overheads

    B   part of prime cost

    C   direct labour costs

    D   administrative overheads   LO 1c

3   Wage payments for idle time of direct workers within a production department are classified as

    A   direct labour cost

    B   prime cost

    C   administration overhead

    D   factory overhead   LO 1c

4   Grant Leeve is an assembly worker in the main assembly plant of Gonnaway Co.

    Details of his gross pay for the week are as follows.

Basic pay for normal hours worked: 38 hours at £5 per hour	£190
Overtime: 8 hours at time and a half	£60
Gross pay	£250

    Although he is paid for normal hours in full, Grant had been idle for 10 hours during the week because of the absence of any output from the machining department.

    The indirect labour costs that are included in his total gross pay of £250 are

    A   £20

    B   £50

    C   £70

    D   £110   LO 1c

5   Which of the following would be classified as indirect costs for a food product manufacturer?

(1)   Food label on a tin of beans

(2)   Maintenance materials used to repair production machinery

(3)   Cleaner's wages in the factory

A   (1) only

B   (2) and (3) only

C   All of them

D   None of them

LO 1c

6   A small engineering company that makes generators specifically to customers' own designs has had to purchase some special tools for a particular job. The tools will have no further use after the work has been completed and will be scrapped.

Which one of the following options is the correct cost classification for these tools?

A   Variable production overheads

B   Fixed production overheads

C   Indirect expenses

D   Direct expenses

LO 1c

7   Which of the following statements about a direct cost are correct?

(1)   A direct cost can be traced in full to the product, service or department that is being costed.

(2)   A cost that is a direct cost of one cost object might be an indirect cost of a different cost object.

(3)   A direct cost might also be referred to as an overhead cost.

(4)   Expenditure on direct costs will probably vary every period.

A   (1) and (2) only

B   (1) and (3) only

C   (1), (2) and (4) only

D   All of them

LO 1c

8   Which of the statements is true?

A   Total direct costs are always greater than total indirect costs.

B   Indirect costs are alternatively called overheads.

C   Fixed costs per unit are the same at all levels of production.

D   A direct cost will always be a variable cost.

LO 1c

9 A shop carries out repairs on customers' electrical items, eg, televisions, DVD players.

From the point of view of costing individual repair jobs, identify the most appropriate description for each cost.

Repair person paid a fixed wage per week

A   Direct and variable

B   Direct and fixed

C   Indirect and fixed

Replacement electrical components

D   Direct and variable

E   Direct and fixed

F   Indirect and fixed

Rent of the repair shop

G   Direct and variable

H   Direct and fixed

I   Indirect and fixed   LO 1c

10 A company pays £1 per unit as a royalty to the designer of a product which it manufactures and sells.

When costing units of the company's product, the royalty charge is classified as a

A   direct expense

B   production overhead

C   administrative overhead

D   selling overhead   LO 1c

11 Cigar Co had the following entries in its materials control account:

Opening inventory	£13,000
Closing inventory	£18,000
Deliveries from suppliers	£250,000
Returns to suppliers	£25,000

The value of the issue of materials to production is

A   £220,000

B   £225,000

C   £230,000

D   £270,000   LO 1c

12 Which **three** of the following are recognised and possibly acceptable methods of valuing inventory?

    A   First in, Last out (FILO)

    B   First in, First out (FIFO)

    C   Last in, First out (LIFO)

    D   Future anticipated cost

    E   Standard cost

LO 1c

13 A wholesaler had an opening inventory of 750 units of geronimo valued at £80 each on 1 February.

The following receipts and sales were recorded during February.

4 February	Received 180 units at a cost of	£85 per unit
18 February	Received 90 units at a cost of	£90 per unit
24 February	Sold 852 units at a price of	£110 per unit

Using the FIFO valuation method, what was the cost of the units of geronimo sold on 24 February?

    A   £68,160

    B   £68,670

    C   £69,960

    D   £93,720

LO 1c

14 A wholesaler had an opening inventory of 750 units of product A valued at £80 each on 1 February.

The following receipts and sales were recorded during February.

4 February	Received 180 units at a cost of	£85 per unit
18 February	Received 90 units at a cost of	£90 per unit
24 February	Sold 852 units at a price of	£110 per unit

Using the LIFO valuation method (to the nearest £), what was the gross profit earned from the product A sold on 24 February?

    A   £17,040

    B   £23,760

    C   £69,960

    D   £93,720

LO 1c

15 A wholesaler had an opening inventory of 330 units of mavis valued at £75 each on 1 February.

The following receipts and sales were recorded during February.

4 February	Received 180 units at a cost of	£80 per unit
18 February	Received 90 units at a cost of	£85 per unit
24 February	Sold 432 units at a price of	£90 per unit

Using the cumulative weighted average cost method of valuation, what was the cost of the mavis' sold on 24 February?

A £33,696

B £34,560

C £35,280

D £38,880

LO 1c

16 At the beginning of week 15 there were 200 units of pixie held in the stores. 80 of these had been purchased for £7.55 each in week 14 and 120 had been purchased for £7.91 each in week 13.

On day 3 of week 15 a further 60 pixies were received into stores at a purchase cost of £7.96 each.

The only issue of pixies occurred on day 4 of week 15, when 75 pixies were issued to production.

Using the LIFO valuation method, what was the total cost of the pixies issued on day 4?

A £566.25

B £590.85

C £593.25

D £597.00

LO 1c

17 At the beginning of week 12 there were 500 units of component J held in the stores. 200 of these components had been purchased for £6.25 each in week 11 and 300 had been purchased for £6.50 each in week 10.

On day 3 of week 12 a further 150 components were received into stores at a purchase cost of £6.60 each.

The only issue of component J occurred on day 4 of week 12, when 90 units were issued to production.

Using the FIFO valuation method, what was the value of the closing inventory of component J at the end of week 12?

A £585

B £594

C £3,596

D £3,605

LO 1c

18 In a period of falling prices, four students have recorded the cost of sales of commodity X. One student has used the FIFO method of inventory valuation and one has used the LIFO method. The other two students have used an average cost method, using the periodic and cumulative weighted average basis respectively.

The gross profits recorded by the students were as follows:

Student	Recorded gross profit £
A	12,600
B	13,400
C	14,500
D	15,230

Which student was using the LIFO method of inventory valuation?

A   Student A

B   Student B

C   Student C

D   Student D

LO 1c

19 Which of the following are true?

(1) With FIFO, the inventory valuation will be close to replacement cost.

(2) With LIFO, inventories are issued at a price which is close to the current market value.

(3) Decision-making can be difficult with both FIFO and LIFO because of the variations in prices.

(4) A disadvantage of the weighted average method of inventory valuation is that the resulting issue price is rarely an actual price that has been paid and it may be calculated to several decimal places.

A   (1) and (2) only

B   (1), (2) and (4) only

C   (1) and (3) only

D   (1), (2), (3) and (4)

LO 1c

20 For many years Sunny has faced rising prices on his main raw material. He maintains inventories of this material at a constant volume. He uses the FIFO method of inventory valuation. If he had used the LIFO method this would have resulted in

A   higher cost of sales and lower inventory value

B   higher cost of sales and higher inventory value

C   lower cost of sales and lower inventory value

D   lower cost of sales and higher inventory value

LO 1c

The following information relates to questions 21 and 22.

G Ltd makes the following purchases and sales:

1 January	Purchases	4,000 units for £10,000
31 January	Purchases	1,000 units for £2,000
15 February	Sales	3,000 units for £13,000
28 February	Purchases	1,500 units for £3,750
14 March	Sales	500 units for £1,200

21 At 31 March which of the following closing inventory valuations using FIFO is correct?

    A   £8,000

    B   £7,500

    C   £7,000

    D   £6,500   LO 1c

22 At 31 March which of the following closing inventory valuations using LIFO is correct?

    A   £6,500

    B   £7,000

    C   £7,500

    D   £8,000   LO 1c

23 With all average price systems where it is required to keep prices up to date, the average price must be re-calculated

    A   each time an issue is made

    B   each accounting period

    C   each time a purchase is made

    D   each time an inventory count is carried out   LO 1c

The following information relates to questions 24 and 25

Inventory Item 2362 X

Date		Units	Receipts Price per unit £	Value £	Units	Issues Price per unit £	Value £
1 June	Opening inventory	100	5.00	500			
3 June	Receipts	300	4.80	1,440			
5 June	Issues				220		
12 June	Receipts	170	5.20	884			
24 June	Issues				300		

24 Using the cumulative weighted average price method of inventory valuation, the cost of the materials issued on 5 June was

A £1,056

B £1,067

C £1,078

D £1,100

LO 1c

25 Using the cumulative weighted average price method of inventory valuation, the value of closing inventory on 30 June was

A £248

B £250

C £251

D £260

LO 1c

26 A wholesaler buys and resells a range of items, one of which is the Kay. Each Kay is resold for £3 per unit and opening inventory for June was 400 units valued at £1.80 per unit. The wholesaler purchased a further 600 units on 10 June for £2.10 per unit, and sold 800 units on 25 June.

What gross profit would be recorded for the sale of Kays during June, using the FIFO method of inventory valuation?

FIFO gross profit

A £780

B £960

C £840

D £1,560

LO 1c

27 A wholesaler buys and resells a range of items, one of which is the Kay. Each Kay is resold for £3 per unit and opening inventory for June was 400 units valued at £1.80 per unit. The wholesaler purchased a further 600 units on 10 June for £2.10 per unit, and sold 800 units on 25 June.

What gross profit would be recorded for the sale of Kays during June, using the LIFO method of inventory valuation?

LIFO gross profit

A £840

B £720

C £780

D £1,620

LO 1c

28 At the beginning of week 5 there were 600 units of material M held in inventory, valued at £6 per unit.

The following purchases and issues occurred during the subsequent four week period.

Week	Purchases Units	Cost per unit £	Issues to production Units
5		–	350
6	400	8	–
7	–	–	300
8	100	9	–

Inventory is valued using a periodic weighted average price calculated at the end of each four week period.

To the nearest £, the value of the inventory at the end of week 8 is

A £3,150

B £3,431

C £3,450

D £3,690

LO 1c

Chapter 3: Calculating unit costs (Part 2)

1   Which of the following decribes a cost centre?

   A   Units of a product or service for which costs are ascertained

   B   Amounts of expenditure attributable to various activities

   C   Functions or locations for which costs are ascertained and related to cost units for control purposes

   D   A section of an organisation for which budgets are prepared and control is exercised   LO 1c

2   Which of the following is a valid reason for calculating overhead absorption rates?

   A   To reduce the total overhead expenditure below a predetermined level

   B   To ensure that the total overhead expenditure does not exceed budgeted levels

   C   To attribute overhead costs to cost units

   D   To attribute overhead costs to cost centres   LO 1c

3   Which of the following is known as spreading common costs over cost centres on the basis of benefit received?

   A   Overhead absorption

   B   Overhead apportionment

   C   Overhead allocation

   D   Overhead analysis   LO 1c

4   The process of overhead apportionment is carried out so that

   A   costs may be controlled

   B   cost units gather overheads as they pass through cost centres

   C   whole items of cost can be charged to cost centres

   D   common costs are shared among cost centres   LO 1c

5   The following information is available for the two production departments (machining and assembly) and one service department (the canteen) at Wilmslow.

	Machining	Assembly	Canteen
Budgeted overheads	£15,000	£20,000	£5,500
Number of staff	30	20	5

After reapportionment of the service cost centre costs, what will be the overhead cost of the machining department cost centre?

A   £3,300

B   £17,750

C   £18,000

D   £18,300

LO 1c

6   The works manager of a company is fully occupied in running the production lines in the factory. The logistics manager spends some time on production and some time organising distribution.

How would their salaries be dealt with when calculating a fixed overhead absorption rate for the factory?

Works manager

A   Allocated to factory

B   Apportioned to factory

Logistics manager

C   Allocated to factory

D   Apportioned to factory

LO 1c

7   The following extract of information is available concerning the four cost centres of EG Limited.

	Production cost centres			Service cost centre
	Machinery	Finishing	Packing	Canteen
Number of direct employees	7	6	2	–
Number of indirect employees	3	2	1	4
Overhead allocated and apportioned	£28,500	£18,300	£8,960	£8,400

The overhead cost of the canteen is to be re-apportioned to the production cost centres on the basis of the number of employees in each production cost centre.

After the re-apportionment, the total overhead cost of the packing department, to the nearest £, will be

A   £1,200

B   £9,968

C   £10,080

D   £10,160

LO 1c

8   Which **three** of the following statements on the determination of overhead absorption rates are correct?

   A   Costs can be allocated where it is possible to identify which department caused them.

   B   Supervisors' salaries are likely to be apportioned rather than allocated.

   C   Costs need to be apportioned where they are shared by more than one department.

   D   There is no need for a single product company to allocate and apportion overheads in order to determine overhead cost per unit.

   E   Apportionment always produces the correct result.   LO 1c

9   Which of the following bases of apportionment would be most appropriate for apportioning heating costs to production cost centres?

   A   Floor space occupied in square metres

   B   Volume of space occupied in cubic metres

   C   Number of employees

   D   Labour hours worked   LO 1c

10   A company makes three products in a period.

	Quantity (units)	Labour hours per unit
Product A	1,000	4
Product B	2,000	6
Product C	3,000	3
Total	6,000	

Overheads for the period are £30,000 and they are absorbed on the basis of labour hours. What is the fixed overhead cost absorbed by a unit of Product B?

   A   £30.00

   B   £5.00

   C   £7.20

   D   £1.20   LO 1c

The following information relates to questions 11 and 12

Budgeted information relating to two departments in JP Ltd for the next period is as follows.

Department	Production overhead £	Direct material cost £	Direct labour cost £	Direct labour hours	Machine hours
1	27,000	67,500	13,500	2,700	45,000
2	18,000	36,000	100,000	25,000	300

Individual direct labour employees within each department earn differing rates of pay, according to their skills, grade and experience.

11   What is the most appropriate production overhead absorption rate for department 1?

A   40% of direct material cost

B   200% of direct labour cost

C   £10 per direct labour hour

D   £0.60 per machine hour

LO 1c

12   What is the most appropriate production overhead absorption rate for department 2?

A   50% of direct material cost

B   18% of direct labour cost

C   £0.72 per direct labour hour

D   £60 per machine hour

LO 1c

13   Budgeted fixed overheads for cost centre 1 during the last accounting period were £64,800 for apportioned overheads and £95,580 for allocated overheads. A predetermined machine hour rate is used to absorb fixed overheads into product costs. Budgeted machine hours during the period were 1,800. Actual fixed overheads were £178,200 and actual machine hours for the period were 1,782.

What was the fixed overhead absorption rate per machine hour?

A   £89.10

B   £90.00

C   £99.00

D   £100.00

LO 1c

14   The following information is recorded in the machinery department relating to activity levels and overheads in period 1.

	Machine hours	Overheads £
Budget	22,000	460,000
Actual	27,000	390,000

Overheads are absorbed on the basis of machine hours.

What is the overhead absorption rate for the machinery department to two decimal places?

A   £14.44

B   £17.04

C   £17.73

D   £20.91

LO 1c

15 Which of the following statements about overhead absorption rates are true?

(1) They are usually determined in advance for each period.

(2) They are used to charge overheads to products.

(3) They are normally based on actual data for each period.

(4) They are used to control overhead costs.

A (1) and (2) only

B (1), (2) and (4) only

C (2), (3) and (4) only

D (3) and (4) only

LO 1c

16 A product requires four hours of direct labour at £5.25 per hour, and requires direct expenses of £53.50. In its production, it requires 24 minutes of complex welding.

Possible overhead absorption rates have been calculated to be £7.10 per direct labour hour or £41.50 per welding machine hour.

Using the direct labour hour basis of overhead absorption, calculate to the nearest penny the total product cost.

A £81.90

B £91.10

C £102.90

D £119.50

LO 1c

17 Lerna Ltd produces hydras in three production departments and needs to apportion budgeted monthly overhead costs between those departments. Budgeted costs are as follows.

	£
Rent of factory	2,000
Rates for factory	1,000
Machine insurance	1,000
Machine depreciation	10,000
Factory manager's salary	7,000
	21,000

The following additional information is available.

	Department A	Department B	Department C
Area (square metres)	3,800	3,500	700
Value of machinery (£'000)	210	110	80
Number of employees	34	16	20

The total budgeted monthly overhead cost for Department C is

A £1,837.50

B £4,462.50

C £6,000.00

D £7,000.00

LO 1c

18 A company manufactures two products, J and K, in a factory divided into two production cost centres, Primary and Finishing. In order to determine a budgeted production overhead cost per unit of product, the following budgeted data are available.

	Primary	Finishing
Allocated and apportioned production overhead costs	£96,000	£82,500
Direct labour minutes per unit		
Product J	36	25
Product K	48	30

Budgeted production is 6,000 units of product J and 7,500 units of product K. Production overheads are to be absorbed on a direct labour hour basis.

The budgeted production overhead cost per unit for product K is

A   £10.00

B   £13.20

C   £14.00

D   £14.60

LO 1c

19 Which of the following statements about predetermined overhead absorption rates are true?

(1) Using a predetermined absorption rate avoids fluctuations in unit costs caused by abnormally high or low overhead expenditure or activity levels.

(2) Using a predetermined absorption rate offers the administrative convenience of being able to record full production costs sooner.

(3) Using a predetermined absorption rate avoids problems of under/over absorption of overheads because a constant overhead rate is available.

A   (1) and (2) only

B   (1) and (3) only

C   (2) and (3) only

D   (1), (2) and (3)

LO 1c

20 Bumblebee Co absorbs production overhead costs on a unit basis. For the year just ended, Bumblebee Co's production overhead expenditure was budgeted at £150,000 but was actually £148,000 while the budgeted activity level (production units) was 30,000 units and 29,000 units were actually produced.

Which of the following is true?

A   Fixed overheads were under absorbed by £5,000, this being the difference between budgeted expenditure and 29,000 units at £5 per unit.

B   Fixed overheads were under absorbed by £5,000, this being the difference between budgeted and actual production at £5 per unit.

C   Fixed overheads were over absorbed by £3,000, this being partly the difference between budgeted and actual expenditure and partly the production shortfall of 1,000 units.

D   Fixed overheads were under absorbed by £3,000, this being partly the difference between budgeted and actual expenditure and partly the production shortfall of 1,000 units.

LO 1c

21 A manufacturing company, Leyton Friday, has three production departments X, Y and Z. A predetermined overhead absorption rate is established for each department on the basis of machine hours at budgeted capacity. The overheads of each department consist of the allocated costs of each department plus a share of the service department's overhead costs. All overheads are fixed costs.

The table shows incomplete information available relating to the period just ended.

	Production department Z
Budgeted allocated overhead expenses	£61,500
Budgeted service department apportionment	£42,000
Budgeted machine capacity (hours)	?
Pre-determined absorption rate per machine hour	?
Actual machine utilisation (hours)	10,000
Over/(under) absorption of overhead	£(11,500)

Actual overhead expenditure incurred in each department was as per budget.

Budgeted capacity and the absorption rate per hour in department Z were

A   Budgeted capacity 11,111 hours, absorption rate per hour of £10.35

B   Budgeted capacity 11,111 hours, absorption rate per hour of £9.20

C   Budgeted capacity 11,250 hours, absorption rate per hour of £10.35

D   Budgeted capacity 11,250 hours, absorption rate per hour of £9.20   LO 1c

22 The budgeted overhead absorption rate for variable production overheads in department X of Lublin's factory is £3.00 per direct labour hour and for fixed overhead is £4.50 per direct labour hour. Actual direct labour hours worked exceeded the budget by 500 hours.

If expenditures were as expected for variable and fixed overheads, the total over-absorbed overhead for the period would be

A   £507.50

B   £1,500.00

C   £2,250.00

D   £3,750.00   LO 1c

23 The finishing department has budgeted labour hours of 3,250 and budgeted overhead costs of £14,950.

The actual labour hours were 3,175 and actual overheads were £14,810.

The overheads for the period were

A   under-absorbed by £140

B   over-absorbed by £140

C   under-absorbed by £205

D   over-absorbed by £205   LO 1c

24 A company absorbs overheads on a machine hour basis. Actual machine hours were 20,000, actual overheads were £480,000 and there was over absorption of overheads of £95,000.

What is the overhead absorption rate?

A £19.25 per unit

B £19.25 per hour

C £28.75 per unit

D £28.75 per hour

LO 1c

25 Budgeted and actual data for the year ended 31 December 20X1 is shown in the following table.

	Budget	Actual
Production (units)	5,000	4,600
Fixed production overheads	£10,000	£9,500
Sales (units)	4,000	4,000

Fixed production overheads are absorbed on a per unit basis.

Why did under/over absorption occur during the year ended 31 December 20X1?

A The company sold fewer units than it produced.

B The company sold fewer units than it produced and spent less than expected on fixed overheads.

C The company produced fewer units than expected.

D The company produced fewer units than expected and spent less on fixed overheads. LO 1c

26 Budgeted overheads for a period were £340,000. At the end of the period the actual labour hours worked were 21,050 hours and the actual overheads were £343,825.

If overheads were over absorbed by £14,025, how many labour hours were budgeted to be worked?

A 20,000

B 20,225

C 21,050

D 21,700

LO 1c

27 The budgeted absorption rate for variable production overhead in department X of Wiggipen Ltd's factory is £2.50 per direct labour hour and for fixed overhead is £4 per direct labour hour. Actual direct labour hours worked fell short of budget by 1,000 hours.

If expenditures for the actual level of activity were as expected for variable and fixed overheads, the total under or over absorbed overhead for the period would be

A £4,000 under-absorbed

B £4,000 over-absorbed

C £6,500 under-absorbed

D £6,500 over-absorbed

LO 1c

28 AB produces two products, A and B. Budgeted overhead expenditure for the latest period was £54,500. Overheads are absorbed on the basis of machine hours. Other data for the period are as follows:

	Product A Units	Product B Units
Actual results:		
Opening inventory	400	700
Sales	1,800	2,400
Closing inventory	500	500
Production	1,900	2,200
Budgeted results:		
Production	1,700	2,500
Machine hours per unit	2	3

If actual overhead expenditure for the period was £55,400, what was the under or over absorption of overhead for the period?

A   £900 under-absorbed

B   £900 over-absorbed

C   £3,400 under-absorbed

D   £3,400 over-absorbed   LO 1c

---

29 In activity based costing (ABC), what is a cost driver?

A   A mechanism for accumulating the costs of an activity

B   An overhead cost that is caused as a direct consequence of an activity

C   A factor which causes the costs of an activity

D   A cost relating to more than one product or service   LO 1c

---

30 Which **two** of the following statements are correct?

A   Just-in-time (JIT) purchasing requires the purchase of large quantities of inventory items so that they are available immediately when they are needed in the production process.

B   Activity based costing (ABC) is concerned only with production overhead costs.

C   Activity based costing (ABC) derives accurate product costs because it eliminates the need for arbitrary cost apportionment.

D   Activity based costing (ABC) involves tracing resource consumption and costing final outputs.

E   Just-in-time (JIT) systems are referred to as 'pull' systems because demand from a customer pulls products through the production process.   LO 1c 1d

31 Which of the following is an aspect of a just-in-time (JIT) system?

(1) The use of small frequent deliveries against bulk contracts

(2) Flexible production planning in small batch sizes

(3) A reduction in machine set-up time

(4) Production driven by demand

A (1) only

B (1), (2), (3) and (4)

C (1), (2) and (4) only

D (1) and (4) only

LO 1d

32 Which **two** of the following statements are correct?

A When target costing is used, the selling price of a product or service determines its target cost.

B An activity based costing (ABC) system makes some use of volume-related cost drivers.

C A JIT system tends to cause increased storage costs because high inventories are held to ensure that materials are available just as they are needed in production.

D Life cycle costing does not track costs that are incurred once production has ceased, since there are no revenues against which to match the costs.

E A product's target cost takes no account of the external market conditions.

LO 1d

33 Which of the following would **not** normally result from the adoption of a JIT purchasing system?

A Closer relationship with the suppliers

B Lower levels of inventory

C Lower levels of receivables

D Better quality supplies obtained

LO 1d

34 Select the costing method that would be appropriate in each of the following industries.

Brewing	Motorway construction
A Process	D Job
B Job	E Batch
C Batch	F Contract
Plumbing repairs	Shoe manufacture
G Process	J Process
H Job	K Job
I Contract	L Batch

LO 1d

35 Which **two** of the following statements are correct?

    A   In process and batch costing the cost per unit of output is found indirectly by dividing total costs by the number of units produced.

    B   In process and job costing the cost per unit of output is found directly by accumulating costs for each unit.

    C   Costing is irrelevant because the same level of detailed information can be extracted from the financial accounts.

    D   The procedures used to calculate unit costs in manufacturing industries can equally be applied to service industries.

LO 1d

36 Which **two** of the following items used in costing batches are normally contained in a typical batch cost?

    A   Actual material cost

    B   Actual manufacturing overheads

    C   Absorbed manufacturing overheads

    D   Budgeted labour cost

LO 1d

37 Which of the following industries would **not** normally use process costing?

    A   The brewing industry

    B   The oil industry

    C   The steel industry

    D   The construction industry

LO 1d

38 Which of the following statements about contract costing are correct?

    (1)   Work is undertaken to customer's special requirements

    (2)   Work is usually undertaken on the contractor's premises

    (3)   Work is usually of a relatively long duration

    A   (1) and (2) only

    B   (1) and (3) only

    C   (2) and (3) only

    D   (1), (2) and (3)

LO 1d

39 A firm makes special assemblies to customers' orders and uses job costing, with overheads being absorbed based on direct labour cost.

The data for a period are:

	Job A £	Job B £	Job C £
Opening work in progress	26,800	42,790	0
Material added in period	17,275	0	18,500
Labour for period	14,500	3,500	24,600

Job B was completed during the period, during which actual overheads were the same as the budgeted figure of £126,000.

What was the approximate value of closing work-in progress at the end of the period?

A £58,575

B £101,675

C £217,323

D £227,675

LO 1d

40 Job number 352 requires 270 hours of active labour. It is expected that 10% of labour's total time will be idle time. The wage rate is £8 per hour.

What is the labour cost for the job?

A £300

B £2,160

C £2,376

D £2,400

LO 1d

41 For each of the following industries select the appropriate method to establish the cost of products.

Oil refining		Clothing		Car repairs	
A	Process	D	Process	G	Process
B	Job/contract	E	Job/contract	H	Job/contract
C	Batch	F	Batch	I	Batch

LO 1d

Chapter 4: Marginal costing and absorption costing

1 The following cost details relate to one unit of product MC.

	£ per unit
Variable materials	9.80
Variable labour	8.70
Production overheads	
Variable	1.35
Fixed	9.36
Selling and distribution overheads	
Variable	7.49
Fixed	3.40
Total cost	40.10

In a marginal costing system the value of a closing inventory of 4,300 units of product MC will be

A £85,355

B £117,562

C £125,603

D £172,430

LO 1c

2 A company manufactures product S and product T.

The following information relates to the latest period.

	Product S	Product T
Variable labour cost per unit	£60	£48
Other variable production costs per unit	£70	£50
Budgeted production units	3,400	4,000
Labour hours	17,000	16,000

Variable labour is paid at £12 per hour.

Fixed production overhead incurred of £214,500 was the same as budgeted for the period. Fixed production overhead is absorbed on the basis of labour hours.

Fixed production overhead absorption rate = £214,500/(17,000 + 16,000)

= £6.50 per labour hour

The value of the closing inventory of product S using absorption costing was £65,000.

If marginal costing had been used the value of this inventory would have been

A £52,000

B £53,150

C £260,000

D £442,000

LO 1c

3   Ticktock Ltd makes clocks with a selling price of £50 per clock. Budgeted production and sales volume is 1,000 clocks per month. During September 1,000 clocks were made and 800 clocks were sold. There was no opening inventory.

The variable cost per clock is £25. Fixed costs in September were, as budgeted, £5,000.

Using marginal costing the contribution and profit for September would be calculated as

A   Contribution: £25,000, Profit: £20,000

B   Contribution: £20,000, Profit: £15,000

C   Contribution: £20,000, Profit: £16,000

D   Contribution: £25,000, Profit: £16,000   LO 1c

4   Which **three** of the following statements concerning marginal costing are true?

A   Marginal costing is an alternative method of costing to absorption costing.

B   Contribution is calculated as sales revenue minus fixed cost of sales.

C   Closing inventories are valued at full production cost.

D   Fixed costs are treated as a period cost and are charged in full to the income statement of the accounting period in which they are incurred.

E   Marginal cost is the cost of a unit which would not be incurred if that unit were not produced.

                                                                             LO 1c

5   Which **two** of the following statements concerning marginal costing systems are true?

A   Such systems value finished goods at the variable cost of production.

B   Such systems incorporate fixed overheads into the value of closing inventory.

C   Such systems necessitate the calculation of under- and over-absorbed overheads.

D   Such systems write off fixed overheads to the income statement in the period in which they were incurred.   LO 1c

6   A company budgets during its first year of operations to produce and sell 15,900 units per quarter of its product at a selling price of £24 per unit.

Budgeted costs are as follows:

	£ per unit
Variable production costs	8.50
Fixed production costs	2.50
Variable selling costs	6.00

In the first quarter the unit selling price, variable unit cost and expenditure on fixed production costs were as budgeted. The sales volume was 16,000 units and closing inventory was 400 units.

The absorption costing profit for the quarter was

A   £110,750

B   £112,000

C   £112,250

D   £113,250   LO 1c

7   Which of the following statements about profit measurement under absorption and marginal costing is true (assuming unit variable and fixed costs are constant)?

A   Profits measured using absorption costing will be higher than profits measured using marginal costing.

B   Profits measured using absorption costing will be lower than profits measured using marginal costing.

C   Profits measured using absorption costing will be either lower or higher than profits measured using marginal costing.

D   Profits measured using absorption costing may be the same as, or lower than, or higher than profits measured using marginal costing.
                                                                                                LO 1c

8   If the number of units of finished goods inventory at the end of a period is greater than that at the beginning, marginal costing inventory will result in (assuming unit variable and fixed costs are constant)

A   less operating profit than the absorption costing method

B   the same operating profit as the absorption costing method

C   more operating profit than the absorption costing method

D   more or less operating profit than the absorption costing method depending on the ratio of fixed to variable costs
                                                                                                LO 1c

9   Adams Ltd's budget for its first month of trading, during which 1,000 units are expected to be produced and 800 units sold, is as follows:

	£
Variable production costs	95,500
Fixed production costs	25,800

Selling price is £250 per unit

The profit calculated on the absorption cost basis compared with the profit calculated on the marginal cost basis is

A   £24,260 lower

B   £5,160 higher

C   £5,160 lower

D   £24,260 higher
                                                                                                LO 1c

10   Bright makes and sells boats. The budget for Bright's first month of trading showed the following:

	£
Variable production cost of boats	45,000
Fixed production costs	30,000
Production cost of 750 boats	75,000
Closing inventory of 250 boats	(25,000)
Production costs of 500 boats sold	50,000
Sales revenue	90,000
Production cost of boats sold	(50,000)
Variable selling costs	(5,000)
Fixed selling costs	(25,000)
Profit	10,000

The budget has been produced using an absorption costing system. If a marginal costing system were used, the budgeted profit would be

A   £22,500 lower

B   £10,000 lower

C   £10,000 higher

D   £22,500 higher

LO 3f

---

11   A company produces a single product for which cost and selling price details are as follows:

	£ per unit	£ per unit
Selling price		28
Variable material	10	
Variable labour	4	
Variable overhead	2	
Fixed overhead	5	
		21
Profit per unit		7

Last period, 8,000 units were produced and 8,500 units were sold. The opening inventory was 3,000 units and profits reported using marginal costing were £60,000.

The profits reported using an absorption costing system would be

A   £47,500

B   £57,500

C   £59,500

D   £62,500

LO 1c

---

12 Typo Ltd's budget for the year ended 31 December 20X8 is as follows.

	Units	£
Sales	1,200	24,000
Opening inventory	500	
Production	1,000	
	1,500	
Closing inventory	(300)	
Sold	1,200	
Marginal cost per unit	£15	(18,000)
Contribution		6,000
Fixed overhead		(7,000)
Loss		(1,000)

For absorption costing purposes, the fixed overhead absorption rate is set at £7 per unit for 20X8.

If absorption costing were to be used in inventory valuation throughout 20X8, what would the profit (or loss) be for 20X8?

A   £400 loss

B   £400 profit

C   £2,400 profit

D   £2,400 loss

LO 3f

13 A company had opening inventory of 48,500 units and closing inventory of 45,500 units. Profits based on marginal costing were £315,250 and on absorption costing were £288,250.

What is the fixed overhead absorption rate per unit?

A   £5.94

B   £6.34

C   £6.50

D   £9.00

LO 1c

14 In March, a company had a marginal costing profit of £78,000. Opening inventories were 760 units and closing inventories were 320 units. The company is considering changing to an absorption costing system.

What profit would be reported for March, assuming that the fixed overhead absorption rate is £5 per unit?

A   £74,200

B   £75,800

C   £76,400

D   £80,200

LO 1c

15 When comparing the profits reported under marginal and absorption costing when the levels of inventories increased (assuming unit variable and fixed costs are constant)

A   absorption costing profits will be lower and closing inventory valuations higher than those under marginal costing

B   absorption costing profits will be lower and closing inventory valuations lower than those under marginal costing

C   absorption costing profits will be higher and closing inventory valuations lower than those under marginal costing

D   absorption costing profits will be higher and closing inventory valuations higher than those under marginal costing

LO 1c

16 Which **two** of the following statements are advantages of marginal costing as compared with absorption costing?

A   It complies with accounting standards

B   It ensures the company makes a profit

C   It is more appropriate for short-term decision-making

D   Fixed costs are treated in accordance with their nature (ie, as period costs)

E   It is more appropriate when there are strong seasonal variations in sales demand

LO 1c

17 When comparing the profits reported under marginal and absorption costing when the levels of inventories decreased (assuming unit variable and fixed costs are constant)

A   absorption costing profits will be lower and closing inventory valuations higher than those under marginal costing

B   absorption costing profits will be lower and closing inventory valuations lower than those under marginal costing

C   absorption costing profits will be higher and closing inventory valuations lower than those under marginal costing

D   absorption costing profits will be higher and closing inventory valuations higher than those under marginal costing

LO 1c

18 Which **two** of the following statements are correct?

A   Absorption unit cost information is the most reliable as a basis for pricing decisions.

B   A product showing a loss under absorption costing will also make a negative contribution under marginal costing.

C   When closing inventory levels are higher than opening inventory levels and overheads are constant, absorption costing gives a higher profit than marginal costing.

D   In a multi-product company, smaller volume products may cause a disproportionate amount of set up overhead cost.

E   Marginal unit cost information is normally the most useful for external reporting purposes.

LO 1c

19 Iddon Ltd makes two products, Pye and Tan, in a factory divided into two production departments, Machining and Assembly. Both Pye and Tan need to pass through the Machining and Assembly departments. In order to find a fixed overhead cost per unit, the following budgeted data are relevant:

		Machining	Assembly
Fixed overhead costs		£120,000	£72,000
Labour hours per unit:	Pye	0.5 hours	0.20 hours
	Tan	1.0 hours	0.25 hours

Budgeted production is 4,000 units of Pye and 4,000 units of Tan (8,000 units in all) and fixed overheads are to be absorbed by reference to labour hours.

What is the budgeted fixed overhead cost of a unit of Pye?

A   £18

B   £20

C   £24

D   £28   LO 1c

20 Norbury plc has just completed its first year of trading. The following information has been collected from the accounting records:

	£
Variable cost per unit	
Manufacturing	6.00
Selling and administration	0.20
Fixed costs	
Manufacturing	90,000
Selling and administration	22,500

Production was 75,000 units and sales were 70,000 units. The selling price was £8 per unit throughout the year.

Calculate the net profit for the year using absorption costing.

A   £13,500

B   £19,500

C   £21,000

D   £22,500   LO 1c

Management Information: Question Bank

Chapter 5: Pricing calculations

1   Product X is produced in two production cost centres. Budgeted data for product X are as follows:

	Cost centre A	Cost centre B
Direct material cost per unit	£60.00	£30.30
Direct labour hours per unit	3	1
Direct labour rate per hour	£20.00	£15.20
Production overhead absorption rate per direct labour hour	£12.24	£14.94

General overheads are absorbed into product costs at a rate of 10% of total production cost.

If a 20% return on sales is required from product X, its selling price per unit should be

A   £271.45

B   £282.31

C   £286.66

D   £298.60   LO 1e

2   A company manufactures two products for which budgeted details for the forthcoming period are as follows:

	Product L £ per unit	Product T £ per unit
Materials	6.00	9.00
Labour (£15 per hour)	30.00	22.50

Production overhead of £61,200 is absorbed on a labour hour basis. Budgeted output is 4,000 units of product L and 6,000 units of product T.

The company adds a mark up of 20% to total production cost in order to determine its unit selling prices.

The selling price per unit of product L is

A   £47.52

B   £51.84

C   £54.00

D   £61.56   LO 1e

3 Print Ltd manufactures ring binders which are embossed with the customer's own logo. A customer has ordered a batch of 300 binders. The following data illustrate the cost for a typical batch of 100 binders:

	£
Variable materials	30
Wages (paid on a per binder basis)	10
Machine set up (fixed per batch)	3
Design and artwork (fixed per batch)	15
	58

Print Ltd absorbs production overhead at a rate of 20% of variable wages cost. A further 5% is added to the total production cost of each batch to allow for selling, distribution and administration overhead.

Print Ltd requires a profit margin of 25% of sales value.

The selling price for a batch of 300 binders should be

A £189.00

B £193.20

C £201.60

D £252.00

LO 1e

4 A firm makes special assemblies to customers' orders and uses job costing.

The data for a period are:

	Job A £	Job B £	Job C £
Opening work in progress	26,800	42,790	0
Material added in period	17,275	0	18,500
Labour for period	14,500	3,500	24,600

The budgeted overheads for the period were £126,000 and these are absorbed on the basis of labour cost.

Job B was completed and delivered during the period and the firm wishes to earn a 33 1/3% profit margin on sales.

What should be the selling price of job B?

A £69,435

B £75,523

C £84,963

D £258,435

LO 1e

5   Halcow Ltd operates a job costing system and its standard net profit margin is 20% of sales value.

The estimated costs for job 173 are as follows:

Direct materials   5 metres @ £20 per metre
Direct labour   14 hours @ £8 per hour

Variable production overheads are recovered at the rate of £3 per direct labour hour.

Fixed production overheads for the year are budgeted to be £200,000 and are to be recovered on the basis of the total of 40,000 direct labour hours for the year.

Other overheads, in relation to selling, distribution and administration, are recovered at the rate of £80 per job.

The selling price to be quoted for job 173 is

A   £404

B   £424

C   £485

D   £505   LO 1e

6   An item priced at £90.68, including local sales tax at 19%, is reduced in a sale by 20%.

The new price before sales tax is added is

A   £58.76

B   £60.96

C   £72.54

D   £76.20   LO 1e

7   Three years ago a retailer sold electronic calculators for £27.50 each. At the end of the first year he increased the price by 5% and at the end of the second year by a further 6%. At the end of the third year the selling price was £29.69 each.

The percentage price change in year three was a

A   2.7% decrease

B   3.0% increase

C   3.0% decrease

D   3.4% decrease   LO 1e

8   At a sales tax rate of 12%, an article sells for £84, including sales tax.

If the sales tax rate increases to 17.5%, the new selling price will be

A   £75.00

B   £86.86

C   £88.13

D   £88.62   LO 1e

9   A greengrocer sells apples either for 45p per kg, or in bulk at £9 per 25kg bag.

The percentage saving per kg from buying a 25kg bag is

A   9%

B   11.25%

C   20%

D   25%

LO 1e

10   A skirt which cost a clothes retailer £50 is sold at a profit of 25% on the selling price.

The profit is therefore

A   £12.50

B   £16.67

C   £62.50

D   £66.67

LO 1e

11   Sunita sells an item for £240 on which there is a mark-up of 20%.

What profit was made on this transaction?

A   £40

B   £48

C   £192

D   £200

LO 1e

12   A company calculates the prices of jobs by adding overheads to the prime cost and then adding 30% to total costs as a profit mark up. Job number Y256 was sold for £1,690 and incurred overheads of £694.

What was the prime cost of the job?

A   £489

B   £606

C   £996

D   £1,300

LO 1e

13   A company prices its product at the full cost of £4.75 per unit plus 70%. A competitor has just launched a similar product selling for £7.99 per unit. The company wishes to change the price of its product to match that of its competitor.

The product mark up percentage should be changed to

A   1.1%

B   1.8%

C   40.6%

D   68.2%

LO 1e

14 Details from a retailer's records concerning product D for the latest period are as follows.

	£
Sales revenue	60,000
Purchases	40,000
Opening inventory	12,000
Closing inventory	2,000

The profit margin for product D is

A   16.7%

B   20.0%

C   33.3%

D   50.0%   LO 1e

15 The following data relate to the Super.

Material cost per unit	£15.00
Labour cost per unit	£52.05
Production overhead cost per machine hour	£9.44
Machine hours per unit	7
General overhead absorption rate	8% of total production cost

The capital invested in manufacturing and distributing 953 units of the Super per annum is estimated to be £136,200.

If the required annual rate of return on capital invested in each product is 14%, the selling price per unit of the Super must be

A   £102.62

B   £153.14

C   £163.79

D   £163.91   LO 1e

 16 A product's marginal costs are 60% of its fixed costs. Selling prices are set on a full cost basis to achieve a margin of 20% of selling price.

To the nearest whole number, which percentage mark up on marginal costs would produce the same selling price as the current pricing method?

A   67%

B   108%

C   220%

D   233%   LO 1e

 17 A company determines its selling prices by adding a mark up of 100% to the variable cost per unit.

If the selling price is increased by 50%, the quantity sold each period is expected to reduce by 40% but the variable cost per unit will remain unchanged.

Which of the following statements is correct?

A   The total revenue will increase and the total contribution will increase.

B   The total revenue will increase and the total contribution will decrease.

C   The total revenue will decrease and the total contribution will increase.

D   The total will decrease and the total contribution will decrease.   LO 1e

18 The following information is available for the latest period.

Fixed costs   £160,000
Variable cost per unit   £4
Profit   £10,000

A 2% increase in selling price would not alter the number of units sold each period but the profit would increase by £5,000.

The current selling price per unit is

A   £0.08

B   £10.00

C   £12.50

D   £12.75

LO 1e

19 A contract is agreed between a supplier and a buyer. The contract will take four weeks to complete and the price to be charged will be agreed upon at the point of sale as the actual costs incurred plus an agreed percentage mark up on actual costs. The buyer is to be granted four weeks credit from the point of sale.

Which of the following best describes how the risk caused by inflation will be allocated between the supplier and the buyer?

A   The supplier and the buyer will each bear some of the inflation risk but not necessarily equally.

B   The supplier and the buyer will each bear equal amounts of the inflation risk.

C   Only the supplier will bear the inflation risk.

D   Only the buyer will bear the inflation risk.

LO 1e

20 Which of the following statements is correct?

A   A cost-plus pricing method will enable a company to maximise its profits.

B   A selling price in excess of full cost will always ensure that an organisation will cover all its costs.

C   The percentage mark up with full cost plus pricing will always be smaller than the percentage mark up with marginal cost-plus pricing.

D   Since it is necessary to forecast output volume to determine the overhead absorption rate, full cost-plus pricing takes account of the effect of price on quantity demanded.   LO 1e

21 The following data relate to Bailey plc, a manufacturing company with several divisions. Division X produces a single product which it sells to division Y and also to external customers.

	Sales to division Y £	External sales £
Sales revenue		
At £25 per unit		250,000
At £20 per unit	100,000	
Variable costs at £12 per unit	(60,000)	(120,000)
Contribution	40,000	130,000
Fixed costs	(20,000)	(50,000)
Profit	20,000	80,000

A supplier offers to supply 5,000 units at £18 each to division Y.

If division Y buys from the external supplier and division X cannot increase its external sales, the change in total profit of Bailey plc will be a

A   £10,000 decrease

B   £30,000 decrease

C   £10,000 increase

D   £30,000 increase   LO 1f

22 Which **two** of the following criteria should be fulfilled by a transfer pricing system?

    A   Should encourage dysfunctional decision-making

    B   Should encourage output at an organisation-wide profit-maximising level

    C   Should encourage divisions to act in their own self interest

    D   Should encourage divisions to make entirely autonomous decisions

    E   Should enable the realistic measurement of divisional profit   LO 1f

23 Which of the following best describes a dual pricing system of transfer pricing?

    A   The receiving division is charged with the market value of transfers made and the supplying division is credited with the standard variable cost.

    B   The receiving division is credited with the market value of transfers made and the supplying division is charged with the standard variable cost.

    C   The receiving division is charged with the standard variable cost of transfers made and the supplying division is credited with the market value.

    D   The receiving division is credited with the standard variable cost of transfers made and the supplying division is charged with the market value.   LO 1f

24 A company has two divisions, A and B. Division A transfers one third of its output to B and sells the remainders to the external market for £14 per unit. The transfers to division B are made at the transfer price of cost plus 20%.

Division B incurs costs of £4 per unit in converting the transferred units before selling them to external customers for £20 per unit.

Division A costs amount to £10 per unit and the budgeted total output for the period is 270 units. There is no budgeted change in inventories for either division.

The reported profits for the period will be

	Division A	Division B
A	£900 profit	£360 profit
B	£900 profit	£720 profit
C	£900 profit	£1,440 profit
D	£1,332 profit	£72 loss

LO 1f

25 Division P produces plastic mouldings, all of which are used as components by Division Q. The cost schedule for one type of moulding, item 103, is shown below.

Direct material cost per unit	£3.00
Direct labour cost per unit	£4.00
Variable overhead cost per unit	£2.00
Fixed production overhead costs each year	£120,000
Annual demand from Division Q is expected to be	20,000 units

Two methods of transfer pricing are being considered:

(1) Full production cost plus 40%

(2) A two-part tariff with a fixed fee of £200,000 each year

The transfer price per unit of item 103 transferred to Division Q using both of the transfer pricing methods listed above is:

	(1) Full production cost plus 40%	(2) Two-part tariff with a fixed fee of £200,000 each year
A	£12.60	£9
B	£12.60	£19
C	£21.00	£9
D	£21.00	£19

LO 1f

26 A and B are two divisions of company C. A manufactures two products, the X and the Y. The X is sold outside the company. The Y is sold only to division B at a unit transfer price of £410. The unit cost of the Y is £370 (variable cost £300 and absorbed fixed overhead £70). Division B has received an offer from another company to supply a substitute for product Y at a price of £330 per unit. Assume Division A and B have spare operating capacity.

Which of the following statements is correct with regard to the offer from the other company?

A The offer is not acceptable from the point of view of company C and the manager of Division B will make a sub-optimal decision.

B The offer is not acceptable from the point of view of company C and the manager of Division B will not make a sub-optimal decision.

C The offer is acceptable from the point of view of company C and the manager of Division B will make a sub-optimal decision.

D The offer is acceptable from the point of view of company C and the manager of Division B will not make a sub-optimal decision.   LO 1f

27 Division J manufactures product K incurring a total cost of £50 per unit. Product K is sold to external customers in a perfectly competitive market at a price of £57, which represents a mark up of 90% on marginal cost.

Division J also transfers product K to division R. If transfers are made internally then division J does not incur variable selling costs which amount to 5% of the total variable cost.

Assuming that the total demand for product K exceeds the capacity of division J, the optimum transfer price per unit between division J and division R is

A £54.50

B £55.50

C £56.72

D £57.00   LO 1f

28 In a contract to sell a commodity the selling price is agreed between the supplier and the buyer to be the actual costs incurred by the supplier plus a profit mark-up using a fixed percentage on actual costs. No credit period is offered by the supplier.

Which of the following best describes how the risk caused by inflation will be allocated between the supplier and the buyer?

A The supplier and the buyer will each bear some of the inflation risk but not necessarily equally

B Only the supplier will bear the inflation risk

C Only the buyer will bear the inflation risk

D The supplier and the buyer will each bear equal amounts of the inflation risk   LO 1e

29 F and G are two divisions of a company. Division F manufactures one product, Rex. Unit
    production cost and the market price are as follows:

	£
Variable materials	24
Labour	16
Variable fixed overhead	8
	48
Prevailing market price	£64

Product Rex is sold outside the company in a perfectly competitive market and also to division G. If
sold outside the company, Rex incurs variable selling costs of £8 per unit.

Assuming that the total demand for Rex is more than sufficient for division F to manufacture to
capacity, what is the price per unit (in round £s) at which the company would prefer division F to
transfer Rex to division G?

A   £64

B   £56

C   £40

D   £48

LO 1f

30 A company estimates indirect costs to be 40% of direct costs and it sets its selling prices to recover
    the full cost plus 50%.

What percentage represents the mark-up on direct costs that would give rise to the same selling
price as using the method described above?

A   90%

B   110%

C   190%

D   210%

LO 1e

31 The master budget for Serse Ltd, a single-product firm, for the current year is as follows:

	£	£
Sales		480,000
Variable materials (20,000 tonnes at £10 per tonne)	200,000	
Variable labour	96,000	
Variable overhead	48,000	
Fixed overhead	72,000	
Total cost		(416,000)
Budgeted net profit		64,000

Serse Ltd has substantial excess production capacity. A sales enquiry has been received, late in the year, which will increase sales and production for the year by 25% over budget.

The extra requirement for 5,000 tonnes of material will enable the firm to purchase 7,000 tonnes at a discount of 5% on its normal buying price. The additional 2,000 tonnes will be used to complete the year's budgeted production.

What price should Serse Ltd charge for the special order in order to earn the same budgeted net profit for the year of £64,000?

A £83,500

B £100,500

C £82,500

D £101,500   LO 1e

---

32 Gabba sets up in business to clean carpets. She will charge £30 per carpet cleaned and estimates the direct variable and fixed costs per carpet cleaned to be £9 and £6 respectively. She also estimates her variable and fixed advertising costs per carpet cleaned to be £2 and £3 respectively.

What is the contribution per carpet cleaned and the mark up on total costs?

	Contribution £	Mark-up %
A	21	50
B	19	100
C	10	100
D	19	50

LO 1e

33 Next month's budget for a single product company is shown below.

	£	£
Sales of 1,200 units		600,000
Manufacturing costs:		
Variable	216,000	
Fixed	60,000	
Selling costs:		
Variable	132,000	
Fixed	78,000	
Administration costs (fixed)	36,000	
		(522,000)
Net profit		78,000

The company's variable manufacturing cost per unit is now expected to increase by 10%, but all other costs remain unchanged.

Assuming an unchanged volume of sales, calculate the selling price per unit that would maintain the contribution ratio.

A £531

B £733

C £550

D £518

LO 1e

34 Delta and Gamma are two divisions of a company. Delta manufactures two products X and Y. X is sold outside the company. Y is sold only to division Gamma at a unit transfer price of £176. Unit costs for product Y are:

	£
Variable materials	60
Variable labour	40
Variable overhead	40
Fixed overhead	20
	160

Division Gamma has received an offer from another company to supply a substitute for Y for £152 per unit.

Assuming division Delta is only operating at 80% of capacity, if Gamma accepts the offer the effect on profits will be

	Division Delta profit	Overall company profit
A	Increase	Increase
B	Increase	Decrease
C	Decrease	Increase
D	Decrease	Decrease

LO 1f

35 Delta and Gamma are two divisions of a company. Delta manufactures two products X and Y. X is sold outside the company. Y is sold only to division Gamma at a unit transfer price of £176. Unit costs for product Y are:

	£
Variable materials	60
Variable labour	40
Variable overhead	40
Fixed overhead	20
	160

Division Gamma has received an offer from another company to supply a substitute for Y for £152 per unit.

Assuming division Delta can sell as much of Product X as it can produce and the unit profitability of X and Y are equal, what will be the effect on profits if Gamma accepts the offer?

	Division Delta profit	Overall company profit
A	No change	Decrease
B	Decrease	No change
C	No change	Increase
D	Increase	No change

LO 1f

---

36 A company currently sets its selling price at £10, which achieves a 25% mark-up on variable cost. Annual production and sales volume is 100,000 units and annual fixed costs are £80,000.

By how much would the selling price need to be increased in order to double profit if costs, production and sales volume remain unchanged?

A 12%

B 17%

C 20%

D 25%

LO 1e

Chapter 6: Budgeting

1   Which of the following would **not** be considered to be an objective of budgeting?

   A   Authorisation

   B   Expansion

   C   Performance evaluation

   D   Resource allocation   LO 2c

2   Which of the following is **not** one of the main purposes of a budget?

   A   To compel planning

   B   To communicate targets to the managers responsible for achieving the budget

   C   To inform shareholders of performance in meeting targets

   D   To establish a system of control by comparing budgeted and actual results   LO 2c

3   Which **two** of the following statements relating to budgets are correct?

   A   A budget covers periods longer than one year and is used for strategic planning.

   B   The budget committee coordinates the preparation and administration of budgets.

   C   The budget committee is responsible for the preparation of functional budgets.

   D   A budget manual will contain instructions governing the preparation of budgets.

   E   A budget is usually prepared by the shareholders of a company.   LO 2c

4   When preparing the master budget, which of the following tasks would normally be carried out first?

   A   Calculate the overhead absorption rate

   B   Establish the organisation's long-term objectives

   C   Identify the principal budget factor

   D   Prepare the sales budget   LO 2b

5   Which **three** of the following are steps in the preparation of a budget?

   A   Arrange overdraft facilities

   B   Identify the principal budget factor

   C   Prepare a budgeted income statement

   D   Budget the resources for production

   E   Complete the audit of the prior year's results   LO 2b

6 Which of the following is a principal budget factor?

   A   The highest value item of cost

   B   A factor which limits the activities of an undertaking

   C   A factor common to all budget centres

   D   A factor controllable by the manager of the budget centre

   LO 2b

7 Which of the following could be principal budget factors?

   (1)   Sales demand

   (2)   Machine capacity

   (3)   Key raw materials

   (4)   Cash flow

   A   (1) and (2) only

   B   (1), (2), (3) and (4)

   C   (1), (2) and (3) only

   D   (1), (2) and (4) only

   LO 2b

8 Which of the following is **not** a functional budget?

   A   Purchases budget

   B   Cash budget

   C   Sales budget

   D   Marketing cost budget

   LO 2b

9 For a company that does not have any production resource limitations, which **one** of the following sets out the correct sequence for budget preparation?

   A   Production budget, finished goods inventory budget, sales budget, then materials usage budget

   B   Sales budget, finished goods inventory budget, production budget, then materials usage budget

   C   Sales budget, production budget, finished goods inventory budget, then materials usage budget

   D   Sales budget, finished goods inventory budget, materials usage budget, then production budget

   LO 2b

10 Which **two** of the statements below correctly complete the following sentence?

The master budget

   A   will include a budgeted balance sheet and a budgeted income statement prepared on the accruals basis

   B   will include a cash budget

   C   is usually prepared before the functional budgets

   D   details the timetable for the preparation of the various budgets

   E   includes the instructions for the completion of the budget forms and the responsibilities of the personnel involved

   LO 2c

11 Which of the following expressions is correct?

   A   Opening inventory + sales − closing inventory = production (in units)

   B   Opening inventory + sales + closing inventory = production (in units)

   C   Closing inventory + sales − opening inventory = production (in units)

   D   Closing inventory − sales − opening inventory = production (in units)

   LO 2b

12 A company is preparing its production budget for product Z for the forthcoming year.

   Budgeted sales of product Z are 1,500 units. Opening inventory is 120 units and the company wants to reduce inventories at the end of the year by 10%.

   The budgeted number of units of product Z to be produced is

   A   1,392

   B   1,488

   C   1,500

   D   1,512

   LO 2b

13 Research Ltd purchases a chemical and refines it before onward sale. Budgeted sales of the refined chemical are as follows.

	Litres
January	40,000
February	50,000
March	30,000

   (1) The target month-end inventory of unrefined chemical is 30% of the chemical needed for the following month's budgeted production.

   (2) The targeted month-end inventory of refined chemical is 30% of next month's budgeted sales.

   Calculate the budgeted purchases of unrefined chemical for January.

   A   56,200 litres

   B   49,750 litres

   C   48,250 litres

   D   43,300 litres

   LO 2b

14 When preparing a material purchases budget, which of the following is the quantity to be purchased?

    A   Materials required for production – opening inventory of materials – closing inventory of materials

    B   Materials required for production – opening inventory of materials + closing inventory of materials

    C   Opening inventory of materials + closing inventory of materials – materials required for production

    D   Opening inventory of materials – materials required for production – closing inventory of materials

LO 2b

15 Barlow plc manufactures two products, Vip and Bip. It intends to produce 2,000 units of each product in the next year to meet the sales budget.

    Each Vip requires 2 kg of material Z and 1 kg of material Y and each Bip requires 3 kg of material Z and 4 kg of material Y.

    At present there are 200 kg of Z and 500 kg of Y in inventory.

    Barlow plc intends to increase the inventory levels of these materials by the end of the year to 600 kg of Z and 800 kg of Y.

    Material Z costs £4 per kg and material Y costs £5 per kg.

    What is the total materials purchases for the next year?

    A   £86,900

    B   £90,000

    C   £93,100

    D   £96,400

LO 2b

16 A retailing company makes a gross profit of 25% on sales. The company plans to increase inventory by 10% in June. The budgeted sales revenue for June is £25,000. Opening inventory on 1 June is valued at £5,000.

    What are the budgeted inventory purchases for June?

    A   £18,250

    B   £19,125

    C   £19,250

    D   £25,500

LO 2b

17 Budgeted sales of X for December are 18,000 units. At the end of the production process for X, 10% of production units are scrapped as defective. Opening inventories of X for December are budgeted to be 15,000 units and closing inventories will be 11,400 units. All inventories of finished goods must have successfully passed the quality control check.

The production budget for X for December, in units, is

A   12,960

B   14,400

C   15,840

D   16,000
LO 2b

18 The quantity of material in the material purchases budget is greater than the quantity of material in the material usage budget.

Which of the following statements can be inferred from this situation?

A   Wastage of material occurs in the production process.

B   Finished goods inventories are budgeted to increase.

C   Raw materials inventories are budgeted to increase.

D   Raw materials inventories are budgeted to decrease.
LO 2b

19 George has been asked by his bank to produce a budgeted income statement for the six months ending on 31 March 20X4.

He forecasts that monthly sales will be £3,000 for October, £4,500 for each of November and December and £5,000 per month from January 20X4 onwards.

Selling price is fixed to generate a margin on sales of 33 1/3%.

Overhead expenses (excluding depreciation) are estimated at £800 per month.

He plans to purchase non-current assets on 1 October costing £5,000, which will be paid for at the end of December and are expected to have a five-year life, at the end of which they will possess a nil residual value.

The budgeted net profit for the six months ending 31 March 20X4 is

A   £3,200

B   £3,700

C   £3,950

D   £8,200
LO 2b

20 At the beginning of March 20X2, a company has an opening balance of £60,000 on its receivables ledger. Sales of £160,000 have been budgeted for March and it is budgeted that 60% of these will be settled in March after a cash discount of 2.5%.

If 23% of the opening receivables are still outstanding at the end of March, what will be the budgeted receivables figure at that date?

A £76,200

B £77,800

C £80,200

D £110,200

LO 2b

21 A retailing company budgets to maintain inventories at the end of each month which are sufficient to meet the budgeted sales requirements for the following month. Two months' credit will be received from suppliers of inventory.

Budgeted sales, which earn a gross profit margin of 20% of sales value, are as follows:

	£
January	28,300
February	26,100
March	33,800
April	30,690

The budgeted balance sheet as at the end of March will show a payables balance of

A £47,920

B £51,592

C £59,900

D £64,490

LO 2b

22 A company's master budget contains the following budgeted income statement.

	£	£
Sales revenue (5,000 units)		120,000
Variable materials cost	24,000	
Variable labour cost	32,500	
Variable overhead	13,000	
Fixed overhead	41,000	
		110,500
Budgeted net profit		9,500

The company's management are considering a change in the materials specification. This would reduce the materials cost per unit by 10%. The reduced product quality would necessitate a 2% reduction in the selling price and the sales volume would fall by 5%.

The revised budgeted net profit for the period would be

A £3,620

B £6,975

C £9,025

D £9,375

LO 2b

23 Which **two** of the following statements are correct?

    A   A forecast and a budget are essentially the same thing.

    B   A budget must be quantified if it is to be useful for planning and control purposes.

    C   A budget provides the basic unit rates to be used in the preparation of standards for control purposes.

    D   The sales budget must always be prepared first.

    E   An organisation's long term plan provides the framework within which an annual budget is set.

                  LO 2a

---

24 A company has recorded the following costs over the last six months.

Month	Total cost £	Units produced
1	74,000	3,000
2	72,750	1,750
3	73,250	2,000
4	75,000	2,500
5	69,500	1,500
6	72,750	2,000

Using the high-low method, which of the following represents the total cost equation?

    A   Total cost = 61,250 + (1.25 × quantity)

    B   Total cost = 65,000 + (3 × quantity)

    C   Total cost = 65,000 + (1.25 × quantity)

    D   Total cost = 61,250 + (3 × quantity)

                  LO 2a

---

25 A company has recorded the following costs over the last four months.

Month	Cost £	Production (Units)
1	21,995	1,050
2	19,540	1,090
3	19,000	750
4	17,200	700

Using the high-low method, the expected cost of producing 950 units is

    A   £17,030

    B   £18,700

    C   £20,625

    D   £23,343

                  LO 2a

26 The following estimates of possible sales revenue and cost behaviour for a one-year period relate to one of AB Company's products:

Activity level	60%	100%
Sales and production (units)	36,000	60,000
	£	£
Sales revenue	432,000	720,000
Production costs		
Variable and fixed	366,000	510,000
Sales distribution and administration costs		
Variable and fixed	126,000	150,000

The budgeted level of activity for the current year is 60,000 units, and fixed costs are incurred evenly throughout the year.

There was no inventory of the product at the start of the first quarter, in which 16,500 units were made and 13,500 units were sold. Actual fixed costs were the same as budgeted.

AB Company uses absorption costing. You may assume that sales revenue and variable costs per unit are as budgeted.

What is the value of the fixed production costs that were absorbed by the product in the first quarter?

A £33,750

B £37,500

C £41,250

D £66,000

LO 2a

27 The following data have been extracted from the budget working papers of BL Ltd.

Production volume	1,000	2,000
	£/unit	£/unit
Variable materials	4.00	4.00
Variable labour	3.50	3.50
Production overhead – department 1	6.00	4.20
Production overhead – department 2	4.00	2.00

The total fixed cost and variable cost per unit is

	Total fixed cost	Variable cost per unit
	£	£
A	3,600	9.90
B	4,000	11.70
C	7,600	7.50
D	7,600	9.90

LO 2a

28 Which of the following would affect the reliability of a forecast using linear regression?

(1) The amount of data on which the regression line is based

(2) The assumption that the trend line applies outside the range of X values used to establish the line in the first place

(3) The assumption that there is a linear relationship between the two variables

(4) The coefficient of correlation

A (1) and (2) only

B (1), (2) and (3) only

C (1), (2), (3) and (4)

D (2) and (4) only

LO 2a

29 Which of the following is **not** an underlying assumption of forecasts made using regression analysis?

A A linear relationship exists between the two variables

B The value of one variable can be predicted or estimated from the value of one other variable

C A perfect linear relationship between the two variables

D What has happened in the past will provide a reliable guide to the future

LO 2a

30 A company's weekly costs (£C) were plotted against production level (P) for the last 50 weeks and a regression line calculated to be C = 100 + 20P.

Which of the following statements about the breakdown of weekly costs is true?

A Fixed costs are £100. Variable costs per unit are £20.

B Fixed costs are £20. Variable costs per unit are £100.

C Fixed costs are £20. Variable costs per unit are £5.

D Fixed costs are £100. Variable costs per unit are £4.

LO 2a

31 Which **two** of the following statements are correct?

A Positive correlation means that low values of one variable are associated with low values of the other, and high values of one variable are associated with high values of the other.

B Positive correlation means that low values of one variable are associated with high values of the other, and high values of one variable are associated with low values of the other.

C Negative correlation means that low values of one variable are associated with low values of the other, and high values of one variable are associated with high values of the other.

D Negative correlation means that low values of one variable are associated with high values of the other, and high values of one variable are associated with low values of the other. LO 2a

32 Examine the following graphs:

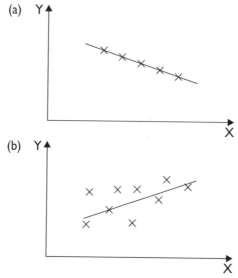

Which of the following statements is correct?

A   Diagram (a) represents perfect positive correlation; diagram (b) represents negative correlation.

B   Diagram (b) represents perfect positive correlation; diagram (a) represents negative correlation.

C   Diagram (a) represents perfect negative correlation; diagram (b) represents imperfect positive correlation.

D   Diagram (b) represents perfect negative correlation; diagram (a) represents perfect positive correlation.

LO 2a

33 The correlation coefficient between two variables, x and y, is +0.72.

The proportion of variation in y that is explained by variation in x is (to two decimal places).

A   0.52

B   0.72

C   0.85

D   1.44

LO 2a

34 Which **two** of the following statements are correct?

A   The coefficient of determination must always fall between 0 and +1.

B   The correlation coefficient must always fall between –1 and +1.

C   An advantage of the high-low method of cost estimation is that it takes into account the full range of available data.

D   A cost estimate produced using the high-low method can be used to reliably predict the cost for any level of activity.

LO 2a

35 The correlation coefficient between advertising expenditure and sales revenue is calculated to be 0.85.

Which of the following statements is true?

A   There is a weak relationship between advertising expenditure and sales revenue.

B   85% of the variation in sales revenue can be explained by the corresponding variation in advertising expenditure.

C   72% of the variation in sales revenue can be explained by the corresponding variation in advertising expenditure.

D   Sales revenue will increase by 85% more than advertising expenditure will increase.   LO 2a

 36 The linear relationship between advertising in thousands of pounds (X) and sales in tens of thousands of pounds (Y) is given by Y = 5 + 2X.

Which **two** of the following statements are correct?

A   For every £1,000 spent on advertising, sales revenue increases by £50,000 on average.

B   When nothing is spent on advertising the average level of sales is £50,000.

C   For every £1,000 spent on advertising, sales revenue increases by £20,000 on average.

D   When nothing is spent on advertising, the average level of sales is £20,000.   LO 2a

37 Which of the following is the best description of a 'top-down' budgeting process?

A   The process starts with sales, then progresses to production, materials usage and other functional budgets.

B   Top management prepare a budget with little or no input from operating personnel.

C   A series of budgets is prepared, from the most optimistic performance down to the most pessimistic.

D   The top level budget is non-financial, but more detailed budgets are progressively in more financial terms.   LO 2c

38 Which **two** of the following are advantages of a 'bottom-up' style of budgeting?

A   Increase operational managers' commitment to organisational objectives

B   Enhance the coordination between the plans and objectives of divisions

C   Reduce the incidence of budgetary slack

D   Based on information from employees most familiar with day to day activities

E   Decrease the period of time taken to prepare the budgets   LO 2c

39 Which of the following is **not** a criticism of incremental budgeting?

A   It is time consuming because it involves starting each budget from scratch

B   It encourages slack

C   It includes past inefficiencies as cost levels are not scrutinised

D   It encourages wasteful spending   LO 2c

40 Which of the following best describes incremental budgeting?

  A   Increments of expenditure are compared with the expected benefits to be received.

  B   Budgeted capacity is increased in increments until it is just sufficient to satisfy budgeted production requirements.

  C   The budget for each period is based on the current year's results, modified for changes in activity levels.

  D   The budget is updated in regular increments, by adding the budget for a further accounting period when the earliest accounting period has expired.

                                                                                                 LO 2c

41 Which **two** of the following are characteristics of rolling budgets?

  A   Each item of expenditure has to be justified in its entirety in order to be included in the next year's budget.

  B   A new accounting period, such as a month or a quarter, is added as each old one expires.

  C   The budget is more realistic and certain as there is a short period between the preparation of budgets.

  D   Updates to the fixed annual budget are made only when they are foreseeable.

                                                                                                 LO 2c

42 Which of the following best describes 'zero-based budgeting'?

  A   A budget method where an attempt is made to make expenditure under each cost heading as close to zero as possible.

  B   A method of budgeting whereby all activities are re-evaluated each time a budget is formulated.

  C   A method of budgeting where the sum of costs and revenues for each budget centre equals zero.

  D   A method of budgeting that distinguishes fixed and variable cost behaviour with respect to changes in output and the budget is designed to change appropriately with such fluctuations.

                                                                                                 LO 2c

43   Three separate newly-formed companies are currently designing their budgetary planning and control systems.

Company A will manufacture a wide range of products of varying flexibility. Some of the products will be mass produced, others will be low volume. The degree of non-production support required for each product differs widely.

Company B will manufacture a single product and has employed a specialist to manage each of its production and non-production activities.

Company C will manufacture a small range of diverse products and the cost and revenue responsibilities will differ for each product.

Indicate which budget structure would be most appropriate for each organisation.

Product based budget

A   Company A

B   Company B

C   Company C

Responsibility based budget

D   Company A

E   Company B

F   Company C

Activity based budget

G   Company A

H   Company B

I   Company C   LO 2c

44   Which **two** of the following statements about budgeting are correct?

A   A forecast is an attempt to predict what will happen.

B   A budget is a plan of what is intended to happen.

C   All budgets are prepared in financial terms.

D   The master budget consists of a budgeted income statement and a budgeted balance sheet.

E   A flexible budget adjusts both fixed and variable costs for the level of activity.   LO 2c

45   A firm that uses zero-based budgeting for its overheads has

A   zero as the starting point for budgeting the coming year's overheads

B   a zero variance between budgeted and actual overhead

C   an assumed sales level of zero as the starting point for budgeting the coming year's overheads

D   an overhead budget of zero   LO 2c

46 The high-low method of cost estimation is useful for

    A   calculating the budgeted cost for the actual activity

    B   calculating the highest and lowest costs in the budget period

    C   measuring the actual cost for the budgeted activity

    D   predicting the range of costs expected in the budget period   LO 2a

---

47 An extract from next year's budget for a manufacturing company is shown below.

	Month 3 £	Month 4 £
Closing inventory of raw materials	22,000	12,000

The manufacturing cost of production is £116,000 in both month 3 and month 4. Materials costs represent 40% of manufacturing cost.

The budgeted material purchases for month 4 are

    A   £36,400

    B   £42,400

    C   £46,400

    D   £56,400   LO 2b

---

48 You are given the following budgeted cost information for Verlaine plc for January.

Sales	£120,000
Unit selling price	£2
Gross profit	30% margin on sales
Opening inventory	6,000 units

Sales volumes are increasing at 20% per month and company policy is to maintain 10% of next month's sales volume as closing inventory.

The budgeted cost of production for January is

    A   £84,000

    B   £85,680

    C   £120,000

    D   £122,400   LO 2b

Chapter 7: Working capital

1   Claw is preparing its cash flow forecast for the next quarter.

Which of the following items should be excluded from the calculations?

A   The receipt of a bank loan that has been raised for the purpose of investment in a new rolling mill

B   Depreciation of the new rolling mill

C   A tax payment that is due to be made, but which relates to profits earned in a previous accounting period

D   Disposal proceeds from the sale of the old rolling mill   LO 2d

2   A cash budget has been drawn up as follows:

	January £	February £	March £
Receipts			
Credit sales	10,000	11,000	12,500
Cash sales	5,000	4,500	6,000
Payments			
Suppliers	6,500	4,200	7,800
Wages	2,300	2,300	3,000
Overheads	1,500	1,750	1,900
Opening cash	500		

The closing cash balance for March is budgeted to be

A   £5,800

B   £12,450

C   £17,750

D   £18,250   LO 2d

3   A machine that was bought in January 20X1 for £44,000 and has been depreciated by £8,000 per year, is expected to be sold in December 20X3 for £17,600.

What is the net cash inflow or (outflow) that will appear in the cash budget for December 20X3?

A   £9,000 inflow

B   £15,200 inflow

C   £17,600 inflow

D   £17,600 outflow   LO 2d

4   Jason is preparing a cash budget for July. His actual credit sales are:

April	£40,000
May	£30,000
June	£20,000
July	£25,000

His recent debt collection experience has been as follows:

Current month's sales	20%
Prior month's sales	60%
Sales two months prior	10%
Cash discounts taken	5%
Bad debts	5%

How much should Jason budget to collect from customers during July?

A   £19,750

B   £20,000

C   £22,000

D   £26,000

LO 2d

5   Lotsa plc has budgeted that sales will be £101,500 in January 20X2, £580,500 in February, £215,000 in March and £320,500 in April.

Half of sales will be credit sales. 80% of customers are expected to pay in the month after sale, 15% in the second month after sale, while the remaining 5% are expected to be bad debts.

Customers who pay in the month after sale can claim a 4% early settlement discount.

What level of sales receipts should be shown in the cash budget for March 20X2 (to the nearest £)?

A   £338,025

B   £347,313

C   £568,550

D   £587,125

LO 2d

6   A company has a two month receivables cycle. It receives in cash 45% of the total gross sales value in the month of invoicing.

Bad debts are 7% of total gross sales value and there is a 10% discount for settling accounts within 30 days.

What percentage of the first month's sales will be received as cash in the second month?

A   38%

B   43%

C   48%

D   58%

LO 2d

7   From the customer collection records of Low Ltd, it is possible to determine that 60% of invoices are paid in the month after sale, 30% in the second month after sale and 5% in the third month after sale. Invoices are raised on the last day of each month and 5% become bad debts.

Customers who settle in the month after sale are entitled to a 4% settlement discount. Budgeted credit sales in January 20X6 are £221,500, in February £332,000, in March £175,000 and in April £384,000.

What is the amount budgeted to be received in April from credit sales (to the nearest £)?

A   £211,475

B   £215,675

C   £290,284

D   £299,500   LO 2d

8   A company anticipates that 10,000 units of product Z will be sold during August.

Each unit of Z requires two litres of raw material W.

Actual inventories as at 1 August and budgeted inventories as at 31 August are:

	1 August	31 August
Product Z (units)	14,000	15,000
Raw materials W (litres)	20,000	15,000

A litre of W costs £1.50. If the company pays for all purchases in the month of acquisition, what is the payment for August purchases of W?

A   £17,000

B   £25,500

C   £33,000

D   £34,500   LO 2d

OP − CP + (S)

9   Sam is a trading company that holds no inventories. Each month the following relationships hold:

Gross profit	40% of sales
Closing trade payables	30% of cost of sales

Sales are budgeted to be £48,500 in April and £36,500 in May.

How much cash is budgeted to be paid in May to suppliers?

A   £19,740

B   £21,900

C   £23,340

D   £24,060   LO 2d

10 The budgeted sales for the first six months of Bendy Ltd's business are:

	£
January	60,000
February	75,000
March	84,000
April	90,000
May	90,000
June	87,000

Bendy Ltd (Bendy) wishes to maintain inventory levels, as at the end of each month, to cover sales for the following three months. Purchases are made at the beginning of each month, and suppliers are to be paid after two months. Bendy will operate a 40% mark-up on costs.

The payment to be made to suppliers in May is (to the nearest £)

A £52,200

B £62,143

C £64,286

D £87,000

LO 2d

11 The following is an extract from an entity's budget for next month.

Sales	£520,000
Gross profit on sales	30%
Increase in trade payables over the month	£15,000
Decrease in cost of inventory held over the month	£22,000

The budgeted payment to trade payables is

A £327,000

B £357,000

C £371,000

D £401,000

LO 2d

12 A company is preparing the budget for a product, and the following data has been provided:

	Month 1	Month 2	Month 3	Month 4
Planned sales (units)	2,000	2,200	2,500	2,600

Closing inventory in each month must be 50% of the next month's sales. Suppliers are paid in the month following purchase. The standard cost of materials is £4 per unit.

What is the budgeted payment to suppliers in month 3?

A £8,200

B £9,400

C £10,000

D £10,200

LO 2d

The following information relates to questions 13 and 14

Each unit of product Zeta requires 3kg of raw material and four direct labour hours. Material costs £2 per kg and the direct labour rate is £7 per hour.

The production budget for Zeta for April to June is as follows:

	April	May	June
Production units	7,800	8,400	8,200

13 Raw material opening inventories are budgeted as follows:

	April	May	June
	3,800kg	4,200kg	4,100kg

The closing inventory budgeted for June is 3,900kg.

Material purchases are paid for in the month following purchase.

The figure to be included in the cash budget for June in respect of payments for purchases is

A   £25,100

B   £48,800

C   £50,200

D   £50,600   LO 2d

14 Wages are paid 75% in the month of production and 25% in the following month.

The figures to be included in the cash budget for May in respect of wages is

A   £222,600

B   £231,000

C   £233,800

D   £235,200   LO 2d

15 Aaron Products is considering the implementation of a revised receivables policy, which will result in an increase in the average collection period from the current 60 days to 90 days. This is expected to lead to a 20% increase in annual sales revenue, currently £960,000, resulting in additional inventories and trade payables of £30,000 and £15,000 respectively. It is expected that all customers will take advantage of the extended credit period.

The net increase in working capital investment that would result from the change in policy, assuming a 360-day year, is

A   £31,000

B   £95,000

C   £113,000

D   £143,000   LO 2d

16 In order to improve operational cash flows indicate whether a business needs to increase or decrease each of the following.

Receivables

A   Increase

B   Decrease

Inventory

C   Increase

D   Decrease

The credit period from trade suppliers

E   Increase

F   Decrease

LO 2g

---

17 Which **two** of the following actions would be appropriate if the cash budget identified a short-term cash deficit?

A   Issue shares

B   Pay suppliers early

C   Arrange an overdraft

D   Implement better credit control procedures

E   Replace non-current assets

LO 2g

---

18 A company's cash budget for the next six months is shown below.

	Jan £'000	Feb £'000	Mar £'000	Apr £'000	May £'000	Jun £'000
Cash receipts						
From customers	5	8	10	15	14	15
Investment maturing	–	–	5	–	–	–
	5	8	15	15	14	15
Cash payments						
To suppliers	6	8	12	10	8	4
Tax	–	–	4	–	–	–
Wages and other	4	4	4	3	4	4
Capital expenditure	–	5	–	–	–	–
Loan repayment	–	–	–	2	–	–
	10	17	20	15	12	8
Net inflow/(outflow)	(5)	(9)	(5)	–	2	7
Balance b/f	2	(3)	(12)	(17)	(17)	(15)
Balance c/f	(3)	(12)	(17)	(17)	(15)	(8)

The company's overdraft facility is only for £15,000.

It has been proposed to reschedule the cash flows by delaying payment of 50% of the supplier payments in each of the first five months by one month.

The maximum overdraft and the overdraft at the end of June will now be

	Maximum	End of June
A	£18,000	£8,000
B	£12,000	£6,000
C	£18,000	£6,000
D	£12,000	£8,000

LO 2d

19 A telephone business has annual sales of £1.1m and a gross profit margin of 10%. It is currently experiencing short-term cash flow difficulties, and intends to delay its payments to trade suppliers by one month.

To the nearest £, the amount by which the cash balance will benefit in the short term from this change in policy, assuming sales are spread evenly over the year, and inventory levels remain constant throughout, is

A   £82,500

B   £83,333

C   £91,667

D   £100,833   LO 2d

20 A company's cash budget highlights a short-term surplus in the near future.

Which **two** of the following actions would **not** be appropriate to make use of the surplus?

A   Increase inventories and receivables to improve customer service

B   Buy back the company's shares

C   Increase payables by delaying payments to suppliers

D   Invest in a short term deposit account   LO 2g

21 A company has annual sales of £3m and its gross profit is 60% of sales. Inventory turnover is 60 days, customers take an average of 35 days to pay and the company pays its suppliers after 25 days.

Defining working capital as average inventories plus average receivables minus average trade payables and using a 365-day year for your calculations, to the nearest £1,000, the company's working capital will be

A   £280,000

B   £403,000

C   £567,000

D   £699,000   LO 2e

22 The following information relates to a business:

Debt collection period	11 weeks
Raw material inventory holding period	3 weeks
Suppliers' credit period	6 weeks
Production period	2 weeks
Finished goods inventory holding period	7 weeks

What is the working capital (operating) cycle of the business?

A   6 weeks

B   7 weeks

C   17 weeks

D   29 weeks   LO 2e

23 Using the table below and a 365-day year, calculate the length of the working capital cycle (operating cycle).

		£
Inventories:	Raw materials	250,000
	Work in progress	115,000
	Finished goods	186,000
Purchases		1,070,000
Cost of goods sold		1,458,000
Sales		1,636,000
Receivables		345,000
Trade payables		162,000

A   174 days

B   182 days

C   193 days

D   293 days

LO 2e

24 Which **two** of the following might be associated with a lengthening cash cycle?

A   Lower net operating cash inflow

B   Lower investment in working capital

C   Taking longer to pay trade suppliers

D   Slower inventory turnover

E   Higher net asset turnover

LO 2e

25 The following information is available for a wholesale business for the latest year.

	Opening balance £'000	Closing balance £'000
Receivables	200	220
Inventory	120	220
Payables	170	130

The cost of goods sold during the year was £2m and the company earns a margin of 20% of sales. Half of all sales are credit sales and the remainder are cash sales.

Using a 365-day year in your calculations, what is the length of the cash operating cycle in respect of credit sales?

A   65 days

B   66 days

C   68 days

D   118 days

LO 2e

26 A company has liquidity ratio (receivables divided by payables and bank overdraft) equal to 0.5. The directors believe that the company has to reduce its bank overdraft and have agreed to alter the company's credit terms to customers from two months to one month.

What would be the effects on the company's cash operating cycle and liquidity ratio if this change were to be achieved?

	Cash operating cycle	Liquidity ratio
A	Decrease	Decrease
B	Decrease	No change
C	Decrease	Increase
D	Increase	Increase

LO 2e

27 From the following extracts from a draft balance sheet, calculate the quick (liquidity) ratio

	£m	£m
Assets		
Non-current assets		10.5
Inventories	4.2	
Receivables	2.8	
Cash in hand	0.3	
		7.3
		17.8
Liabilities		
Trade payables	2.6	
Other short-term payables	0.8	
Loan repayable in five years	6.5	
		9.9

A   0.31

B   0.91

C   1.80

D   2.15

LO 2d

28 A company's liquidity (quick or acid test) ratio, which includes receivables, cash and payables, is 0.5.

Consideration is being given to two changes:

Proposal 1   offer a 2% cash discount to customers for early settlement,

Proposal 2   delay payment to all suppliers.

All other things being equal, what will be the effects of the proposed change on the liquidity ratio?

Proposal 1

A   Increase

B   Decrease

C   No change

Proposal 2

D   Increase

E   Decrease

F   No change

LO 2d

29 If an increase in inventory levels is funded by an increase in the bank overdraft, what will be the effect on the quick (liquidity) ratio?

A Increase

B Decrease

C Remain the same

D Increase, decrease or remain the same depending on the initial size of the quick ratio   LO 2d

30 A company has a current ratio greater than 1:1 and a quick (liquidity) ratio less than 1:1. If the company uses cash to reduce trade payables, how will these payments affect each of the ratios?

Current ratio

A Increase

B Decrease

C No change

Quick (liquidity) ratio

D Increase

E Decrease

F No change   LO 2d

31 A retailing company's current assets and current liabilities consist of inventory at cost £2,100, receivables, cash and trade payables. Its financial ratios include the following:

Quick (liquidity) ratio	2:1
Rate of inventory turnover	10 times p.a.
Gross profit margin	30%
Receivables collection period	1 month
Payables payment period	1.6 months

The opening inventory, receivables and payables balances are the same as the closing balances.

The closing cash in hand balance will be

A £3,100

B £2,170

C £1,000

D £100   LO 2d

32 Fenton Ltd's projected revenue for 20X1 is £350,000. It is forecast that 12% of sales will occur in January and remaining sales will be equally spread among the other eleven months. All sales are on credit. Receivables accounts are settled 50% in the month of sale, 45% in the following month, and 5% are written off as bad debts after two months.

The budgeted cash collections for March are

A £24,500

B £26,600

C £28,000

D £32,900   LO 2d

33 A retail company extracts the following information from its accounts at 30 June 20X6:

	£
Average inventory	490,000
Average receivables	610,000
Average payables	340,000
Cost of sales	4,500,000
Purchases	4,660,000
Gross profit margin	32%

The number of days in the company's cash operating cycle is

A   34 days

B   44 days

C   47 days

D   51 days

LO 2e

34 Fraser Ltd manufactures leather bags. The company buys raw materials from suppliers that allow the company 2.5 months credit. The raw materials remain in inventory for 1 month and it takes Fraser Ltd 2 months to produce the goods, which are sold immediately production is completed. Customers take an average 1.5 months to pay.

Fraser Ltd's cash operating cycle is

A   1 month

B   1.5 months

C   2 months

D   6 months

LO 2e

35 Trant plc has a two-stage trading process:

Stage 1: buy a large quantity of goods on credit

Stage 2: immediately sell them on credit at a profit

Which of the following will increase after Stage 1?

A   Receivables and inventory

B   Current assets and non-current assets

C   Payables and cash

D   Current assets and current liabilities

LO 2f

36   Merlion plc is an international company based in Malaysia. It manufactures and sells items for a wide variety of outdoor leisure pursuits including wind surfing, camping and mountain biking. A summary of the ratios provided by the chief accountant is as follows:

Ratio	20X4	20X5	20X6
Receivables collection period	49 days	38 days	35 days
Payables payment period	51 days	35 days	30 days
Inventory turnover period	23 days	25 days	29 days

What are the figures for Merlion plc's cash operating cycle for each of the three years?

Cash operating cycle in 20X4

A   21 days

B   28 days

C   34 days

Cash operating cycle in 20X5

D   21 days

E   28 days

F   34 days

Cash operating cycle in 20X6

G   21 days

H   28 days

I   34 days

LO 2f

37   Shrier plc is trying to decide on its optimal level of current assets. The company's management face a trade-off between

A   profitability and risk

B   liquidity and risk

C   equity and debt

D   short-term and long-term borrowing

LO 2f

38   There are a number of motives that influence how much a business wishes to hold in cash. When a company holds cash in order to make the payments that are necessary to keep the business going, such as wages, taxes and payments to suppliers, the motive behind this is

A   the transactions motive

B   the finance motive

C   the precautionary motive

D   the speculative motive

LO 2f

39 If a business is suffering from liquidity problems, the aim must be to reduce the length of the cash operating cycle. Which **three** of the following actions would achieve this?

A   Reducing the credit period extended to receivables

B   Reducing the payables payment period

C   Extending the period of credit taken from suppliers

D   Reducing the production period

E   Extending the inventory holding period   LO 2f

40 If a company moves from a defensive working capital policy to an aggressive working capital policy, it should expect

A   liquidity to decrease, whereas expected profitability would increase

B   expected profitability to increase, whereas risk would decrease

C   liquidity would increase, whereas risk would also increase

D   risk and profitability to decrease   LO 2f

41 Albert's Autos is a small garage providing car servicing. Business is good, there is a steady stream of income from repeat customers and breakdown recoveries. There are no significant cash reserves and there is no need for an overdraft. Now the organisation that passes on most of the breakdown recovery work offers Albert a contract to supply recovery services over a 50-mile radius. It is seeking 60 days credit rather than Albert's usual 30 days. Albert is keen but has been warned to look for signs of overtrading.

Which **two** of the following are most likely to be symptoms of overtrading?

A   A lengthening of the cash operating cycle

B   A rapid reduction in sales

C   Increase in the level of the current ratio

D   A rapid increase in sales

E   A shortening of the cash operating cycle   LO 2f

42 Apart from the actual cost of buying inventory, there are other inventory costs to consider.

Which **two** of the following are inventory holding costs?

A   Clerical and administrative expenses

B   Insurance

C   Opportunity cost of capital tied up

D   Production stoppages due to lack of raw materials

E   The cost of inventory packaging materials   LO 2f

43   The different functions within a company (finance, production, marketing, etc) often have differing views about what is an 'appropriate' level of inventory. Essentially, two inventory problems need to be answered – how much to order and when to order?

If we order inventory more frequently which of the following can we expect?

A   Lower ordering costs and lower average inventory

B   Lower ordering costs and higher average inventory

C   Higher ordering costs and lower average inventory

D   Higher ordering costs and higher average inventory   LO 2f

44   The Economic Order Quantity (EOQ) can be expressed as follows: $\sqrt{\dfrac{2cd}{h}}$

What does **h** describe in this formula?

A   The cost of holding one unit of inventory for one period

B   The cost of placing one order

C   The cost of a unit of inventory

D   The customer demand for the item   LO 2f

45   Fruit & Nut Ltd is re-evaluating its inventory control policy. Its daily demand for wooden boxes is steady at 40 a day for each of the 250 working days (50 weeks) of the year. The boxes are currently bought weekly in batches of 200 from a local supplier for £2 each. The cost of ordering the boxes from the local supplier is £64 per order, regardless of the size of the order. The inventory holding costs, expressed as a percentage of inventory value, are 25% pa. The Economic Order Quantity (EOQ) can be expressed as follows: $\sqrt{\dfrac{2cd}{h}}$

Identify the correct EOQ

A   101 boxes

B   253 boxes

C   1,600 boxes

D   2,262 boxes   LO 2f

46   Kate Osmond works for a company manufacturing industrial fasteners, so the company has several thousand types of inventory item. The company wants to introduce a new inventory control system and Kate is reviewing what is available.

Identify the most suitable system for an organisation with so many inventory items.

A   Re-order level system

B   Periodic review system

C   ABC system

D   Just-in-time system   LO 2f

47 The key trade-off that lies at the heart of working capital management is that between

   A   business stability and solvency

   B   debtors and creditors

   C   current assets and current liabilities

   D   liquidity and profitability   LO 2f

48 Identify whether the following tasks are normally undertaken by the treasury department of a large business.

Credit control

   A   Yes

   B   No

Short-term investment

   C   Yes

   D   No

Capital investment appraisal

   E   Yes

   F   No   LO 2f

49 Total usage of one item of Archer Ltd's inventory for the next month is estimated to be 100,000 units. The costs incurred each time an order is placed are £180. The carrying cost per unit of the item each month is estimated at £2. The purchase price of each unit is £4. The economic order quantity formula is:

$$\sqrt{(2cd)/h}$$

When using this formula to find the optimal quantity to be ordered, identify the amounts that are included in the calculation.

Cost per order (£180)

   A   Included

   B   Not included

Carrying cost per unit per month (£2)

   C   Included

   D   Not included

Purchase price per unit (£4)

   E   Included

   F   Not included   LO 2f

50 Rust Ltd invoices customers at the beginning of the month following the month in which a sale is made. All of the cash to be received in respect of these invoices occurs within two calendar months of invoicing. The company receives in cash 45% of the total gross sales value in the month of invoicing. Because Rust Ltd operates in a market where there is poor creditworthiness bad debts are 20% of total gross sales value, but there is a 10% discount for settling accounts within a calendar month of invoicing.

What percentage of the sales invoiced in the first month will be received as cash in the second month by Rust Ltd?

A   55.0%

B   35.0%

C   39.5%

D   30.0%   LO 2f

51 Youri plc has the following opening and closing balances on its trade receivables budget for next year, 20X7:

	£
Opening balance on trade receivables (invoiced on 31 December 20X6)	56,000
Closing balance on trade receivables (invoiced on 30 November 20X7)	72,000

In 20X7 credit sales are expected to be £276,000. The company offers a 10% discount on all amounts paid within one month of the invoice date. In 20X7 the company expects 50% of eligible trade customers to take advantage of this discount.

How much cash does Youri plc expect to receive from customers during the year?

A   £247,000

B   £243,400

C   £260,000

D   £276,000   LO 2f

Chapter 8: Performance management

1 Shown below is a diagram of a simple control cycle. What should be in the box marked 'X'?

A Feedback

B Fixed costs

C Activity levels

D Budgets and standards   LO 3c

2 Which of the following is **not** a feature of effective feedback reports?

A Made available in a timely fashion

B Produced on a regular basis

C Distributed to as many managers as possible

D Sufficiently accurate for the purpose intended   LO 3d

3 Which of the following describes exception reporting?

A Reporting of exceptional activities within an organisation

B Reporting only controllable matters to managers

C Reporting only of variances which exceed a certain value

D Reporting of all variances to the relevant manager   LO 3a

4 Which **two** of the following statements about management control reports are correct?

A Reports should be completely accurate.

B Reports should be clear and comprehensive.

C Reports should not include information about uncontrollable items.

D Based on the information contained in reports, managers may decide to do nothing.   LO 3a

5   Which of the following is **not** an example of budget bias?

A   A manager overestimates costs when setting the budget, to guard against overspending during the period.

B   A manager's advertising budget is disproportionately large in comparison with the budgeted revenue to be generated.

C   A manager underestimates revenues when setting the budget to ensure that the budget target can be easily exceeded.

D   A manager overestimates revenues when setting the budget in order to make a favourable impression on senior managers.   LO 3a

6   Which of the following statements is correct?

A   Since management accounts are prepared for a different purpose from that of external financial reports, there is no need for any convergence between the two.

B   The setting of appropriate performance measures will ensure that an organisation's performance management is effective.

C   Since the board of directors is not concerned with the day to day management of a business they do not require regular management reports.

D   Management control activity might involve a comparison of the latest forecast results with the original budget.   LO 3a

7   Which of the following is **not** a style of performance evaluation identified in Hopwood's studies?

A   Budget constrained

B   Non-accounting

C   Revenue focused

D   Profit conscious   LO 3a

8   Select which of the following styles of using budgetary information is most likely to lead to each of the situations described.

Job related tension is caused by which of the following styles:

A   Budget constrained

B   Profit conscious

C   Non-accounting

Less focus on cost control is caused by which of the following styles:

D   Budget constrained

E   Profit conscious

F   Non-accounting

Incidence of budget bias is caused by which of the following styles:

G   Budget constrained

H   Profit conscious

I   Non-accounting   LO 3a

9   A company have recently implemented a new budgetary planning and control system after several years of trading.

Having made a significant investment in the new system, the company's management team were surprised to learn that it is not designed to do which of the following?

A   Improve control of actual performance

B   Improve co-ordination of activities

C   Improve gross profit

D   Improve communication of ideas and plans   LO 3d

10   Which of the following is a reason for adopting a decentralised rather than a centralised organisational structure?

A   Improved goal congruence between the goals of divisional management and the goals of the organisation

B   Rapid management response to changes in the trading environment

C   Availability of objective performance measures

D   Improved communication of information between the group's managers   LO 3a

11   Division P is an investment centre within PC Ltd. Over which of the following is the manager of division P likely to have control?

(1)   Transfer prices

(2)   Level of inventory in the division

(3)   Discretionary fixed costs incurred in the division

(4)   Apportioned head office costs

A   (1), (2), (3) and (4)

B   (1), (2) and (3) only

C   (1) and (2) only

D   (1) only   LO 3b

12 The manager of a trading division has complete autonomy regarding the purchase and use of non-current assets. The division operates its own credit control policy in respect of its customers but the group operates a central purchasing function through which the division places all orders with suppliers and invoices are paid by head office.

Inventories of goods for sale are kept in central stores, from which local divisions call off requirements for local sales on a monthly basis into a local inventory.

Divisional performance is assessed on the basis of controllable residual income. The company requires a rate of return of 'R'.

Using the following symbols:

Divisional non-current assets	N
Apportioned net book value of central stores	S
Divisional working capital	
Receivables	D
Local inventory	I
Bank	B
Payables	(P)
	W
Divisional net assets	T
Divisional contribution	C
Controllable fixed costs	(F)
Head office charges	(H)
Divisional net income	G

Which of the following formulae calculates the division's controllable residual income?

A $[C - F] - [(N + D + B) \times R]$

B $[C - F] - [(N + D + I + B) \times R]$

C $C - [(N + D) \times R]$

D $G - (T \times R)$

LO 3b

13 Division D of Distan Ltd is considering a project which will increase annual profit by £15,000 but will require average receivables levels to increase by £100,000. The company's target return on investment is 10% and the imputed interest cost of capital is 9%. Division D currently earns a return on investment of 13%.

Would the return on investment (ROI) and residual income (RI) performance measures motivate the manager of Division D to act in the interest of the Distan company as a whole?

ROI

A   Manager would wish to act in the interest of Distan Ltd

B   Manager would not wish to act in the interest of Distan Ltd

RI

C   Manager would wish to act in the interest of Distan Ltd

D   Manager would not wish to act in the interest of Distan Ltd

LO 3b

14 Division B of a national house-building group is projected to earn profits of £4.5m in the current year on capital employed at the year end of £25m. The division has been set a target return on investment (ROI) of 20%.

The manager of division B is considering disposing of some slow-moving houses which have a full market value of £16m, but are held in the books at cost of £12m, for a reduced figure of £14m.

Which of the following statements is true?

A   The revised divisional ROI will be below 20% and the manager will make a goal congruent decision.

B   The revised divisional ROI will be above 20% and the manager will not make a goal congruent decision.

C   The revised divisional ROI will be below 20% and the manager will not make a goal congruent decision.

D   The revised divisional ROI will be above 20% and the manager will make a goal congruent decision.

LO 3b

15 On the last day of the financial year a division has net assets with a total carrying amount of £300,000. The return on investment for the division is 18%.

The division manager is considering selling a non-current asset immediately before the year end. The non-current asset has a carrying amount of £15,000 and will sell for a profit of £5,000.

What would be the division's return on investment (ROI) immediately after the sale of the asset at the end of the year?

A   17.7%

B   19.3%

C   20.3%

D   20.7%

LO 3b

16 Which of the following is not a perspective that is monitored by the balanced scorecard approach to performance measurement?

A   Financial

B   Customer

C   Supplier

D   Innovation and learning

LO 3b

17   Indicate which of the following statements are true.

(1)   If a company uses a balanced scorecard approach to the provision of information it will not use ROI or residual income as divisional performance measures.

(2)   The residual income will always increase when investments earning above the cost of capital are undertaken.

(3)   The internal business perspective of the balanced scorecard approach to the provision of information is concerned only with the determination of internal transfer prices that will encourage goal congruent decisions.

(4)   An advantage of the residual income performance measure is that it facilitates comparisons between investment centres.

A   (1) only

B   (2) only

C   (3) only

D   (1) and (4) only   LO 3b

18   Which of the following describes a flexible budget?

A   A budget comprising variable production costs only

B   A budget which is updated with actual costs and revenues as they occur during the budget period

C   A budget which shows the costs and revenues at different levels of activity

D   A budget which is prepared using a computer spreadsheet model   LO 3e

19   Which of the following statements is/are correct?

(1)   Fixed budgets are not useful for control purposes.

(2)   A prerequisite of flexible budgeting is a knowledge of cost behaviour patterns.

(3)   Budgetary control procedures are useful only to maintain control over an organisation's expenditure.

A   (1), (2) and (3)

B   (1) and (2) only

C   (1) and (3) only

D   (2) only   LO 3e

20 A company manufactures a single product and has drawn up the following flexed budget for the year.

	60% £	70% £	80% £
Variable materials	120,000	140,000	160,000
Variable labour	90,000	105,000	120,000
Production overhead	54,000	58,000	62,000
Other overhead	40,000	40,000	40,000
Total cost	304,000	343,000	382,000

What would be the total cost in a budget that is flexed at the 77% level of activity?

A   £330,300

B   £370,300

C   £373,300

D   £377,300   LO 3e

21 Within decentralised organisations there may be cost centres, investment centres and profit centres. Which of the following statements is true?

A   Cost centres have a higher degree of autonomy than profit centres.

B   Investment centres have the highest degree of autonomy and cost centres have the lowest.

C   Investment centres have the lowest degree of autonomy.

D   Profit centres have the highest degree of autonomy and cost centres have the lowest. LO 3a

22 A manager of a trading division of a large company has complete discretion over the purchase and use of non-current assets and inventories. Head Office keeps a central bank account, collecting all cash from receivables and paying all suppliers. The division is charged a management fee for these services. The performance of the manager of the division is assessed on the basis of her controllable residual income. The company requires a rate of return of 'R'. Using the following symbols:

Divisional non-current assets		F
Divisional working capital		
Receivables	D	
Inventory	S	
Payables	(L)	
		$\frac{W}{Z}$
Divisional net assets		
Divisional profit		P
Head office management charges		(M)
Divisional net profit		$\underline{\underline{N}}$

Which of the following is the correct formula for calculating the controllable residual income of the division?

A   P − [(F + S) × R]

B   N − [(F + S) × R]

C   N − (Z × R)

D   P − (Z × R)   LO 3b

23 Which of the following sentences best describes what is necessary for a responsibility accounting system to be successful?

A Each manager should know the criteria used for evaluating his or her own performance.

B The details on the performance reports for individual managers should add up to the totals on the report of their superior.

C Each employee should receive a separate performance report.

D Service department costs should be apportioned to the operating departments that use the service.

LO 3a

24 Information concerning three divisions of Haughton plc is shown below.

Division	Capital invested	Return on investment
P	£1,100,000	12%
Q	£1,200,000	13%
R	£1,500,000	14%

Select the percentage that is the highest rate for the imputed cost of capital that would produce the same ranking for these three divisions using residual income instead of return on investment.

A 11.9%

B 13.9%

C 17.9%

D 23.9%

LO 3b

25 A division has a residual income of £480,000 and a net profit before imputed interest of £1,280,000.

If it uses a rate of 10% for computing imputed interest on its invested capital, what is its return on investment?

A 10%

B 22%

C 6%

D 16%

LO 3b

26 Division X of Martext Ltd produced the following results in the last financial year:

	£'000
Net profit	400
Average net assets	2,000

For evaluation purposes all divisional assets are valued at original cost. The division is considering a project which will increase annual net profit by £30,000, but will require average inventory levels to increase by £100,000 and fixed assets to increase by £100,000. Martext Ltd imposes a 16% capital charge on its divisions.

Given these circumstances, will the evaluation criteria of return on investment (ROI) and residual income (RI) motivate division X managers to accept the project?

	ROI	RI
A	No	Yes
B	Yes	Yes
C	No	No
D	Yes	No

27   A division currently has an annual return on investment (ROI) of 20% on its investment base of £1,200,000. The following additional projects are being considered:

Project	Investment outlay £'000	Annual profit £'000	ROI %
K	300	100	33
L	700	210	30
M	500	130	26
N	200	44	22

Which combination of investments will maximise the division's return on investment assuming unlimited capital is available?

A   K, L, M and N

B   K, L and M only

C   K and L only

D   K only

LO 3b

28   Ulster plc estimates that the net cash flows associated with a new piece of equipment will be equal in each of the five years of the asset's life.

In assessing performance, Return on Investment (ROI) is used, but the figures for capital employed and accounting profit have come under scrutiny.

Which methods of stating these two components of ROI will provide figures which are constant from year to year over the five-year life of this new asset?

	Capital employed	Accounting profit
A	Gross book value	Profit after charging depreciation on a reducing balance basis
B	Gross book value	Profit after charging depreciation on a straight-line basis
C	Net book value	Profit after charging depreciation on a straight-line basis
D	Net book value	Profit after charging depreciation on a reducing balance basis

LO 3b

Management Information: Question Bank

Chapter 9: Standard costing and variance analysis

1 Which of the following would **not** be used to estimate standard material prices?

    A   The availability of bulk purchase discounts

    B   Purchase contracts already agreed

    C   The forecast movement of prices in the market

    D   Performance standards in operation   LO 3e

2 Which of the following statements about budgets and standards is/are correct?

    (1)   Budgets can be used in situations where output cannot be measured but standards cannot be used in such situations.

    (2)   Budgets can include allowances for inefficiencies in operations but standards use performance targets which are attainable under the most favourable conditions.

    (3)   Budgets are used for planning purposes, standards are used only for control purposes.

    A   (1), (2) and (3)

    B   (1) and (2) only

    C   (1) only

    D   (2) and (3) only   LO 3e

3 Which of the following is **not** a cause of variances?

    A   Actual prices are different from budgeted prices

    B   Actual resource usage is different from planned resource usage

    C   Actual production volume is different from budgeted production volume

    D   Actual prices are different from forecast prices   LO 3e

The following information relates to questions 4 and 5

Telgar plc uses a standard costing system, with its material inventory account being maintained at standard cost. The following details have been extracted from the standard cost card in respect of materials.

8 kg @ £0.80/kg = £6.40 per unit

Budgeted production in April was 850 units.

The following details relate to actual materials purchased and issued to production during April when actual production was 870 units.

| Materials purchased | 8,200 kg costing £6,888 |
| Materials issued to production | 7,150 kg |

4   The material price variance for April was

    A   £286 adverse

    B   £286 favourable

    C   £328 adverse

    D   £328 favourable

LO 3e

5   The material usage variance for April was

    A   £152.00 favourable

    B   £152.00 adverse

    C   £159.60 adverse

    D   £280.00 adverse

LO 3e

The following information relates to questions 6 and 7

Revue plc uses a standard costing system. The budget for one of its products for September includes labour cost (based on 4 hours per unit) of £117,600. During September 3,350 units were made which was 150 units less than budgeted. The labour cost incurred was £111,850 and the number of labour hours worked was 13,450.

6   The labour rate variance for the month was

    A   £710 favourable

    B   £1,130 favourable

    C   £1,130 adverse

    D   £5,750 adverse

LO 3e

7   The labour efficiency variance for the month was

    A   £415.80 adverse

    B   £420.00 adverse

    C   £420.00 favourable

    D   £710.00 favourable

LO 3e

The following information relates to questions 8 to 10

Extracts from Verona Ltd's records for June are as follows.

	Budget	Actual
Production	520 units	560 units
Variable production overhead cost	£3,120	£4,032
Labour hours worked	1,560	2,240

8   The variable production overhead total variance for June is

   A   £240 adverse

   B   £672 adverse

   C   £672 favourable

   D   £912 adverse   LO 3e

9   The variable production overhead expenditure variance for June is

   A   £448 favourable

   B   £448 adverse

   C   £672 adverse

   D   £912 adverse   LO 3e

10   The variable production overhead efficiency variance for June is

   A   £1,008 adverse

   B   £1,120 adverse

   C   £1,120 favourable

   D   £1,360 adverse   LO 3e

11   The following information is available for Mentamint Ltd, which makes one product.

Budgeted fixed overhead per unit	£10
Budgeted output	1,000 units
Actual output	1,200 units
Actual fixed overheads	£11,200

   What is the fixed overhead expenditure variance?

   A   £1,200 adverse

   B   £800 favourable

   C   £1,200 favourable

   D   £800 adverse   LO 3e

12 The following information relates to Product M, made and sold by Nan Ltd.

	Standard £ per unit	Actual £ per unit
Selling price	20	22
Material	6	8
Labour	3	4
Variable overhead	2	4
Total variable costs	(11)	(16)
Contribution	9	6

Nan Ltd budgeted for a sales volume of 1,000 units, but actually sold 100 units less than this.

Which of the following shows the correct calculation of the sales price and contribution volume variances?

A   Sales price variance   = £1,800 favourable

    Sales volume variance = £2,000 adverse

B   Sales price variance   = £2,000 favourable

    Sales volume variance = £900 adverse

C   Sales price variance   = £2,000 favourable

    Sales volume variance = £2,000 adverse

D   Sales price variance   = £1,800 favourable

    Sales volume variance = £900 adverse

LO 3e

---

13 To reconcile the budgeted contribution to the actual contribution, which of the following must be accounted for?

A   All sales variances and all marginal cost variances

B   All sales variances

C   All marginal cost variances

D   Neither sales nor marginal cost variances

LO 3e

---

14 A company budgets to make and sell 83,000 units of its product each period. The standard contribution per unit is £8.

The following variances (A = adverse; F = favourable) were reported for the latest period.

Variances	£
Sales volume contribution	42,400 (A)
Sales price	7,310 (F)
Material total	7,720 (F)
Material price	10,840 (F)
Labour total	6,450 (A)
Variable overhead total	4,250 (A)
Fixed overhead expenditure	8,880 (F)

The budgeted fixed overhead expenditure for the period was £210,000.

The actual profit for the period was

A   £424,810

B   £435,650

C   £483,190

D   £634,810

LO 3f

15   In a period, 11,280 kg of material were used at a total standard cost of £46,248. The material usage variance was £492 adverse.

What was the standard allowed weight of material for the production achieved?

A   10,788 kg

B   11,160 kg

C   11,280 kg

D   11,400 kg   LO 3e

16   During a period, 17,500 labour hours were worked at a standard cost of £6.50 per hour. The labour efficiency variance was £7,800 favourable.

How many standard hours should have been worked?

A   1,200

B   16,300

C   17,500

D   18,700   LO 3e

17   The following information relates to material costs for the latest period.

Actual material purchased and used	210,000 kg
Standard material for actual output	175,000 kg
Total actual materials cost	£336,000
Materials price variance	£21,000 adverse

What was the standard materials price per kg?

A   £1.50

B   £1.70

C   £1.80

D   £2.04   LO 3e

18   Consider the following statements:

(1) Favourable variances are always good for an organisation.

(2) Variance reporting is the comparison of the actual results with the original budget.

Which of the following is correct with regards to the statements above?

A   Both statements are correct

B   Both statements are incorrect

C   Statement 1 is correct but statement 2 is incorrect

D   Statement 1 is incorrect but statement 2 is correct   LO 3e

19   Variances which are simply random deviations can be described as which of the following?

   A   Controllable

   B   Uncontrollable

   C   Either controllable or uncontrollable

   D   Marginal costs

LO 3e

20   Consider the following factors for investigating a variance.

   (1)   Controllability of variance

   (2)   Cost of investigation

   (3)   Personnel involved

   (4)   Trend of variance

   Which of these would be a factor that would affect a decision as to whether to investigate the variance?

   A   (2) and (4) only

   B   (2), (3) and (4) only

   C   (1), (2) and (3) only

   D   (1), (2) and (4) only

LO 3e

21   Which of the following would **not** help to explain a favourable materials usage variance?

   A   Using a higher quality of materials than specified in the standard

   B   Achieving a lower output volume than budgeted

   C   A reduction in quality control checking standards

   D   A reduction in materials wastage rates

LO 3e

22   Select the likely impact of the following actual events on the materials price variance.

   The standard material price was set too low.

   A   Adverse

   B   Favourable

   C   No impact

   Discounts were taken from suppliers for early settlement of invoices.

   D   Adverse

   E   Favourable

   F   No impact

   The material purchased was of a higher quality than standard.

   G   Adverse

   H   Favourable

   I   No impact

LO 3e

23 Which of the following could cause a favourable variable overhead efficiency variance?

    A   Using less material than the flexed materials usage budget predicts

    B   Working fewer hours than the flexed labour hours budget predicts

    C   Variable overhead cost per hour being less than the standard variable overhead cost per hour

    D   Fixed overhead expenditure being less than budgeted   LO 3e

---

24 The labour total variance for the latest period was favourable. Which of the following are, together, certain to have caused this variance?

    A   Lower hourly rates than standard and higher than budgeted labour hours

    B   Lower hourly rates than standard and lower than budgeted labour hours

    C   Lower hourly rates than standard and lower than standard labour hours for the actual production

    D   Lower hourly rates than standard and higher than standard labour hours for the actual production   LO 3e

---

25 A business has a budgeted materials cost of £7 per kg. During the month of June 2,500 kg of the material was purchased and used at a cost of £18,750 in order to produce 1,250 units of the product. The budgeted materials cost of £14,000 had been based upon budgeted production of 1,000 units of the product.

What was the materials total variance?

    A   £1,250 adverse

    B   £1,250 favourable

    C   £4,750 adverse

    D   £4,750 favourable   LO 3e

---

26 A business has a budgeted labour cost per unit of £15.50. During the month of December production details were as follows:

Budget	12,600 units
Actual	12,000 units

The actual labour cost for the month was £199,400

What was the labour total variance as a percentage of the flexed budgeted figure?

    A   2.1% adverse

    B   2.1% favourable

    C   7.2% adverse

    D   7.2% favourable   LO 3e

27 A company's actual output for the period was 22,000 units and variable overhead costs were in line with budget. The budgeted variable overhead cost per unit was £3 and total overhead expenditure of £108,000 meant that fixed overheads were £8,000 under budget.

What was the budgeted level of fixed overheads for the period?

A   £34,000

B   £50,000

C   £66,000

D   £116,000
LO 3e

28 When absorbing variable overheads on the basis of machine hours, the total variable overhead variance can be worked out by comparing actual variable overheads in a period with the product of the absorption rate and which of the following?

A   (Planned output) × (Standard machine hours per unit)

B   (Actual output) × (Actual machine hours per unit)

C   (Planned output) × (Actual machine hours per unit)

D   (Actual output) × (Standard machine hours per unit)
LO 3e

29 A product requires raw material with a standard cost of 50p per kg. In February, 2,500 kg of raw material were purchased at a cost of £1,500 of which 2,300 kg of raw material were used in that month's production.

If raw material inventory is valued at standard cost and there was no opening inventory of raw material, which of the following represents the material price variance for February?

A   £250 adverse

B   £230 adverse

C   £230 favourable

D   £250 favourable
LO 3e

30 The following is extracted from Proteus Ltd's monthly management reporting:

Performance report for October

	Adverse £	Favourable £	£
Budgeted contribution (10,000 units)			172,000
Variances			
Labour rate	3,600		
Labour efficiency		8,000	
Material price	10,800		
Material usage		4,800	
	14,400	12,800	(1,600)
Actual contribution (10,000 units)			170,400

The purchasing manager decided to buy a superior quality material that was more expensive than the standard material for use in October. This superior material causes less waste. Labour was able to convert this superior material into the final product in less than the standard time. A wage rise, agreed in July and implemented at the beginning of October, also impacted on the results.

The decision to buy the superior quality materials caused the profit in October to change. Select which of the following best describes that change.

A   Fall by £1,600

B   Rise by £4,800

C   Fall by £6,000

D   Rise by £2,000   LO 3f

---

31 The following data are available with regard to a product for a given period:

	Actual	Budget
Sales (units)	10,100	10,000
	£	£
Sales value	105,040	102,000
Variable costs at standard	86,860	86,000
Contribution	18,180	16,000

The favourable sales volume variance was

A   £1,020

B   £1,040

C   £180

D   £160   LO 3e

32   The following information relates to a firm's labour costs for the year:

Standard rate per hour   £2.00
Actual rate per hour   £4.00
Actual hours worked   130,000
Labour efficiency variance   £10,000 favourable

The standard number of labour hours for actual output were

A   125,000 hours

B   127,500 hours

C   132,500 hours

D   135,000 hours

LO 3e

33   Would each of the following actual events during the year lead to a sales volume variance being **adverse** or **favourable** or have **no impact** on it?

Sales prices increased

A   Adverse

B   Favourable

C   No impact

Successful advertising campaign

D   Adverse

E   Favourable

F   No impact

Increased labour pay rates

G   Adverse

H   Favourable

I   No impact

LO 3e

Chapter 10: Breakeven analysis and limiting factor analysis

1 The Finance Assistant from Castle Associates has recently returned from a management accounting seminar at which she was introduced to some new management accounting terms and formulae. She has now got several of the terms and formulae mixed up in her mind.

The contribution required to breakeven is best given by which of the following?

A Unit selling price less unit variable cost

B Unit contribution × number of units sold

C Total fixed costs

D Total fixed costs/contribution ratio

LO 4a

2 Which **two** of the following show how the breakeven point in units can be calculated?

A Total fixed costs/contribution per unit

B Contribution required to break even/contribution per unit

C Contribution/sales

D Fixed costs/costs to sales ratio

LO 4a

3 A company makes a single product and incurs fixed costs of £30,000 per month. Variable cost per unit is £5 and each unit sells for £15. Monthly sales demand is 7,000 units.

The breakeven point in terms of monthly sales units is

A 2,000 units

B 3,000 units

C 4,000 units

D 6,000 units

LO 4a

4 A company manufactures a single product for which cost and selling price data are as follows:

Selling price per unit	£12
Variable cost per unit	£8
Fixed costs per month	£96,000
Budgeted monthly sales (units)	30,000

The margin of safety, expressed as a percentage of budgeted monthly sales, is

A 20%

B 25%

C 73%

D 125%

LO 4a

5   Uula plc makes a single product, which it sells for £16 per unit. Fixed costs are £76,800 per month and the product has a contribution ratio of 40%.

In a month when actual sales were £224,000, Uula plc's margin of safety, in units, was

A   2,000

B   12,000

C   14,000

D   32,000

LO 4a

6   A company has budgeted sales revenue of £500,000 for Period 1, with an associated contribution of £275,000. Fixed production costs are £137,500 and fixed selling costs are £27,500.

What is the breakeven sales revenue?

A   £165,000

B   £250,000

C   £300,000

D   £366,667

LO 4a

7   A company has calculated its margin of safety to be 20% of budgeted sales. Budgeted sales are 5,000 units per month and budgeted contribution is £25 per unit.

What are the budgeted fixed costs per month?

A   £25,000

B   £100,000

C   £125,000

D   £150,000

LO 4a

8   Doer Ltd makes a single product, the Whizzo. This product sells for £15, and makes a contribution of £5 per unit. Total fixed costs per annum are £11,125.

If Doer Ltd wishes to make an annual profit of £11,875 how many Whizzos do they need to sell?

A   1,533 units

B   2,225 units

C   2,375 units

D   4,600 units

LO 4a

9   Jackson plc expects a new venture to yield a gross profit of 50% on sales.

Fixed salary costs are expected to be £23,520 per month and other expenses are expected to be 8% of sales.

Calculate the sales revenue necessary to yield a monthly profit of £58,800.

A   £56,000

B   £140,000

C   £164,640

D   £196,000

LO 4a

10   Bandido Ltd manufactures and sells a single product, with the following estimated costs for next year.

	Unit cost	
	100,000 units of output	150,000 units of output
	£	£
Variable materials	20.00	20.00
Variable labour	5.00	5.00
Production overheads	10.00	7.50
Marketing costs	7.50	5.00
Administration costs	5.00	4.00
	47.50	41.50

Fixed costs are unaffected by the volume of output.

Bandido Ltd's management think they can sell 150,000 units per annum if the sales price is £49.50.

The breakeven point, in units, at this price is

A   36,364

B   90,000

C   101,020

D   225,000

LO 4a

11   Xena Ltd generates a 12% contribution on its weekly sales of £280,000. A new product, Z, is to be introduced at a special offer price in order to stimulate interest in all the company's products, resulting in a 5% increase in weekly sales of the company's other products. Product Z will incur a variable unit cost of £2.20 to make and £0.15 to distribute. Weekly sales of Z, at a special offer price of £1.90 per unit, are expected to be 3,000 units.

The effect of the special offer will be to increase the company's weekly profit by:

A   £330

B   £780

C   £5,700

D   £12,650

LO 4a

12   JJ Ltd manufactures a product which has a selling price of £14 and a variable cost of £6 per unit. The company incurs annual fixed costs of £24,400. Annual sales demand is 8,000 units.

New production methods are under consideration, which would cause a 30% increase in fixed costs and a reduction of £1 in the variable cost per unit. The new production methods would result in a superior product and would enable the sales price to be increased to £15 per unit.

If the organisation implements the new production methods and wishes to achieve the same profit as that under the existing method, the number of units to be produced and sold annually would be

A   3,960

B   4,755

C   7,132

D   8,915

LO 4a

13

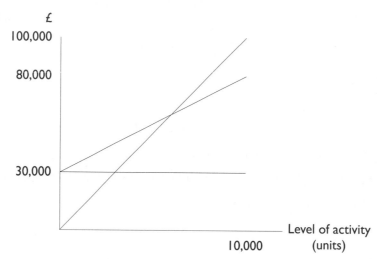

The above breakeven chart has been drawn for a company's single product. Which of the following statements about the product are correct?

(1)   The product's selling price is £10 per unit.

(2)   The product's variable cost is £8 per unit.

(3)   The product incurs fixed costs of £30,000 per period.

(4)   The product earns a profit of £70,000 at a level of activity of 10,000 units.

A   (1), (2) and (3) only

B   (1) and (3) only

C   (1), (3) and (4) only

D   (3) and (4) only

LO 4a

14 Which **two** of the following statements about traditional breakeven charts are correct?

   A   The fixed costs are depicted by a straight line parallel to the vertical axis.

   B   The sales revenue line passes through the origin.

   C   The total cost line cuts the vertical axis at the point which is equal to the period fixed costs.

   D   The breakeven point is the point where the sales revenue line crosses the fixed cost line.

LO 4a

15 When using limiting factor analysis in order to calculate maximum profit, which **three** of the following assumptions should be made?

   A   Fixed costs per unit are not changed by increases or decreases in production volume.

   B   Fixed costs in total are not changed by increases or decreases in production volume.

   C   Variable costs per unit are not changed by increases or decreases in production volume.

   D   Variable costs in total are not changed by increases or decreases in production volume.

   E   Estimates of sales demand, prices and resources required for each product are known with certainty.

LO 4a

16 A company produces a single product for which standard cost details are as follows.

	£ per unit
Material (£2 per kg)	8
Labour (£6 per hour)	18
Production overhead	9
Total production cost	35

The item is perishable and no inventories are held.

Demand for next period will be 6,000 units but only 19,000 hours of labour and 22,000 kg of material will be available.

What will be the limiting factor next period?

   A   Material only

   B   Labour only

   C   Material and labour

   D   Sales demand

LO 4b

17   A company makes three products to which the following budget information relates:

	B £ per unit	A £ per unit	T £ per unit
Selling price	100	120	145
Labour at £20 per hour	40	40	60
Materials at £10 per kg	10	20	30
Fixed overheads	30	40	20
Profit	20	20	35

The marketing department says the maximum annual demand is for 1,000 units of Product B, 1,200 units of product A and 1,500 units of product T, and the factory has budgeted to produce that number of units. It has just been discovered that next year materials will be limited to 5,000 kg and labour to 10,000 hours.

If the company wishes to maximise profit, the priority in which the products should be made and sold is

A   B then A then T

B   A then B then T

C   T then A then B

D   T then B then A

LO 4b

---

18   A company makes three products and has produced the following standard cost cards.

	X £ per unit	Y £ per unit	Z £ per unit
Selling price	100	80	70
Variable costs			
Material	20	30	5
Labour	30	10	5
Fixed overheads	40	10	40
Profit	10	30	20

The same labour is used to make all three products, but in different quantities.

Assume that the company can make and sell any combination of products.

In a month where expenditure on labour is restricted to £50,000, what is the maximum contribution and profit that can be earned?

A   Contribution: insufficient information to calculate, Profit: insufficient information to calculate

B   Contribution: Insufficient information to calculate, Profit: £200,000

C   Contribution: £600,000, Profit: Insufficient information to calculate

D   Contribution: £600,000, Profit: £200,000

LO 4b

19 Brian Ltd produces three products which have the following unit contributions and labour requirements.

Product	Unit contribution	Labour requirement
	£	Hours
Scratch	6	2
Purr	7	3
Buzz	8	3

Due to industrial action only 2,600 labour hours are available next period, when expected demand is 700 units of each product. Fixed costs are £1,700 for the period.

What is the maximum profit that can be achieved next period?

A   £5,062

B   £5,700

C   £6,100

D   £13,000

LO 4b

20 Using the following data Chin has correctly selected the plan which will maximise profit for next month, assuming 15,000 labour hours are available.

	Product M		Product Q	
	£ per unit	£ per unit	£ per unit	£ per unit
Selling price		171		235
Less Variable costs				
Materials	26		45	
Labour (at £10 per hour)	60		80	
		86		125
Contribution		85		110
Maximum demand (units)		1,000		1,200

If an extra 48 hours were available (at the normal hourly rate of £10) and allocated optimally, profit for next month would be expected to increase by

A   £180

B   £660

C   £680

D   £880

LO 4b

21 MNP plc produces three products from a single raw material that is limited in supply. Product details for period 6 are as follows:

	Product M	Product N	Product P
Maximum demand (units)	1,000	2,400	2,800
Optimum planned production	720	nil	2,800
Unit contribution	£4.50	£4.80	£2.95
Raw material cost per unit (£0.50 per kg)	£1.25	£1.50	£0.75

The planned production optimises the use of 6,000 kg of raw material that is available from MNP plc's normal supplier at the price of £0.50 per kg. However, a new supplier has been found that is prepared to supply a further 1,000 kg of the material.

The maximum price that MNP plc should be prepared to pay for the additional 1,000 kg of the material is

Pay Maic = Conw. - Malul

A £1,740

B £1,800

C £2,240

D £2,300

LO 4b

22 Jethro Ltd manufactures three products, the selling prices, maximum demand and cost details of which are as follows.

	X £	Y £	Z £
Unit selling price	150	190	190
Unit costs			
Materials (£10/kg)	20	10	30
Labour (£8/hr)	32	48	40
Variable overheads	16	24	20
Fixed overheads	48	72	60
Maximum demand (units)	590	840	660

In the forthcoming period direct materials are restricted to 1,400 kg and the company has contracted to supply 100 units of Z and 130 units of Y to a customer (included in the maximum demand figures above).

What is the profit-maximising production plan?

	X Units	Y Units	Z Units
A	130	840	100
B	280	840	Nil
C	Nil	2	466
D	1	840	186

LO 4b

23 Green Ltd manufactures two components, the Alpha and the Beta, using the same machines for each. The budget for next year requires the production of 4,000 units of each component.

The variable production cost per component is as follows:

	Machine hours per unit	Variable production cost (£ per unit)
Alpha	3	20
Beta	2	36

Only 16,000 machine hours will be available next year. A sub-contractor has quoted the following unit prices to supply components: Alpha £29; Beta £40.

The optimum plan to obtain the components required is

	Component Alpha		Component Beta	
	Produce	Purchase from sub-contractor	Produce	Purchase from sub-contractor
	Units	Units	Units	Units
A	0	4,000	0	4,000
B	2,000	2,000	0	4,000
C	2,666	1,334	4,000	0
D	4,000	0	2,000	2,000

LO 4b

24 Blue plc manufactures two components, the Aura and the Venta, using the same machines for each. The budget for next year requires the production of 400 units of each component.

The variable production cost per component is as follows:

	Machine hours per unit	Variable production cost (£ per unit)
Aura	30	360
Venta	20	360

A maximum of 15,000 machine hours will be available next year. A sub-contractor has quoted the following unit prices to supply components: Aura £390; Venta £400.

The optimum plan to obtain the components required is

	Component Aura		Component Venta	
	Produce	Purchase from sub-contractor	Produce	Purchase from sub-contractor
	Units	Units	Units	Units
A	400	0	150	250
B	250	150	375	25
C	233	167	400	0
D	0	400	0	400

LO 4b

25 A company has only 6,000 kg of an irreplaceable raw material called Grunch. Grunch can be used to make three possible products X, Y and Z, details of which are given below:

	X	Y	Z
Maximum demand (units)	4,000	3,000	5,000
Constant unit selling price (£/unit)	£3.00	£4.00	£5.00
Constant unit variable cost (£/unit)	£1.50	£2.40	£2.60
Fixed costs (£/unit)	£1.80	£2.20	£2.40
Quantity of raw material Grunch to make one unit of product (kg)	0.30	0.40	0.80

If the company's objective is to maximise profit, which of the following production schedules should be chosen?

	X Units	Y Units	Z Units
A	2,666	3,000	5,000
B	4,000	3,000	5,000
C	4,000	2,000	5,000
D	4,000	3,000	4,500

LO 4b

---

26 A company makes large plastic containers for storing chemicals. An extract from the 20X7 budget based on a sales volume of 10,000 units is given below.

	£ per unit	£ per unit
Selling price		200
Variable cost	80	
Fixed overhead cost	20	
Total cost		(100)
Profit		100

Actual results for 20X7 were in line with this budget except that 12,000 units were produced and sold.

For 20X8 all costs are expected to increase by 10%, although selling price increases are expected to be restricted to 5%.

What level of sales must be achieved in 20X8 in order to maintain the actual profit at the 20X7 level?

A   12,400 units

B   11,639 units

C   12,000 units

D   11,967 units

LO 4a

Chapter 11: Investment appraisal techniques

1   A company is considering investing £46,000 in a machine that will be operated for four years, after which time it will sell for £4,000. Depreciation is charged on the straight-line basis. Forecast operating profits/(losses) to be generated by the machine are as follows:

Year	£
1	16,500
2	23,500
3	13,500
4	(1,500)

What are the Payback Period (PP) and the Accounting Rate of Return (ARR), calculated as average annual profits divided by the average investment?

	PP	ARR
A	1.56 years	52.0%
B	2.44 years	56.5%
C	2.44 years	52.0%
D	1.56 years	56.5%

LO 4c

2   A company is currently evaluating a project which requires investments of £5,000 now, and £2,000 at the end of year 1. The cash inflow from the project will be £7,000 at the end of year 2 and £6,000 at the end of year 3.

The cost of capital is 16%.

What are the Discounted Payback Period (DPP) and the Net Present Value (NPV)?

	DPP	NPV
A	2.0 years	£3,013
B	2.4 years	£2,323
C	2.0 years	£2,323
D	2.4 years	£3,013

LO 4c

3   An investment will generate cash flows of £1,800 each year in years 3 to 7 (ie, first amount to be received three years from now). The discount rate is 15% per annum.

What is the present value of the cash flows?

A   £1,350

B   £3,377

C   £4,561

D   £6,830

LO 4c

4   A leasing agreement is for five years. £10,000 must be paid at the beginning of the first year, to be followed by four equal payments at the beginning of years two, three, four and five. At a discount rate of 8%, the present value of the four equal payments is £26,496.

The total amount to be paid during the lease period is

A   £8,000

B   £32,000

C   £32,480

D   £42,000

LO 4c

5   An investment has a net present value of £4,000 at 10% and one of -£2,000 at 15%. What is the approximate Internal Rate of Return?

A   11.67%

B   12.50%

C   13.33%

D   20.00%

LO 4c

6   Which **two** of the following statements about the Net Present Value (NPV) and Internal Rate of Return (IRR) methods of investment appraisal are correct?

A   The graph of the NPV against the discount rate has a negative slope.

B   If the NPV of an investment at r% is positive, the NPV will be lower at a rate of s% if s% is less than r%.

C   The IRR can be obtained exactly using interpolation whereas the graphical method provides only an approximate rate for the IRR.

D   An estimate of the IRR requires the calculation of the NPV at two different discount rates.

LO 4d

7   Which of the following statements about Net Present Value (NPV) and Internal Rate of Return (IRR) methods are correct?

(1)   An investment with a positive NPV is financially viable.

(2)   NPV is a superior method to IRR.

(3)   The graph of NPV against discount rate has a negative slope for most projects.

(4)   NPV is the present value of expected future net cash receipts less the cost of the investment.

A   (1) and (3) only

B   (2) and (4) only

C   (1), (2) and (3) only

D   (1), (2), (3) and (4)

LO 4d

8   A company is considering investing £160,000 in a project which will generate the following positive cash flows.

Year	Cash flow
1	£31,700
2	£179,000
3	£48,900

The Net Present Value of the project's cash flows, at a cost of capital of 24%, is (to the nearest £500)

A   £167,500

B   –£84,000

C   £38,500

D   £7,500   LO 4c

9   A two-year project has the following annual cash flows:

	£
Initial cost	(400,000)
12 months later	300,000
24 months later	200,000

The cost of capital is estimated at 15% per annum during the first year and 17% per annum during the second year.

What is the net present value of the project (to the nearest £500)?

A   £2,500

B   £9,500

C   £12,000

D   £32,000   LO 4c

10   For a company with the objective of maximising net present value, what is the validity of the following statements for a conventional investment project?

(1)   The accounting rate of return (ARR) method of project appraisal usually gives too little weight to cash flows which occur late in the project's life.

(2)   For a project with a (unique) IRR greater than the opportunity cost of capital, the IRR method of project appraisal usually gives too little weight to cash flows which occur late in the project's life.

	Statement 1	Statement 2
A	True	True
B	True	False
C	False	False
D	False	True

LO 4d

11 Which of the following statements about Net Present Value (NPV) are correct?

    (1) An investment with a positive NPV is viable.

    (2) NPV is a superior appraisal method to Internal Rate of Return.

    (3) NPV is the present value of expected future net cash receipts less the cost of the investment.

    A   (1) and (2) only

    B   (1) and (3) only

    C   (1) only

    D   (1), (2) and (3)   LO 4d

12 Which of the following is **not** an advantage of the payback method of investment appraisal?

    A   Focus on a short payback period enhances liquidity

    B   Investment risk is reduced if the payback period is shorter

    C   It quantifies the effect of the timing of cash flows through the investment

    D   It is useful as an initial screening device   LO 4d

13 Which **two** of the following are **not** advantages of the accounting rate of return (ARR) method of investment appraisal?

    A   It is based on objective accounting profits

    B   The calculation method of ARR is universally agreed

    C   It involves a familiar concept of a percentage return

    D   It takes account of returns over the entire project life   LO 4d

14 In a comparison of the Net Present Value (NPV) and Internal Rate of Return (IRR) techniques, which of the following statements is true?

    A   Both methods give the same accept or reject decision, regardless of the pattern of the cash flows.

    B   IRR is technically superior to NPV and easier to calculate.

    C   The NPV approach is superior if discount rates are expected to vary over the life of the project.

    D   NPV and the accounting rate of return (ARR) can be confused.   LO 4d

15 A company is considering investing in a two-year project. Machine set-up costs will be £150,000 payable immediately. Working capital of £4,000 is required at the beginning of the contract and will be released at the end.

    Given a cost of capital of 10% and rounding to the nearest £1,000, what is the minimum acceptable contract price to be received at the end of the contract?

    A   £151,000

    B   £154,000

    C   £183,000

    D   £187,000   LO 4c

16 A company has identified two mutually-exclusive projects which have an equivalent effect on the risk profile of the company.

	Project I	Project II
Discounted payback period	2.8 years	3.2 years
Net present value	£17,200	£15,700
Internal rate of return	18%	22%
Average accounting rate of return	19%	21%

Cost of capital is 15%.

Assuming that the directors wish to maximise shareholder wealth and that no shortage of capital is expected, which project should the company choose and why?

A   Project I because it has the shorter payback period

B   Project I because it has the higher net present value

C   Project II because it has the higher internal rate of return

D   Project II because it has the higher accounting rate of return   LO 4d

17 A group of projects all involve the same initial outflow followed by a series of constant annual cash inflows. The projects all have the same lives.

What is the validity of the following statements?

(1)   A ranking of the projects by NPV gives the same order as ranking by payback.

(2)   A ranking of the projects by IRR gives the same order as ranking by payback.

	Statement 1	Statement 2
A	True	True
B	True	False
C	False	False
D	False	True

LO 4d

18 Alesme Ltd needs to replace a major item of capital equipment in five years' time. The estimated replacement cost will be £750,000. Funds for the replacement will be provided by setting aside five equal annual sums and investing them at 10%. The first amount will be invested immediately, the last in four years' time.

What is the annual amount to set aside (to the nearest £100)?

A   £111,700

B   £122,800

C   £179,900

D   £197,800   LO 4c

19 An investment of £50,000 to be made on 31 December 20X8 will produce an annual return of £7,000 in perpetuity, with the first income occurring on 1 January 20X9.

What (to the nearest £10) is the net present value of this investment on 31 December 20X7 discounted at 12%?

A   £2,090

B   £7,440

C   £8,330

D   £13,690

LO 4c

---

20 Kennett plc is about to undertake a project requiring an investment of £305,000 to generate equal annual inflows of £61,000 in perpetuity.

If the first inflow from the investment arises at the same time as the initial investment, what is the IRR of the project?

A   20%

B   25%

C   400%

D   500%

LO 4c

---

21 A company is considering investing £400,000 in equipment that will produce annual savings of £116,300 for five years.

If the investment is made on 1 January 20X0 and the savings are receivable from 31 December 20X1 to 31 December 20X5, the internal rate of return of the investment is approximately

A   10%

B   14%

C   16%

D   29%

LO 4c

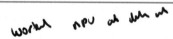

22 Devereaux Ltd is considering investing in a project with the following cash flows:

Year	Cash flow £'000
0	(500)
1	1,150
2	(660)

The project has a negative net present value of £3,401 at a 5% discount rate, and a positive net present value of £945 at 15%.

Which of the following is the approximate internal rate(s) of return of the project?

A   10% only

B   13% only

C   10% and 20%

D   110% and 120%

LO 4c

23 A company is considering a project which has an initial outflow followed by several years of cash inflows, with a cash outflow in the final year.

How many internal rates of return could there be for this project?

A   Only two

B   Either one or two

C   Either zero or two

D   Zero, one or two   LO 4d

24 What is the payback period of the following investment?

Year 0:	£400,000 spent on a new machine
Years 1 to 5:	£70,000 cash inflow per annum
Years 6 to 10:	£50,000 cash inflow per annum
Year 11:	Machine sold for £72,857

A   Seven years

B   Six years

C   Five years

D   Four years   LO 4c

25 Given a cost of capital of 10%, what is the discounted payback period of the following investment?

Year 0:	£300,000 spent on a new machine
Years 1 to 5:	£70,000 cash inflow per annum
Years 6 to 10:	£50,000 cash inflow per annum
Year 11:	Machine sold for £72,857

A   5.25 years

B   6.00 years

C   6.25 years

D   7.00 years   LO 4c

26 A project analyst has just completed the following evaluation of a project which has an initial cash outflow followed by several years of cash inflows:

Internal rate of return (IRR)   15% pa

Discounted payback period (DPP)   7 years

She then realises that the company's annual cost of capital is 12% not 10% and revises her calculations.

Select the option for what will happen to each of the IRR and DPP figures when the calculations are revised.

IRR

A   No change

B   Increase

C   Decrease

DPP

D   No change

E   Increase

F   Decrease   LO 4c

 27 For a project with a normal pattern of cash flows (ie, an initial outflow followed by several years of inflows) the internal rate of return is the interest rate that equates the present value of expected future cash inflows to

A   the project's cost of capital

B   zero

C   the terminal (compounded) value of future cash receipts

D   the initial cost of the investment outlay   LO 4d

28 A project has an initial cash outflow followed by a series of positive future cash inflows where the internal rate of return is unique and the net present value is positive at the opportunity cost of capital.

Which of the following statements is true for this project?

A   The internal rate of return is always greater than the opportunity cost of capital.

B   The internal rate of return is sometimes lower than the opportunity cost of capital.

C   The internal rate of return is always lower than the opportunity cost of capital.

D   The internal rate of return is sometimes greater than the opportunity cost of capital.   LO 4d

29 A company has identified three independent projects, X, Y and Z. It has estimated the cash flows and positive internal rates of return (IRRs) as follows:

Year	Project X £	Project Y £	Project Z £
0	(25,000)	82,000	(50,000)
1	–	(20,000)	127,500
2	–	(20,000)	(78,750)
3	20,000	(20,000)	–
4	40,000	(20,000)	–
5	(27,938)	(20,000)	–
IRRs	10%	7%	5% and 50%

If the three projects are of equivalent risk and the company aims to maximise shareholder wealth, at which of the following costs of capital would all three projects be deemed to be acceptable by the company?

A   12%

B   8%

C   6%

D   4%

LO 4c

30 A company is to spend £60,000 on a machine that will have an economic life of ten years and no residual value. Depreciation is to be charged using the straight-line method. Estimated operating cash flows are:

Year	£
1	– 2,000
2	+ 13,000
3	+ 20,000
4–6	+ 25,000 each year
7–10	+ 30,000 each year

What is the average accounting rate of return (ARR), calculated as average annual profits divided by the average investment?

A   75%

B   55%

C   38%

D   28%

LO 4c

31 A project has an initial investment cost of £200,000. It is expected to generate a net cash inflow of £20,000 at the end of its first year. This will rise to £25,000 at the end of the second year and remain at £25,000 per annum in perpetuity. The relevant cost of capital is expected to be 8% in the first year and 10% in the second and subsequent years.

What is the net present value of the project (to the nearest £100)?

A   £29,000

B   £45,800

C   £50,000

D   £68,500

LO 4c

32 A project can be expected to generate ten annual cash inflows of £30,000 starting **immediately**. The project requires an initial cash outlay of £150,000 and a final cash outlay at the end of ten years of £50,000.

If the annual cost of capital is 10%, what is the net present value of the project (to the nearest £100)?

   A   £15,100

   B   £23,500

   C   £31,600

   D   £33,500

LO 4c

33 A conventional project has a payback period of 5 years and yields a constant annual cash flow. The cost of capital is 20%.

Which of the following statements is true?

   A   The net present value of the project must always be positive.

   B   The net present value of the project must always be negative.

   C   The internal rate of return of the project must equal 20%.

   D   The average accounting rate of return is never less than zero.

LO 4d

34 Soyuz Ltd is considering two separate investment projects. Both projects involve an initial outlay and both are expected to produce positive annual net cash flows throughout their expected lives. The projects are not mutually exclusive. The company uses the net present value (NPV) method and internal rate of return (IRR) method to evaluate its investment projects.

The following statements have been made in relation to the above projects:

   (1)   The IRR method may produce multiple solutions for one or both of the projects.

   (2)   The IRR method and NPV method may not give the same decision concerning acceptance or rejection of the projects.

   (3)   The IRR method and NPV method may not rank the projects in the same order of acceptability.

Which of the above statements are correct?

   A   (1) and (2)

   B   (1) and (3)

   C   (2) and (3)

   D   (3) only

LO 4d

35 Projects X and Y both have an initial outflow followed by a series of inflows. At an interest rate of 15% project Y has the greater Net Present Value (NPV). The discount rate at which both projects have the same NPV is greater than 15%, but less than the Internal Rates of Return of either individual project.

Which diagram best represents the relationship between the NPVs of the projects and the discount rate?

Diagram A

Diagram B

Diagram C

Diagram D

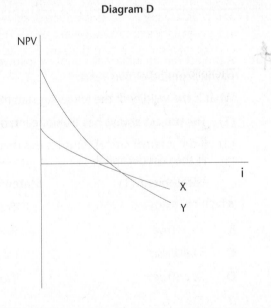

A   Diagram A

B   Diagram B

C   Diagram C

D   Diagram D

LO 4d

36   A project has an initial outflow followed by several years of inflows.

What would be the effects on the internal rate of return (IRR) of the project and its payback period of an increase in the company's cost of capital?

	IRR	Payback period
A	Increase	Increase
B	Increase	No change
C	No change	Increase
D	No change	No change

LO 4c

37   A project has a normal pattern of cash flows (ie, an initial outflow followed by several years of inflows).

What would be the effects on the internal rate of return (IRR) of the project and its discounted payback period (DPP) of an increase in the company's cost of capital?

	IRR	DPP
A	Increase	Decrease
B	Increase	Increase
C	No change	Increase
D	No change	Decrease

LO 4c

 38   A project has an initial cash outflow followed by three annual positive cash inflows and has a payback period of two years.

What is the validity of the following statements?

(1)   The project always has a unique internal rate of return.

(2)   If the internal rate of return is less than the cost of capital then the project has a positive NPV at the cost of capital.

	Statement (1)	Statement (2)
A	False	True
B	True	False
C	False	False
D	True	True

LO 4d

 39   A company is considering a two-year project which has two annual internal rates of return, namely 10% and 25%. The sum of the undiscounted cash flows is positive.

The project will necessarily have a positive net present value, when the annual cost of capital is:

A   More than 25%

B   More than 10%

C   Between 10% and 25%

D   Less than 25%

LO 4c

40 A project with an initial cash outflow of £55,000 was expected to have the following cash inflows which arise at the end of each year:

Year 1   £19,000

Year 2   £19,000

Year 3   £19,000

Year 4   £19,000

Subsequently it was discovered that the cash inflow at the end of Year 3 had been underestimated by £6,000. What would be the effect on the project's internal rate of return (IRR) and its payback period?

	IRR	Payback period
A	Increase	No change
B	Increase	Decrease
C	Decrease	No change
D	Decrease	Decrease

LO 4c

41 A company is considering undertaking a cost reduction project which will require an outlay in one year's time (t_1) of £900,000. Savings in costs are likely to amount to £400,000 at t_2, and £600,000 at t_3. The company's cost of capital is 10% p.a.

If all cash savings are deemed to arise at the end of each year, what (to the nearest £1,000) is the NPV of the project?

A   £(41,000)

B   £(37,000)

C   £41,000

D   £37,000

LO 4c

42 A company has £75,000 in a bank account as at 31 December 20X0. The company then deposits £4,000 in the account at the end of each of the next three years (ie, 20X1, 20X2, 20X3).

If all amounts in the account earn annual interest at 8% per annum, what will be the balance on the account at 1 January 20X3?

A   £82,133

B   £95,800

C   £96,466

D   £107,464

LO 4c

Sunshine Ltd

Sunshine Ltd (Sunshine) manufactures and sells a range of three umbrellas – the Standard, the Easy Opener and the Dome. Production and sales data for April was as follows:

	Standard	Easy Opener	Dome
Selling price	£36 per unit	£10 per unit	£25 per unit
Variable materials	£6 per unit	£2 per unit	£5 per unit
Variable labour	£6 per unit	£2 per unit	£4 per unit
Variable production overhead	£2 per unit	£1 per unit	£2 per unit
Actual production	10,000 units	6,000 units	4,000 units
Closing inventory	1,000 units	1,000 units	1,000 units

The variable labour cost is £10 per hour and Sunshine's fixed overheads for April were £88,000.

Calculate the total value of the closing inventory for each product under marginal costing:

£

Standard   [14,000]

Easy Opener   [5,600]

Dome   [11,000]

Sunshine is considering the impact of changing to absorption costing.

Calculate the fixed overhead absorption rate per labour hour for April:

£ per labour hour

Fixed overhead absorption rate   [9.67]   3

During May the fixed overhead absorption rate was calculated as £15 per labour hour and the value of the closing inventory under marginal costing, and the number of units, was as below. The labour cost per hour and per unit remained at their April values.

	Closing inventory value £	Closing inventory Units
Standard	19,500	1,500
Easy Opener	3,000	500
Dome	5,000	500

Calculate the total value of the closing inventory for May for each product under absorption costing.

£

Standard   [ ]

Easy Opener   [ ]

Dome   [ ]

During June Sunshine sold all of the opening inventory and all the units it manufactured during the month. Sales price and marginal cost information for June was as follows:

	Standard	Easy Opener	Dome
Selling price (per unit)	£36	£10	£25
Marginal cost (per unit) as May	£13	£6	£10

Assuming the same actual production data and fixed production overheads in June as for April, complete the table below which calculates Sunshine's gross profit for June under marginal costing and absorption costing.

	Marginal costing £	Absorption costing £
Sales revenue		
Standard	324,000	324,000
Easy Opener	50,000	50,000
Dome	75,000	75,000
Total sales revenue	449,000	449,000
Total marginal cost of sales	(177,000)	
Total absorption cost of sales		(170,000)
Fixed production overheads	(88,000)	
Gross profit	184,000	279,000

During July sales matched production and Sunshine was again left holding no inventories for any of its products.

Assuming the same actual production data and costs in July as for April, select whether the gross profit in July was

A Higher under marginal costing
B Higher under absorption costing
C Exactly the same under absorption and marginal costing

2 Kingsman Ltd

Kingsman Ltd (Kingsman) started business on 1 September manufacturing a single product, the A356. The budgeted production cost per unit of the A356 is as follows:

	£
Variable materials	78
Variable labour	12
Variable production overheads	6
Fixed production overheads	18

The budget showed production and sales for the first six months of 1,200 units. The budgeted selling price is £170 per unit.

The budgeted selling, distribution and administration costs are as follows:

Fixed	£36,000 per annum
Variable	£2.50 per unit

Inventory at the end of September was 20 units of the A356. In October Kingsman sold 150 units and manufactured 155 units. Budgeted fixed costs are incurred evenly per month. Actual costs and the selling price were as budgeted except for the fixed selling, distribution and administration costs, which were 12.5% lower than budgeted.

Calculate the profit or loss for October using both absorption costing and marginal costing:

Enter costs as negative values

	Absorption £	Absorption £	Marginal £	Marginal £
Sales		25 500		25 500
Variable production costs	-14 880		-14 880	
Fixed production costs absorbed	-2 790		0	
Opening inventory	2 280		1 920	
Closing inventory	2 850		2 400	
Production cost of sales		(17 020)		(14 400)
Under/over absorption		(810)		—
Variable selling, administration and distribution		-375		-375
Fixed selling, administration and distribution		-2 620		-2 545
Fixed production costs		—		-3 600
Profit/loss		4 960		7 100

In the second six months of the year Kingsman plans to introduce the B786, a deluxe version of the A356. The budgeted total absorption cost for the B786 is £420 per unit including £40 per unit for fixed overheads. In order to set a selling price Kingsman plans to use a margin of 25% on the absorption cost.

If there is no inventory of the B786 at the end of the first six months of production, will the profits calculated under marginal costing be higher than, lower than or the same as those calculated under absorption costing?

Use the drop down to select from:

Higher
Lower
Same

Calculate the per cent mark-up for the B786 using marginal costing and the planned selling price.

47	%

3 / Numan Ltd

Numan Ltd (Numan) began manufacturing a new product named Gazza in March. The budgeted data per unit of Gazza was as follows:

	Cost	Resource required
Variable materials	£48 per m^2	5m^2
Variable labour	£16 per hour	3.5 hours
Variable production overheads	£6 per hour	As labour

Calculate the budgeted prime cost per Gazza for March:

£   296   2 S

The budgeted cost and resource requirements for March were all met except for materials price and usage. Owing to higher quality supplies, only 4.5m^2 of material were actually used per Gazza but at a cost of £52 per m^2. Numan absorbs fixed overheads into all its products using a rate of 115% of actual materials cost.

Calculate the actual absorption cost per Gazza for March:

£ 58   2.7   2.5

During April the actual absorption cost per Gazza was £592 and Numan set a target of a 33 1/3% margin on the selling price per Gazza.

Calculate the selling price per Gazza in April:

£ 888   2.5   2.5

During May Numan changed the production process. This resulted in a saving of 30 minutes of labour time per Gazza compared with March. Materials actual price and usage were as in March. Actual labour and variable production overhead costs were as March's budget. Numan decided to absorb fixed overheads at a rate of 60% of prime cost.

Calculate the actual absorption cost per Gazza in May:

£ 479   2S

In June, the materials usage and labour and variable overhead costs were as the March budget but materials were 10% cheaper per m^2. The labour time per unit was the same as in May. The fixed overhead absorption rate was £56 per Gazza and 1,400 units were produced.

Calculate the actual marginal cost per Gazza in June:

£ 338

Before finalising the selling price for July, which was to be based on the June costs, the accountant noticed an error in the costing information and this resulted in the actual marginal cost per unit for June being corrected. The fixed overhead per Gazza remained at its June level. A target mark-up on absorption cost was now set.

Using a corrected marginal cost of £302 and a target mark-up on absorption cost of 22%, calculate the selling price for July:

£ 434   2

Numan's accountant decided to experiment with different ways of calculating the fixed overhead absorption rate in August. In particular she wanted to see the effect of using a blanket absorption rate (based on all of Numan's products) on selling prices. The target mark-up remained at 22%.

The following actual data from August is available:

Data related to Gazzas

Total variable cost per unit	£305
Units produced	1,450
Fixed overheads	£82,650
Labour hours per unit	3

Data related to all of Numan's products

Total fixed overheads	£1,239,500
Total number of units produced	18,500

Calculate the difference in the selling price of Gazzas that results from switching from a fixed overhead absorption rate based on Gazza's labour hours to a blanket fixed overhead absorption rate based on all of Numan's products:

£   12

The budgeted blanket fixed overhead absorption rate for August was £66.25 per unit of output.

Calculate the total under or over absorption of fixed overheads for all of Numan's products using the blanket rate in August:

£ 1387 | Use drop down to select from:
| Under absorption |
| Over absorption |

4 Oaklea plc

Oaklea plc manufactures high quality dining tables. The standard cost per table is as follows:

		£
Materials	4 kg @ £10/kg	40
Labour	12 hours @ £16/hour	192
Variable overheads	12 hours @ £4/hour	48
Fixed overheads	12 hours @ £2.50/hour	30
Total absorption cost		310

The budgeted production and sales for each month are 400 tables selling for £600 each.

In April everything went according to budget except that only 380 tables were sold.

Calculate the difference between the absorption costing and marginal costing profits for April:

Difference   £   600

Actual results for May are as follows:

6% fewer tables than budgeted were produced and sold at a price of £620 each. 1,600 kg of materials were used costing £16,800. Labour was paid £69,020 for 4,060 hours. Fixed and variable overheads were £13,050 and £17,255 respectively.

Complete the table to generate the marginal costing operating statement for May.

Make **one** entry (adverse or favourable) for each variance **and** enter a zero or dash in the other column.

Enter the net total of adverse and favourable variances as either a positive number (favourable total) or negative number (adverse total) in the final column.

Operating statement for May

	Favourable £	Adverse £	£
Budgeted profit			116 000
Sales volume variance		7680	
Sales price variance	7520		
Cost variances			
Materials price		800	
Materials usage		960	
Labour rate		4000	
Labour efficiency	7232		
Variable overhead rate		1015	
Variable overhead efficiency	1808		
Fixed overhead expenditure		1050	
Total variances	16560		975
Actual profit			116975

5 VanHensen plc

VanHensen plc has two production departments (Assembly and Finishing) and two service departments (Stores and Maintenance). Its budgeted overheads for the next quarter (July to September) are as follows:

	£
Rent and rates	80,000
Plant depreciation	100,000
Light and heat	50,000
Canteen costs	85,000
Finishing costs	32,000

These overheads are to be allocated and apportioned as fairly as possible to the four departments using the information contained in the table below.

	Assembly	Finishing	Stores	Maintenance
Plant cost (£)	25,000	60,000	7,500	7,500
Number of employees	10	20	10	10
Floor area (m^2)	2,000	4,000	3,000	1,000

Allocate and apportion the budgeted overheads to the four departments:

	Assembly £	Finishing £	Stores £	Maintenance £
Rent and rates	16000	32000	24000	8000
Plant depreciation	25000	60,000	7500	7500
Light and heat	10,000	20,000	15000	5000
Canteen costs	10,000	20,00	110000	110000
Finishing costs		32000		

In the following quarter (October to December) VanHensen's accountant has already completed the initial allocation and apportionment of budgeted overheads to the four departments and now wishes to reapportion the service department overheads to the production departments. He has provided the following information:

	Assembly *50*	Finishing *20*	Stores	Maintenance *30*
Total overhead (£)	70,000	185,000	65,000	38,000
Plant cost (£)	25,000	60,000	7,500	7,500
Number of employees	10	20	10	10
Floor area (m²)	2,000	4,000	3,000	1,000

Stores works 50% of the time for Assembly, 30% for Maintenance and the balance for Finishing. Its costs should be reapportioned first. Maintenance looks after the plant in each department.

Reapportion the service department overheads (Stores and Maintenance) to the production departments (Assembly and Finishing):

	Assembly £	Finishing £	Stores £	Maintenance £
Total overhead	70,000	185,000	65,000	38,000
Stores reapportionment	32500	13004	(65000)	14800 *3*
Revised total overheads (enter figures in all 4 boxes)	102500	198000	—	57800 *1*
Maintenance reapportionment	16912	40388	—0	(57800) *2*
Revised total overheads (enter figures in all 4 boxes)	119412	238312	—	— *1*

In the next quarter (January to March) the budgeted overhead in Finishing was £243,000 and the budgeted labour hours were 20,250. The budgeted overhead absorption rate was £8 per machine hour in Assembly based on budgeted labour hours of 15,000. In fact 15,876 hours were actually worked.

Calculate the budgeted overhead absorption rate per labour hour in Finishing:

£ 12

Calculate the under or over absorption of overheads in Assembly:

£ 7008	Use the drop down to select from:
	Under absorption
	Over absorption

1
2

6 Basket Ltd

Basket Ltd (Basket) produces a range of three picnic products: Large Hampers, Medium Hampers and Small Hampers. The budgeted data per Large Hamper for January was as follows:

	Cost	Resource required
Variable materials (all imported)	£6 per kg	5 kg
Variable labour	£8 per hour	3 hours
Variable production overheads	£2 per hour	As labour

Calculate the budgeted prime cost per Large Hamper for January:

£ 60

In January a total of 2,400 labour hours were worked, shared equally between the three types of hamper. The actual cost of Medium Hampers was the same as the January budgeted cost of Large Hampers, except for materials usage. Owing to their smaller size Medium Hampers used 4 kg of material per hamper. During January Basket incurred fixed production overheads of £85,000 of which £24,000 related to the manufacture of Medium Hampers. The other two sizes of hampers shared the remaining fixed production overhead equally. The accountant at Basket absorbed each hamper's fixed overheads into output using a rate per labour hour based upon actual labour hours worked.

Calculate the actual absorption cost per Medium Hamper in January:

£ 144

During January the actual absorption cost per Large Hamper was £165 and Basket's accountant recommended setting all its selling prices using a target mark-up of 40% on the actual absorption cost per unit.

Calculate the selling price per Large Hamper in January:

£ 231

During February, Basket took delivery of new weaving equipment that resulted in a 22% reduction in the labour time per unit for each hamper size from the January level. However, as a result of the new equipment, February's fixed production overheads were 10% higher than their level in January. Material costs and usage and variable overheads were at the same level as budgeted for January, as was the volume of output for all products.

Calculate the fixed overhead absorption rate per labour hour in February for Large Hampers:

£ 53

During March, the materials usage and variable overhead costs for Large Hampers were the same as February but due to movements in foreign exchange rates the materials cost was 15% higher per kg. The labour time per unit was the same as the January budget adjusted for the saving made in February. The fixed overhead absorption rate was £48 per hamper.

Calculate the absorption cost per Large Hamper in March:

£ 106

When preparing the monthly cost reports for March, Basket's accountant calculated the absorption cost per Small Hamper to be £84. In order to stimulate demand a target margin of 20% was set.

Calculate the selling price per Small Hamper for March:

£ 105

Basket's board asked the accountant to demonstrate the effect of calculating the fixed overhead absorption rate in different ways. In particular it wanted to see the effect of using a blanket absorption rate (based on all of Basket's hampers) on selling prices. The target margin remained at 20%.

During April Basket manufactured 1,000 hampers of each size (3,000 in total) and the variable cost per Large Hamper was £100. Total fixed overheads were £88,000 of which 30% were attributable to Large Hampers. Labour hours per unit were 80% of the original January budget.

Calculate the decrease in the selling price per Large Hamper that results from switching to a fixed overhead rate absorption rate based on the labour hours for Large Hamper's from a blanket fixed overhead absorption rate based on all three hamper sizes:

£ 4

The budgeted company wide blanket fixed overhead absorption rate for April was £38 per hamper.

Calculate the total under or over absorption of fixed overheads for all three hamper sizes using Basket's wide blanket absorption rate in April:

£ 26,000	Use drop down to select from:
	Under absorption
	Over absorption

7 Geartop plc

Geartop plc (Geartop) manufactures components for the car industry. Data for three of its products for July was as follows:

	AVX12	PUH78	YTF65
Selling price per unit	£45	£60	£70
Variable materials per unit	£15	£14	£21
Variable labour per unit	£6	£8	£9
Variable production overhead per unit	£2	£3	£4
Actual production (units)	3,000	2,500	1,800

Closing inventory (in units) for each product was 10% of July's production. The variable labour rate is £12 per hour and Geartop's fixed overheads for these three products for July were £80,000. There was no opening inventory of any of the products.

Calculate the total value of the cost of sales for each product for July using marginal costing:

	£
AVX12	62 100
PUH78	58 000
YTF65	55 080

Geartop's accountant now wishes to change to absorption costing.

Calculate the fixed overhead absorption rate as a percentage of the labour cost for July:

	% of labour cost
Fixed overhead absorption rate	147

During August the fixed overhead absorption rate was calculated as £18 per labour hour and the value of the closing inventory using absorption costing, and number of units, was as below. The labour cost per hour and per unit remained at their July values.

	Closing inventory £	Closing inventory units
AVX12	7,000	200
PUH78	6,000	150
YTF65	5,000	100

Calculate the total value of the closing inventory for each product line for August using marginal costing.

	£
AVX12	5200
PUH78	4200
YTF65	3650

During September Geartop sold all the units it produced during the month together with the entire opening inventory of the three product lines. Sales price, absorption cost, production and inventory information for September was as follows:

	AVX12	PUH78	YTF65
Selling price (per unit)	£45	£60	£70
Total absorption cost (per unit) as of August	£35	£40	£50
Actual production (units)	3,000	2,500	1,800
Opening inventory (units)	200	150	100

Assuming fixed production overheads of £81,300 were incurred during September and that there was a total of £4,950 of fixed production overheads included in the absorption costing value of opening inventory, complete the table below which calculates Geartop's profit for September under marginal costing and absorption costing.

	Marginal costing £	Absorption costing £
Sales revenue		
AVX12		
PUH78		
YTF65		
Total sales revenue		
Total marginal cost of sales		
Total absorption cost of sales		
Fixed production overheads	(81,300)	
Gross profit		

In October Geartop sold all the units of each product that it produced.

Assuming the same actual production data and costs in October as for September, select whether the gross profit in October was:

A Higher under marginal costing
B Higher under absorption costing
C Exactly the same under absorption and marginal costing

8 Borehole Ltd

Borehole Ltd (Borehole) is a specialist manufacturer of water pumps for the water extraction industry. Borehole produces three types of pumps and data for these for May was as follows:

	High Load	Standard Load	Low Load
Actual production (units)	250	400	500
Selling price per unit	£265	£220	£195
Variable materials per unit	£150	£125	£100
Variable labour per unit	£36	£36	£30
Variable production overhead per unit	£20	£18	£16
Closing inventory (units)	25	30	10

Borehole has a variable labour rate of £10 per hour and its fixed overheads for these three pumps for May totalled £22,000. There was no opening inventory of any of the pumps.

Calculate the total value of the cost of sales for each pump for May using marginal costing:

	£
High load	
Standard load	
Low load	

The board of directors of Borehole has decided to stop using marginal costing and instead adopt absorption costing.

Calculate the fixed overhead absorption rate as a percentage of the labour cost for May:

	% of labour cost
Fixed overhead absorption rate	57%

During June Borehole's accountant calculated the company's fixed overhead absorption rate as £6 per labour hour. She also calculated the value of the closing inventory for each pump type using absorption costing as below. The labour cost remained at £10 per hour.

	Closing inventory £	Closing inventory units
High load	4,600	20
Standard load	6,000	30
Low load	800	5

Calculate the total value of the closing inventory for each pump type for June using marginal costing.

	£
High load	4,168
Standard load	5,352
Low load	716

July was a very dry month with almost no rainfall and as a consequence Borehole sold all the pumps it could produce during the month together with the entire opening inventory of the three pump types. Fixed production overheads for July were £31,000 and the sales price, absorption cost, production and inventory information for July was as follows:

	High load	Standard load	Low load
Selling price (per unit)	£270	£230	£195
Total absorption cost (per unit) as June	£230	£200	£160
Opening inventory (units)	20	30	5
Actual production (units)	300	400	600

Assuming there was a total of £1,170 of fixed production overheads included in the absorption costing value of opening inventory, complete the table below which calculates Borehole's profit for July under both marginal costing and absorption costing.

	Marginal costing £	Absorption costing £
Sales revenue		
High load	86,400	86,400
Standard load	98,900	98,900
Low load	117,975	117,975
Total sales revenue	303,275	303,275
Total marginal cost of sales	226,300	
Total absorption cost of sales		256,000
Fixed production overheads	(31,000)	
Gross profit	45,975	46,875

In August the dry weather ended and Borehole did not sell all the pumps that it produced but the month's production data and costs were the same as in July.

Select whether Borehole's profit in August was:

A   Higher under marginal costing
B   Higher under absorption costing
C   Exactly the same under absorption and marginal costing

9 Hector plc

Hector plc (Hector) provides a number of different services from two service departments (Service 1 and Service 2) that are supported by two other departments (Canteen and Administration). Hector's budgeted overheads for the next six months (January to June) are as follows:

	£
Rent and business rates	500,000
Fixtures depreciation	700,000
Electricity, gas and water	175,000
Supervisors' salaries	750,000
Canteen costs	60,000

Canteen takings for the next six months are budgeted at £10,000.

These overheads are to be allocated and apportioned to the four departments using the information gathered below.

	Service 1	Service 2	Canteen	Administration
Floor area (m²)	3,000	4,000	1,500	1,500
Fixtures cost (£'000)	120	80	50	100
Number of employees	40	30	5	25

Allocate and apportion the overheads to the four departments:

	Service 1 £	Service 2 £	Canteen £	Administration £
Rent and rates	150,000	200,000	75,000	75,000
Fixtures depreciation	240,000	160,000	100,000	200,000
Electricity, gas and water	52,500	70,000	26,250	26,250
Supervisors' salaries	300,000	225,000	37,500	187,500
Canteen costs	–	–	50,000	

In the following six months (July to December) Hector's accountant has already completed the initial allocation and apportionment of budgeted overheads to the four departments and now wishes to reapportion the canteen and administration overheads to the two service departments. He has provided the following information:

	Service 1	Service 2	Canteen	Administration
Total apportioned overhead (£)	740,000	650,000	280,000	500,000
Floor area (m²)	3,000	4,000	1,500	1,500
Fixtures cost (£'000)	120	80	50	100
Number of employees	40	30	5	25

Reapportion the Canteen and Administration overheads to Service 1 and Service 2:

	Service 1 £	Service 2 £	Canteen £	Maintenance £
Total overhead	740,000	650,000	280,000	500,000
First reapportionment	214,285	285,713	(280,000)	(500,000)
Revised total overheads (enter figures in all 4 boxes)	900,000	770,000	–	500,000
Second reapportionment	160,000	120,000	(280,000)	–
Revised total overheads (enter figures in all 4 boxes)	1,115,71	914,281	–	– 0

In the first six months of the following year Service 2 had budgeted overhead of £980,000 and budgeted labour cost of £2,940,000. For the same period Service 1 had budgeted and actual overhead of £1,200,000 and budgeted labour hours of 5,000 although actual hours worked were 5,344.

Calculate the budgeted overhead absorption rate as a percentage of labour cost in Service 2:

33	%

Calculate the under or over absorption of overheads in Service 1:

£ 8256	Use drop down to select from:
	Under absorption
	Over absorption

10 Oakbeam Ltd

Oakbeam Ltd (Oakbeam) is a manufacturer of kitchen furniture. It has two production departments (Cabinets and Worktops) that are supported by two non-production departments (Warehousing and Administration). Its budgeted overheads for this year are as follows:

	£
Rent and rates	60,000
Machinery depreciation	60,000
Building utility costs	90,000
Managers' salaries	120,000
Warehousing department costs	175,000
Administration department costs	50,000

These overheads are to be allocated and apportioned to the four departments as fairly as possible and the information below is available to help with this.

	Cabinets	Worktops	Warehousing	Administration
Direct labour cost (£'000)	65	35	50	100
Machinery cost (£'000)	400	300	300	0
Floor area (m²)	2,200	1,800	10,000	1,000

Allocate and apportion the overheads to the four departments:

	Cabinets £	Worktops £	Warehousing £	Administration £
Rent and rates	8800	7200	40	4000
Machinery depreciation	24000	18000	18,000	–
Building utility costs	13000	10800	60,000	6000
Managers' salaries	36000	18366	24000	48000
Warehousing department costs	–	–	175,000	
Administration department costs			–	50000

In the following year, Oakbeam's accountant has already completed an initial allocation and apportionment of budgeted overheads between its four departments. As a second stage she now wishes to reapportion the Warehousing and Administration department overheads to the two other departments. She has provided the following information:

	Cabinets	Worktops	Warehousing	Administration
Total overhead (£)	170,000	70,000	300,000	80,000
Direct labour cost (£'000)	70	30	50	100
Machinery cost (£'000)	400	300	300	-
Floor area (m²)	2,200	1,800	10,000	1,000

Administration costs are to be reapportioned first based on the direct labour cost in each department. Warehousing costs should then be apportioned between the other two departments based on machinery cost.

Reapportion the Warehousing and Administration department overheads to the Cabinets and Worktops departments:

	Cabinets £	Worktops £	Warehousing £	Administration £
Total overhead	170,000	70,000	300,000	80,000
Administration reapportionment				
Revised total overheads (enter figures in all 4 boxes)				—
Warehousing reapportionment				—
Revised total overheads (enter figures in all 4 boxes)			—	—

In the next year the Cabinets department had budgeted overhead of £400,000 and budgeted labour costs of £75,000. For the Worktops department the budgeted overhead absorption rate was £5 per £ of labour cost based on a budgeted labour cost of £35,000, although the actual labour cost turned out to be £33,365.

Calculate the budgeted overhead absorption rate as a percentage of labour cost in the Cabinets department:

	%

Calculate the under or over absorption of overheads in the Worktops department:

£	Use drop down box to select from:
	Under absorption
	Over absorption

11 Jitinder plc

Jitinder plc (Jitinder) started business on 1 January manufacturing a single product, the Gromett. The budget includes the following for production costs per Gromett:

Variable materials: 4kg @ £15/kg
Variable labour: 2.5 hours @ £16/hour
Variable production overheads: £10/unit

The budgeted production and sales for the first year is 4,800 Grometts, selling for a budgeted price of £300 each. Budgeted fixed production overheads are £192,000 per annum. Jitinder uses a pre-determined fixed overhead absorption rate.

Selling, administration and distribution costs are partly fixed and partly variable as follows:

Fixed   £27,000 per quarter
Variable   £7 per unit

Inventory at the end of January was 55 Grometts. In February Jitinder sold 440 Grometts and manufactured 420. Budgeted fixed costs are incurred evenly over the year. Actual costs and the selling price were as budget except for the fixed selling, administration and distribution costs, which were 12% higher than budgeted and fixed production overheads, which were £16,374.

Calculate the profit or loss for February using both absorption costing and marginal costing:

Enter costs as negative values.

	Absorption		Marginal	
	£	£	£	£
Sales		132 000		132 000
Variable production costs	+460200		-46200	
Fixed production costs absorbed	(+ 16800		0	
Opening inventory	8250		6050	
Closing inventory	5250		3850	
Production cost of sales		-66000		(48400
Under/over absorption		(426)		—
Variable selling, administration and distribution		-33000		(33000
Fixed selling, administration and distribution		(-10080		(-10080)
Fixed production costs		—		-16324
Profit/loss		53266		53566

In its second year of business Jitinder plans to introduce a basic version of its product known as the Salis, which is budgeted to have a far greater volume of sales than the Gromett and will be much easier to manufacture. The budgeted total absorption cost for the Salis is £80 per unit using traditional volume based absorption costing. In order to set a selling price Jitinder plans to use either a mark up of 25% or a margin of 25%.

If Jitinder were to switch to using Activity Based Costing (ABC), would the total cost per Salis be higher or lower than the cost calculated using traditional absorption costing?

Use the drop down to select from:

Higher
Lower

Calculate the difference in the price of a Salis from applying either a 25% mark-up or 25% margin.

12 Flag Ltd

Flag Ltd (Flag) has been trading for many years and manufactures just one product, the Standard. Flag's accountant has prepared a budget, for its next quarter (September to November) that shows the following production cost information per unit of Standard:

	£
Variable materials	3.50
Variable labour	6.50
Variable production overheads	1.00
Fixed production overheads	4.00
	15.00

Budgeted sales and production are to equal 4,400 units at a budgeted selling price of £35 per Standard.

Flag's accountant is aware from past experience that the company's sales, administration and distribution costs are partly fixed and partly variable as follows:

Variable element	£3.00 per unit
Fixed element	£12,000 per quarter

Inventory at the end of August was 115 Standards. In the quarter September to November, Flag manufactured 4,200 Standards and sold 4,215. Flag's budgeted fixed costs are incurred evenly throughout its financial year. Flag's actual costs and the selling price were as budget except for the fixed element of the sales, administration and distribution costs, which were 4% higher than budgeted.

Calculate Flag's profit or loss for the quarter September to November under both marginal costing and absorption costing:

Enter costs as negative values.

	Absorption £	Absorption £	Marginal £	Marginal £
Sales		147,565		147,515
Variable production costs	(46,100)		(46,100)	
Fixed production costs absorbed	(16,800)		—	
Opening inventory	1,725		1,265	
Closing inventory	1,500		1,100	
Production cost of sales		(62,925)		(46,305)
Under/over absorption		(800)		—
Variable sales, administration and distribution		(12,645)		(12,645)
Fixed sales, administration and distribution		(12,480)		(12,480)
Fixed production costs		(16,800)		(17,600)
Profit/loss		41,875		58,095

Following extensive market research, Flag has decided to launch a low cost product called the Substandard. The budgeted total absorption cost is £9 per Substandard including £2 per unit for fixed costs. In order to set a selling price Flag's accountant plans to apply a mark up of 60% to the total absorption cost. During the first year of manufacture the Substandard will not be marketed, with all production going into inventory. By the end of the second year of manufacture the aim is to keep inventory levels as close to zero as possible, with production more or less keeping pace with sales.

If there is a high inventory of the Substandard at the end of the first year it is manufactured, but no inventory at the end of the second year, will the profits calculated under absorption costing for the second year be higher or lower than those calculated under marginal costing?

Use the drop down to select from:

Higher
Lower

Calculate the % margin for the Substandard using marginal costing and the planned selling price.

	%

13 Hexabeast plc

Hexabeast plc manufactures up-market model figurines. The standard cost per unit of one of its products, the Grimmbo, is as follows:

		£
Plastic material	2kg @ £12/kg	24.00
Labour	3 hours @ £22/hour	66.00
Variable overheads	3 hours @ £5.50/hour	16.50

Budgeted production and sales for August are 1,200 units selling for £199.50 each. Budgeted fixed overheads are £300,000 per quarter incurred evenly each month.

Actual results for August are as follows:

1,290 units were produced and sold at a price that was £10 per unit less than the budget. The cost of material was £29,025 and there was a favourable usage variance of 0.2kg per unit because better quality plastic was used. Labour worked 3,600 hours and received a 3% pay rise at the start of August. Fixed and variable overheads were £98,765 and £21,600 respectively.

Complete the table below to generate the operating statement for August:

Make **one** entry (adverse or favourable) for each variance **and** enter a zero or dash in the other column.

Enter the net total of adverse and favourable variances as either a positive number (favourable total) or negative number (adverse total) in the final column.

Operating statement for August

	Favourable £	Adverse £	£
Budgeted contribution			111600
Sales volume variance	8376	–	
Sales price variance		12900	
Variable cost variances			
Materials price		1161	
Materials usage	3060		
Labour rate		2376	
Labour efficiency	5400		
Variable overhead rate		1800	
Variable overhead efficiency	1471		
Total variances			10245
Fixed overhead budgeted			100180
Fixed overhead expenditure variance			127
Actual profit			2350

14 Yarn & Co

Yarn & Co (Yarn) is an unincorporated business that manufactures a single type of wool, the Knit. The standard cost for a unit of Knit is as follows:

		£
Skilled labour	4 hours @ £10/hour	40
Raw material	4 metres @ £6/metre	24
Variable overheads	4 hours @ £4/hour	16

Yarn's budget for November is to manufacture and sell 1,200 units of Knit at a selling price of £105 per unit. Yarn has budgeted fixed overheads of £72,000 per annum, which are incurred evenly throughout the year.

Yarn's actual results for November are as follows:

In total 110% of the budgeted number units of Knit were manufactured and sold, although the average selling price achieved was £5 per unit below budget.

The total skilled labour variance was £2,200 adverse, with 5,200 hours worked. The total materials variance was also £2,200 adverse with raw materials usage of 5,100m. Yarn's fixed and variable overheads were £5,500 and £23,400 respectively.

Complete the operating statement table below for the month of November:

Make **one** entry (adverse or favourable) for each variance **and** enter a zero or dash in the other column.

Enter the net total of adverse and favourable variances as either a positive number (favourable total) or negative number (adverse total) in the final column.

	Favourable £	Adverse £	£
Budgeted contribution			60,000
Sales volume variance	3,000		
Sales price variance		(6660)	
Variable cost variances			
Skilled labour rate		(810)	
Skilled labour efficiency	860		
Materials price		(3280)	
Materials usage	1080		
Variable overhead rate	340	(1400)	
Variable overhead efficiency	320		
Total variances	5700	(15481)	(10,280)
Budgeted fixed overheads			(6660)
Fixed overhead expenditure variance			500
Actual profit			20,270

15 Johnson & Redmond plc

A newly established manufacturing company, Johnson & Redmond plc (Johnson & Redmond), manufactures three types of carton: Large, Medium and Small. The budgeted data for cartons for 20X1 was as follows:

	Cost	Resource required
Variable labour (all types of carton)	£8 per hour	2 hours
Variable material – Large	£2 per kg	2 kg
Variable material – Medium	£2 per kg	1.5 kg
Variable material – Small	£2 per kg	1 kg
Variable production overheads	£4 per hour	As labour

Calculate the budgeted prime cost per Large carton for 20X1:

£ 20

In 20X1 Johnson & Redmond worked 30,000 labour hours, split as follows:

	Labour hours
Small	8,000
Medium	12,000
Large	10,000

During the year the company incurred fixed production overheads of £336,000 of which £216,000 related to the manufacture of Large Cartons. Small and Medium cartons shared the remaining fixed production overhead equally. All fixed overheads are absorbed into output using a rate per labour hour based upon actual labour hours worked. Each carton took 2 hours to produce.

Calculate the actual absorption cost per unit of output for Medium cartons in 20X1:

£ 37

During 20X1 the actual absorption cost per Large carton was £44 and the accountant of Johnson & Redmond decided to set all its selling prices using a target mark up of 25% on the absorption cost per unit.

Calculate the selling price Large cartons in 20X1:

£ 55

During the following year, 20X2, Johnson & Redmond introduced a streamlined manufacturing process that resulted in a reduction of 10% in labour time per carton from the level in 20X1. However, as a result of other changes, the fixed production overheads were 5% higher than their level in 20X1. Material costs and usage and variable overheads were at the same level as for 20X1, as was the volume of output for all products.

Calculate the fixed overhead absorption rate per labour hour for Large cartons in 20X2:

£ 25

Johnson & Redmond's budget for the next year, 20X3, is to be set using the materials usage and variable overhead costs for all products as in 20X1 but due to lower import duties the raw materials cost is expected to be 5% lower per kg. The labour time per unit is budgeted to 90% of that in 20X1. The fixed overhead absorption rate for 20X3 is budgeted to be £28 per unit of output.

Calculate the budgeted absorption cost per Medium carton for 20X3:

£ 51

When the actual cost reports for 20X3 became available they showed that the absorption cost per unit for Small cartons was £40. In order to stimulate sales demand for 20X4 a target margin of 15% was set.

Using this data for Small cartons for 20X3 and the target margin, calculate the selling price for 20X4:

£ 47

Johnson & Redmond's managing director asked to see the effect of calculating the fixed overhead absorption rate in different ways. In particular she wanted to see the effect of using a blanket absorption rate (based on all of the company's products) on selling prices. The target margin remained at 15%.

During 20X4 the company manufactured 5,000 cartons of each size and the variable cost for a Medium carton was £50. In 20X4 total fixed overheads were £350,000 of which 35% were attributable to Medium cartons. Labour hours per unit remained in line with the 20X3 budget.

Calculate the decrease in the selling price of a Medium carton achieved by switching from a fixed overhead rate absorption rate based on the specific carton's labour hours to a single blanket fixed overhead absorption rate based on all three carton sizes:

£ 1.32

The budgeted company wide blanket fixed overhead absorption rate for 20X4 was £22.50 per carton.

Calculate the total under or over absorption of fixed overheads for all three carton sizes using the company wide blanket absorption rate in 20X4:

£	Use drop down box to select from:
	Under absorption
	Over absorption

Answer Bank

Chapter 1: The fundamentals of costing

1   A   **A unit of product or service in relation to which costs are ascertained**

The cost per hour of operating a machine and the cost per unit of electricity consumed are examples of the cost of input resources, which might form part of the total cost of a cost unit.

A measure of output of work in a standard hour is an indication of productivity.

2   C   **Dividends received**

Dividends received are not related to the production process. This is income received from investments. Cost accountants are only interested in income and costs relating to production (or manufacturing).

Indirect labour is incorrect. The cost accountant is interested in the cost of indirect labour as it affects the cost per unit of production.

Purchase of raw materials is incorrect. The cost accountant is interested in the cost of raw materials as it affects the cost per unit of production.

Factory rent is incorrect. The cost accountant is interested in factory rent as it affects the cost per unit of production.

3   B   **Be constant per unit of output**

Variable costs are constant per unit of output. As output changes, total variable costs will vary in direct proportion to the level of activity.

Variable costs are not conventionally deemed to be constant in total when the production volume changes. This is a definition of fixed costs, ie, costs which do not change as outputs change.

Variable costs are also not deemed to vary per unit of output as production volumes change. Variable costs are constant per unit regardless of output levels.

Variable costs do not vary, in total, from period to period when production is constant. If production is constant, variable costs will also be constant.

4   D   **Lease payments on a machine**

The decision to take out a lease would have been made by the finance function and not be of relevance to production.

A supervisor would be concerned with material costs because he is responsible for the efficiency with which materials are used.

A supervisor would be concerned with labour costs because he is responsible for the efficiency with which labour work.

A supervisor would be concerned with maintenance costs because he is responsible for the manner in which machines are operated.

SAMPLE PAPER

5   A   A selling and distribution cost

As the deliveries will only occur when a sale has been made it is therefore a selling and distribution cost.

Prime cost is the name given to the total of all the direct production costs, not a cost incurred when distributing goods after they have been sold.

Production overheads are the costs incurred in making goods which cannot be identified directly to the goods made by the company, not a cost incurred when distributing goods after they have been sold.

A direct production expense is incorrect. These are the expenses other than materials and labour costs which are incurred in full as a direct consequence of making the product, not a cost incurred when distributing goods after they have been sold.

6   C   £5.00

Cost per unit   = Total cost/Number of patients treated

                 = £1m/200,000 patients

                 = £5.00 per patient

If you answered £0.20 your calculation was upside down. The figure of £7.50 double counts the payments to doctors, which are already included in total costs. The answer of £2.50 was only the doctors' costs, which is understating the total cost.

7   A   £1,500

The fixed costs are those costs that remain unchanged irrespective of activity levels. The information given in the question regarding the activity levels is therefore irrelevant.

£4,800 is incorrect. You have calculated the total costs incurred at the given activity level, not the fixed costs.

£3,500 is incorrect. The fixed costs are those costs which are unaffected by changes in activity levels, which could be calculated by considering the total costs if both production and sales levels were 0.

£3,300 is incorrect. You have calculated the total variable cost incurred at the given activity level, not the fixed costs.

8   C   £36,744

	Shoe Type A	Shoe Type B
Units	2,100	4,400
Time (hrs)	(× 24 mins) = 840	(× 36 mins) = 2,640
Rate	£3.60 per unit	£6 per unit
Labour cost	£7,560	£26,400
Non productive time (20%)	840 × 0.20 = 168	2,640 × 0.20 = 528
Non productive cost @ £4/hr	£672	£2,112
Total cost	£8,232	£28,512

Therefore the correct answer

      = Total cost of shoe Type A + Total cost of shoe Type B

      = £8,232 + £28,512 = £36,744

If you answered £13,920 you simply calculated an hourly rate for the productive hours but took no account of the rate per unit or the payment for non-productive hours.

If you answered £33,960 you did not add the payment for non-productive hours.

The answer of £50,664 incorrectly allows £4 per hour for all productive hours, in addition to the piece rate payment.

9   A   A semi-variable cost

The basic salary is fixed, but the sales representative also receives commission, which increases as sales increase. The cost is therefore best described as semi-variable.

A fixed cost is incorrect. As the salary is made up of both fixed and variable elements it is a semi-variable cost.

A variable cost is incorrect. The commission is variable, but the sales representative also receives a basic salary which is fixed.

A production cost is incorrect. This cost relates to sales not to production.

10   A   The total of all direct costs

In other words, prime cost is the total of all the costs that can be directly attributed to a cost unit.

Total manufacturing cost would include overheads in addition to the costs that are directly attributable to a cost unit.

Fixed costs attributed to a cost unit are not the prime cost because the variable costs have not been considered.

Any cost which does not vary with changes in output levels is a description of a fixed cost.

11   D   A semi-variable cost

A semi-variable cost contains both fixed and variable components.

A direct cost is affected by changes in the level of activity, but may not be semi-variable.

A variable cost is wholly dependent on the level of activity.

An indirect cost may be fixed and/or variable but is not necessarily made up of both fixed and variable elements.

12   A   Variable costs

For example, fixed costs do not vary with output levels.

13   A   A semi-variable cost

As the salary contains both a fixed element (the basic wage) and a variable element (the £0.10 paid per unit) the wage expense is a semi-variable cost.

It is not a fixed cost, because the total amount paid each week varies with the amount produced during the week, nor a variable cost, as even if no units were produced the supervisor would still receive the basic salary (£100).

And finally it is not a step cost, because it does not remain constant for a given range of output, and then 'step up' to a new level, but increases (by £0.10) for each additional unit produced.

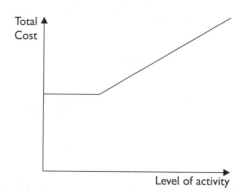

The cost consists of a fixed amount up to a certain level of activity which is represented by a straight horizontal line on the graph. At a certain point a variable element is introduced and the cost line slopes upwards at a constant rate as the level of activity increases.

15   A   A step cost

As the hiring cost remains fixed within certain activity levels it is a step cost.

Although the cost may increase with output it remains constant for certain activity levels. It is therefore not a variable cost.

If the factory made between 1 and 100 toys in one month the cost would be £1,000. However if they made 101 toys they would need two production lines, and therefore two machines. The cost would then be £2,000. As this cost can be seen to increase with output it cannot be fixed.

This cost remains constant within a range of activity levels. It is therefore not a semi-variable cost.

16   D   A fixed administrative cost

As the salary paid to the financial accountant is unlikely to change if output levels change the cost is fixed, and as the expense relates to the business's administration it is an administrative cost.

A variable administrative cost is incorrect. This cost is unlikely to vary as output changes, therefore this cost is more likely to be a fixed cost.

A fixed production cost is incorrect. An accountant's salary is incurred as part of the business's administration not production.

Prime cost is the total of all direct production costs. An accountant's salary is neither a direct cost, nor a production cost, and therefore would not be part of prime cost.

17   A   Electricity bills made up of a standing charge and a variable charge

The cost shown in the graph has a basic fixed element which is payable even at zero activity, with a variable element being added at a constant rate as activity increases. Therefore the correct answer is where electricity bills are made up of a standing charge and a variable charge. The cost depicted is known as a semi-variable cost.

18   A   C = 480 + 0.01T

A standing charge of £40/month is £480 per year. Costs then increase by £0.01/minute.

SAMPLE PAPER

19   A   Fixed costs = 500. Variable costs per unit are constant until output is 30, then additional costs per unit are higher.

The fixed costs are 500 because this is the single point at which the line crosses the y-axis (the cost incurred at zero activity). The gradient of the total cost line becomes steeper when output exceeds 30 units, which indicates a higher cost per unit for output above 30 units.

20 C Management accounts are usually prepared for internal use by an organisation's managers.

The management accounts provide information to managers within a business to help them to manage the business by making planning and control decisions. In contrast, the financial accounts are usually prepared for stakeholders external to the organisation.

The use of cost accounting systems is not restricted to manufacturing operations. Cost accounting information is also used in service industries, public sector bodies and not-for-profit organisations.

The format of management accounts is not regulated by accounting standards. No strict rules govern the way the management accounts are prepared or presented: the format is entirely at managers' discretion.

The financial accounting and cost accounting records are not prepared from different sets of basic data. Both systems record the same basic data for income and expenditure. However, each system has a different purpose and each therefore analyses the data in a different way.

21 D Cost per tonne-kilometre

The most useful cost unit from those described is a tonne-kilometre. This is a composite cost unit which takes account of both the weight carried and the distance travelled.

The cost per tonne carried is not as useful because it is affected by distance travelled. For example, it would not be possible to compare for control purposes the cost per tonne transported on a journey of 500 kilometres with the cost per tonne transported for 10 kilometres.

Similarly, the cost per kilometre travelled would be affected by the weight transported. It would not be as useful as the cost per tonne-kilometre for control by comparison.

The cost per driver hour would not be as useful as a cost per tonne-kilometre because it is distorted both by the weight carried and the distance travelled.

22 D Items (2) and (3) only

It would be appropriate to use the cost per invoice processed and the cost per supplier account for control purposes.

Postage cost, item (1), is an expense of the department but not a suitable unit for cost analysis and control.

23 C The line with the constant upward slope represents total costs; D represents fixed costs

The line with the constant upwards slope represents the total of fixed costs and variable costs, ie, total costs.

The point where the total costs line cuts the y-axis, D, represents the cost incurred at zero activity, ie, the fixed costs.

24 D Variable costs per unit are constant until output reaches Q after which further production incurs higher variable costs per unit

The line representing fixed costs remains horizontal for all levels of output, therefore the first two statements are incorrect.

The increase in the gradient of the total cost line at Q indicates that each unit, from that level of output onwards only, incurs a higher variable cost. Therefore the third statement is incorrect.

25 B,D,I

Labour costs will vary directly in proportion to the number of hours worked and therefore are a true variable cost

The factory rent will not vary even if output levels change and is therefore a fixed cost.

Salary plus profit related pay will contain a fixed element, the basic salary, plus an element that will vary depending upon the profits of the enterprise. Therefore this will be a semi-variable cost.

26   B, D

   A, C and E are all **elements** of cost.

27   D, E

   A, B and C are all cost objects.

28   C   Intimidation

   Threat of disciplinary proceedings or dismissal over a disagreement about the application of accounting principle or the way in which financial information is to be reported is an example of an intimidation threat.

SAMPLE PAPER

29   B   A framework-based approach

   The ICAEW Code of Ethics is a framework or ethics-based approach, which is the opposite of the compliance, rule or tick-box approach seen in other jurisdictions such as the US.

Chapter 2: Calculating unit costs (Part 1)

1   A   The basic pay of production line staff

If overtime is worked at the specific request of a customer then it is treated as a direct labour cost attributable to that job. However the premium paid for general overtime not required for a specific job is generally treated as an indirect cost.

The cost of indirect workers (production line supervisors) will usually be indirect labour costs (ie, overheads) as it will not be possible to trace them in full to individual cost units.

Idle time payments are indirect labour costs because it is not possible to trace them to specific cost units.

2   A   Factory overheads

Overtime premium payments are always classed as factory overheads unless the overtime is worked at the specific request of a customer (in order to complete the specific job more quickly) or worked regularly by a production department in the normal course of operations.

3   D   Factory overhead

Idle time is usually treated as an overhead because it cannot be identified with a specific cost unit. In this case the cost is incurred within the production department and is therefore a factory overhead.

4   C   £70

The indirect labour costs are made up of idle time costs and overtime premiums.

Idle time costs	= 10 hours × £5 per hour
	= £50
Overtime premium	= ½ × £5
	= £2.50 per hour
Overtime premium for 8 hours	= £2.50 × 8 hours
	= £20
Therefore indirect labour costs	= £50 + £20
	= £70

If you selected £20 you calculated the overtime premium correctly but did not add on the cost of idle time payments. Wages paid for idle time cannot be traced to a specific cost unit and are therefore a part of indirect labour cost.

If you selected £50 you classified the idle time payments correctly but did not add on the cost of the overtime premium. If the overtime had been worked for a specific cost unit then the premium could have been a direct labour cost of that unit, but this is not the case here.

If you selected £110 you included all of the overtime cost as an indirect labour cost. However, the basic pay for overtime hours can be traced to specific cost units and is therefore a direct labour cost.

5   B   (2) and (3) only

Labels can be identified with a specific cost unit and form a part of the product. Therefore, the cost of food labels is a direct cost.

Maintenance and cleaning wages (2) and (3) are indirect costs because they cannot be specifically identified with a specific cost unit.

6   D   Direct expenses

The cost of the tools is a **direct cost** of the job because it can be specifically identified with the job.

7   C   (1), (2) and (4) only

Statement (1) is correct. Direct costs are specific and traceable to the relevant product, service or department.

Statement (2) is correct. For example a departmental manager's salary is a direct cost of the department but it is an indirect cost of the individual cost units passing through the department.

Statement (3) is incorrect. This describes an indirect cost which much be apportioned between several cost objects because it cannot be specifically identified with any single one.

Statement (4) is correct. It is likely that if activity changes so will the expenditure on direct costs, as direct costs are usually costs such as materials, labour and other direct expenses.

8   B   Indirect costs are alternatively called overheads

Total direct costs are not always greater than total indirect costs. The relative size of direct and indirect costs varies according to the type of output, the industry, the technology and so on. For example, in highly automated service industries the direct material and direct labour costs are likely to be small relative to the indirect costs.

The fixed costs per unit are not the same at all levels of production. The total fixed cost will remain the same but the fixed cost **per unit** will reduce as output increases.

A direct cost will often be a variable cost, but it will not always be a variable cost. For example, the cost of hiring a special machine for a job is a direct cost of that job but it is also a fixed cost which remains the same irrespective of the level of output.

9   B,D,I

The repair person's wages can be analysed between specific jobs and accordingly would usually be classified as a direct cost. The cost is fixed because it does not vary with the level of activity.

The cost of electrical components can be traced as a direct cost of each job and the cost will increase as the level of activity increases.

The rent of the repair shop is an indirect cost because it cannot be traced to a specific repair job. It is a fixed cost because it does not vary with the level of activity.

10   A   Direct expense

The royalty cost can be traced in full to units of the company's product. Therefore it is a direct expense.

11   A   £220,000

MATERIALS CONTROL ACCOUNT

Opening inventories	£13,000	Returns	£25,000
Deliveries	£250,000	Issue to production	**£220,000**
		Closing inventory	£18,000
	£263,000		£263,000

12   B   First in, First out (FIFO)

     C   Last in, First out (LIFO)

     E   Standard cost

First in, Last out (FILO) and future anticipated cost are not recognised methods of valuing inventory.

13   B   £68,670

The FIFO method uses the cost of the older batches first.

Cost of units sold on 24 February	£
750 units @ £80	60,000
102 units @ £85	8,670
852 units	68,670

If you answered £68,160 you valued all of the units sold at the opening inventory cost of £80 per unit. However there are only 750 units held at this cost. The cost of the remainder of the units sold must be taken from the next batch received.

The option of £69,960 uses the LIFO basis rather than the required FIFO basis.

The option of £93,720 uses the sales revenue, not the cost of the units sold.

14   B   £23,760

The LIFO method uses the cost of the most recent batches first.

Cost of units sold on 24 February	£
90 product A @ £90	8,100
180 product A @ £85	15,300
582 product A @ £80	46,560
852	69,960

	£
Sales revenue = 852 units × £110	93,720
Less cost of units sold	69,960
Gross profit	23,760

The option of £17,040 values all the units sold at the cost of the latest batch received. However, there are only 90 units at this cost. The remaining units must be valued at the cost of earlier batches received.

If you selected the option of £69,960 you calculated the correct cost of goods sold, but the question asks for the gross profit earned.

The option of £93,720 is the sales revenue of the units sold, not the gross profit earned.

15   A   £33,696

Weighted average cost per unit:	£
330 units @ £75	24,750
180 units @ £80	14,400
90 units @ £85	7,650
600	46,800

Weighted average cost per unit	= £46,800/600
	= £78.00
Cost of units sold on 24 February	= £78.00 × 432 units
	= £33,696

The option of £34,560 uses a simple average cost of the three available batches, rather than a weighted average cost.

If you answered £35,280 you based your weighted average on the cost of two batches received in February. You did not take account of the unit cost of the opening inventory.

The option of £38,880 is the sales value of the units sold, not the weighted average cost.

16 B £590.85

		£
60	pixies received on day 3 of week 15 @ £7.96	477.60
15	pixies received in week 14 @ £7.55	113.25
75		590.85

If you selected £566.25 you ignored the receipts on day 3 of week 15 and based your calculations on the opening inventory. However the LIFO method uses the cost of the latest batch first.

The option of £593.25 would have been the correct cost of pixies issued if the FIFO method was used.

If you selected £597.00 you valued all of the pixies issued at the price of the latest batch received. However, there are only 60 units in this batch and the remaining units must be taken from the latest batch in the opening inventory.

17 D £3,605

Components issued on day 4 = 90 from week 10 receipts

Closing inventory week 12:

			£
Remaining	210	components from week 10 @ £6.50	1,365
	200	components from week 11 @ £6.25	1,250
	150	components from week 12 @ £6.60	990
	560		3,605

If you answered £585 you selected the cost of the issues rather than the value of the closing inventory.

The answers of £594 and £3,596 are the cost of the issues and the closing inventory respectively, using the LIFO valuation method.

18 D Student D

The LIFO method charges the latest prices paid to cost of sales. In a period of falling prices the latest prices will be the lowest prices. Therefore the student using the LIFO method would record the lowest cost of sales and the highest gross profit.

19 D (1), (2), (3) and (4)

With FIFO, the oldest prices are charged first to cost of sales and inventory is valued at the latest prices paid, which will be close to replacement cost.

With LIFO, the most recent prices are charged first to cost of sales, therefore inventories are issued at a price which is close to the current market value.

20 A Higher cost of sales and lower inventory value

The LIFO method charges the latest prices paid to cost of sales. In a period of rising prices the cost of sales will be higher than with FIFO. The remaining items in inventory will be valued at the older, lower prices.

Workings for questions 21 and 22

		Units	£/unit	Value FIFO £	Units	£/unit	Value LIFO £
Purchase	1/1	4,000	2.50	10,000	4,000	2.50	10,000
	31/1	1,000	2.00	2,000	1,000	2.00	2,000
		5,000		12,000	5,000		12,000
Sales	15/2	(3,000)	2.50	(7,500)	(1,000)	2.00	(2,000)
					(2,000)	2.50	(5,000)
		2,000		4,500	2,000		5,000
Purchase	28/2	1,500	2.50	3,750	1,500	2.50	3,750
		3,500		8,250	3,500		8,750
Sales	14/3	(500)	2.50	(1,250)	(500)	2.50	(1,250)
		3,000		7,000	3,000		7,500

21   C   £7,000

If you selected the wrong option then check your working carefully against the above table.

22   C   £7,500

If you selected the wrong option then check your working carefully against the above table.

23   C   Each time a purchase is made

Each time a purchase is made this is likely to change the average price of the items held in inventory. If it is required to keep prices up to date, the average price must be re-calculated each time a purchase is made at a different price.

Each time an issue is made is incorrect because the average price of remaining inventory items is not altered when an issue is made at the average price.

Re-calculating the average price at the end of each accounting period would not keep prices up to date.

An inventory count is verification of physical quantities and does not require the re-calculation of average prices.

24   B   £1,067

Date	Received	Issued	Balance	Total inventory value £	Unit cost £
1 June			100	500	5.00
3 June	300			1,440	4.80
			400	1,940	4.85*
5 June		220	180	(1,067)	4.85
				873	4.85
12 June	170			884	5.20
			350	1,757	5.02*
24 June		300		(1,506)	5.02
Closing inventory			50	251	5.02

* A new weighted average price is calculated every time there are receipts into inventory.

From the above records, it can be seen that the cost of material issued on 5 June was £1,067.

If you selected £1,056 you used a unit rate of £4.80, ie, the price of the latest goods received, rather than the average price of £4.85.

If you selected £1,078 you used a simple average price of £4.90, rather than a weighted average price.

If you selected £1,100 you used a unit rate of £5, ie, the price of the oldest items in inventory.

25   C   £251

From the table in solution 25, the closing inventory value is £251.

If you selected £248 you used a periodic weighted average cost of all inventory at the month end, instead of recalculating the average every time there are receipts into inventory.

If you selected £250 you calculated a simple average of all three available prices.

£260 would be the correct solution if the FIFO method of inventory valuation was used.

26   C   FIFO = £840

	£	£
Sales value £3 × 800		2,400
Less cost of sales:		
400 × £1.80	720	
400 × £2.10	840	
		(1,560)
Gross profit		840

If you selected £780 you have used a LIFO calculation.

If you selected £960 you priced all units at the first price of £1.80 for FIFO. However, you must deal with the separate batches of units, taking account of how many were received at each price.

£1,560 is the correct figure for cost of sales, but the question asked for the gross profit.

27   C   LIFO = £780

	£	£
Sales value £3 × 800		2,400
Less cost of sales:		
600 × £2.10	1,260	
200 × £1.80	360	
		(1,620)
Gross profit		780

If you selected £840 you have used a FIFO calculation.

If you selected £720 you priced all units at the latest price of £2.10 for LIFO. However, you must deal with the separate batches of units, taking account of how many were received at each price.

£1,620 is the correct figure for cost of sales, but the question asked for the gross profit.

28   A   £3,150

	Units	Value £
Opening inventory	600	3,600
Week 6	400	3,200
Week 8	100	900
	1,100	7,700

Periodic weighted average price	= £7,700/1,100 = £7 per unit
Closing inventory	= 1,100 – (350 + 300)
	= 450 units
Value of closing inventory	= 450 units × £7
	= £3,150

If you selected £3,431 you used the cumulative weighted average method whereby a new average cost is calculated each time a batch is received into inventory.

If you selected £3,450 you calculated a simple average of the three unit costs available. However, the unit cost calculation must take account of how many units were purchased at each price.

If you selected £3,690 you excluded the value of the opening inventory from your average cost calculations.

1   C   Functions or locations for which costs are ascertained and related to cost units for control purposes

Units of a product or service for which costs are ascertained is a description of a cost unit.

Amounts of expenditure attributable to various activities is a description of overheads.

A section of an organisation for which budgets are prepared and control is exercised is a description of a budget centre.

2   C   To attribute overhead costs to cost units

'To attribute overhead costs to cost centres' describes overhead allocation and apportionment.

'To reduce the total overhead expenditure below a predetermined level' and 'To ensure that the total overhead expenditure does not exceed budgeted levels' are more concerned with cost planning and control than with the costing of individual products or services.

3   B   Overhead apportionment

Overhead absorption is the final process of absorbing the total cost centre overheads into product costs.

Overhead allocation is the allotment of whole items of overhead costs to a particular cost centre or cost unit.

Overhead analysis is the general term used to describe all of the tasks of processing overhead cost data.

4   D   Common costs are shared among cost centres

'Costs may be controlled' is not correct because costs are controlled using budgets and other management information.

'Cost units gather overheads as they pass through cost centres' describes overhead absorption, not overhead apportionment.

'Whole items of cost can be charged to cost centres' describes overhead allocation, not overhead apportionment.

5   D   £18,300

The overheads of the canteen department are reapportioned on the basis of the number of staff working in the production departments only.

Reapportionment of canteen overheads

To machining department $= (30/50) \times £5,500 = £3,300$

Machining department total overheads $= £15,000 + £3,300$

                                        $= £18,300$

If you answered £3,300 you calculated the correct amount of canteen costs to be apportioned to machining. However, you then forgot to add on the original budgeted overheads of £15,000.

If you answered £17,750 you simply apportioned the canteen costs evenly to the two production cost centres. Since we know the number of staff in each cost centre, this is likely to be a more equitable apportionment basis. It is probable that a cost centre with more staff would place a greater burden on the canteen facilities.

The answer of £18,000 bases the apportionment of the canteen costs on all 55 employees. However, the canteen cannot give itself a charge and the correct apportionment basis is the 50 employees in the production cost centres only.

6 A Works manager = Allocated to factory

  D Logistics manager = Apportioned to factory

   The whole of the works manager's salary can be allocated to the factory since the manager is fully occupied in the factory cost centre.

   Part of the logistics manager's salary must be apportioned to the factory since some time is spent on production tasks.

7 D £10,160

Number of employees in packing department	= 2 direct + 1 indirect = 3
Number of employees in all production departments	= 15 direct + 6 indirect
	= 21

Packing department overhead

Canteen cost apportioned to packing department	$= \dfrac{£8,400}{21} \times 3$
	= £1,200
Original overhead allocated and apportioned	= £8,960
Total overhead after apportionment of canteen costs	= £10,160

If you selected £1,200 you forgot to include the original overhead allocated and apportioned to the packing department.

If you selected £9,968 you included the four canteen employees in your calculation, but the question states that the basis for apportionment is the number of employees in each **production** cost centre.

If you selected £10,080 you based your calculation on the direct employees only.

8 A Costs can be allocated where it is possible to identify which department caused them.

  C Costs need to be apportioned where they are shared by more than one department.

  D There is no need for a single product company to allocate and apportion overheads in order to determine overhead cost per unit.

   Although supervisors' salaries might be apportioned over more than one department or cost centre, it is more likely that a supervisor would work in a single cost centre. Therefore, supervisors' salaries are likely to be allocated rather than apportioned.

   The process of apportioning overhead costs is arbitrary. There is no single 'correct' result.

9 B Volume of space occupied in cubic metres

   From the four options available, a basis relating to space occupied would seem to be most appropriate. This eliminates the number of employees and labour hours worked. Since heating is required to warm the whole of the space occupied, from floor to ceiling, the volume of space is more appropriate than the floor space occupied.

10 C £7.20

Total labour hours = (1,000 × 4) + (2,000 × 6) + (3,000 × 3) = 25,000 hours

Overhead per labour hour = £30,000/25,000 = £1.20 per hour

Overhead content per unit of Product B = £1.20 × 6 = £7.20

If you selected £1.20 you calculated the correct absorption rate per labour hour. However, you should then have applied this rate to the number of labour hours per unit of product B.

A fixed overhead cost of £5 per unit is incorrect because it is calculated by simply determining a single rate per unit for all 6,000 units produced. However, the different number of labour hours for each unit of product indicates that each places a different burden on resources. This is reflected in the absorption of overheads on the basis of labour hours.

If you selected £30 you calculated the simple rate of £5 per unit as described above. However, you then went on to take account of the six hours worked on product B and so created a 'hybrid' absorption method which mixes two bases.

11 D £0.60 per machine hour

Department 1 appears to undertake primarily machine-based work, therefore a machine-hour rate would be most appropriate.

$$\frac{£27,000}{45,000} = £0.60 \text{ per machine hour}$$

A rate of 40% of direct material cost is not the most appropriate because it is not time-based, and most items of overhead expenditure tend to increase with time.

The two rates based on direct labour are not the most appropriate because labour activity is relatively insignificant in department 1, compared with machine activity.

12 C £0.72 per direct labour hour

Department 2 appears to be labour-intensive therefore a direct labour-hour rate would be most appropriate.

$$\frac{£18,000}{25,000} = £0.72 \text{ per direct labour hour}$$

The rate of 18% of direct labour cost is based on labour therefore it could be suitable. However, differential wage rates exist and this could lead to inequitable overhead absorption. The machine hour rate is not suitable because machine activity is not significant in department 2.

13 A £89.10

Fixed overhead absorption rate = budgeted overheads/budgeted machine hours

= £(95,580 + 64,800)/1,800

= £89.10

The rate of £100 per machine hour is the actual rate for the period. However, a predetermined rate, based on the budget data both for the overhead expenditure and the activity level, is used to absorb overheads.

14 D £20.91

Overhead absorption rate = £460,000/22,000 = £20.91 per hour

Remember overhead absorption rates are based on budgeted information.

15 A (1) and (2) only

Overhead absorption rates are usually determined in advance for each period, usually based on budgeted data. Therefore statement (1) is correct and statement (3) is incorrect. Overhead absorption rates are used in the final stage of overhead analysis, to absorb overheads into product costs. Therefore, statement (2) is correct. Statement (4) is not correct because overheads are controlled using budgets and other management information.

16 C £102.90

	£
Direct labour £5.25 × 4 hours	21.00
Direct expenses	53.50
Total direct cost	74.50
Overhead absorbed	
£7.10 × 4 hours	28.40
Total production cost	102.90

The answer of £81.90 does not include a direct labour cost. The direct cost is not affected by the basis chosen for the absorption of overheads.

If you selected £91.10 you based the overhead absorption on the rate per welding machine hour, rather than using the direct labour hour basis as requested.

The answer of £119.50 includes too much overhead cost. It uses both bases of absorption together, but only one basis of overhead absorption can be used.

17 B £4,462.50

Apportionment of budgeted overhead costs	£
Rent and rates (area) £3,000 × (700/8,000)	262.50
Plant insurance and depreciation (value of machinery)	
£11,000 × (80/400)	2,200.00
Factory manager's salary (employee numbers) £7,000 × (20/70)	2,000.00
	4,462.50

The option of £1,837.50 apportions all of the costs on the basis of area. More appropriate apportionment bases are available for some of the costs.

Similarly, the option of £6,000 apportions all of the costs on the basis of the number of employees, and suffers from the same inadequacy.

If you selected £7,000 you simply apportioned the overhead costs evenly between the departments. More appropriate apportionment bases are available.

18 D £14.60

	Primary hours	Finishing hours
Product J (6,000 × 36/60) / (6,000 × 25/60)	3,600	2,500
Product K (7,500 × 48/60) / (7,500 × 30/60)	6,000	3,750
Total budgeted direct labour hours	9,600	6,250
Budgeted production overheads	£96,000	£82,500
Production overhead absorption rate	£10 per hour	£13.20 per hour

Production overhead cost absorbed by product K

	£ per unit
Primary cost centre (£10 × 48/60)	8.00
Finishing cost centre (£13.20 × 30/60)	6.60
Total budgeted production overhead cost	14.60

If you selected £10.00 or £13.20 you calculated the correct absorption rate but you should have then applied it to the labour hours worked on product K.

If you selected £14.00 you calculated an absorption rate based on the 13,500 total budgeted production units. This rate takes no account of the different amounts of time taken to produce one unit of each product, and hence of the different resources consumed by each.

19 A (1) and (2) only

Statement (1) is correct because a constant unit absorption rate is used throughout the period. Statement (2) is correct because 'actual' overhead costs, based on actual overhead expenditure and actual activity for the period, cannot be determined until after the end of the period. Statement (3) is incorrect because under/over absorption of overheads is caused by the use of predetermined overhead absorption rates.

20 D Fixed overheads were under absorbed by £3,000, this being partly the difference between budgeted and actual expenditure and partly the production shortfall of 1,000 units.

Overhead absorption rate = £150,000/30,000 = £5 per unit

	£
Absorbed overhead (29,000 units × £5)	145,000
Actual overheads	148,000
Under-absorbed overhead	3,000

The effect of the production shortfall was partly offset by the difference between budgeted and actual expenditure.

21 D Budgeted capacity 11,250 hours, absorption rate per hour of £9.20

To calculate budgeted capacity, calculate the budgeted overheads and the overhead absorption rate. To calculate the overhead absorption rate remember to use the budgeted data.

Department Z	£
Actual overhead expenditure (same as budget, £61,500 + £42,000)	103,500
Under-absorbed overhead	-11,500
Overhead actually absorbed into production costs	92,000
Actual machine hours	10,000 hrs
Absorption rate per hour	£9.20

Budgeted capacity = Budgeted overheads/Absorption rate

= £103,500/£9.20 per hr =   11,250 hrs

22 C £2,250.00

When expenditures are as budgeted, but actual and budgeted production activity levels are different, only fixed overhead can be under or over absorbed.

Over-absorbed overhead = 500 hrs × £4.50

= £2,250

Variable overhead absorbed = (500 × £3.00) = £1,500 more than budgeted in the original budget. However, variable overhead incurred would be £1,500 more as well, leaving neither under nor over absorbed variable overheads.

23 C Under-absorbed by £205

The overhead absorption rate is the
budgeted overhead cost /budgeted hours = £14,950/3,250

= £4.60 per hour

Absorbed overheads (3,175 hours × £4.60) = £14,605

Actual overheads = £14,810

Under absorbed overheads = £205

The overhead is under absorbed because the actual overhead expenditure exceeded the amount absorbed.

If you calculated the under or over absorption as £140 you simply determined the difference between the budgeted and actual overheads. However, the amount of overhead absorbed will depend on the actual level of activity achieved.

24 D £28.75 per hour

	£
Actual overheads incurred	480,000
Over absorbed overheads	95,000
Overheads absorbed	575,000

Overhead absorption rate = £575,000/20,000

= £28.75 per hour

If you selected a rate of £19.25 you deducted the over absorbed overheads from the actual overheads to derive the amount absorbed. However, if the overhead is over absorbed then the amount absorbed must be greater than the actual overhead incurred.

25 C The company produced fewer units than expected.

	£
Overhead absorbed = 4,600 units × £2	9,200
Overhead incurred	9,500
Under absorption	300

The company sold fewer units than it produced is incorrect. It is the levels of production which bring about under/over absorption.

The company sold fewer units than it produced and spent less than expected on fixed overheads is incorrect. The company has under absorbed production overheads because of lower production levels than expected.

Spending less than expected on fixed overheads would, in isolation, lead to over absorption rather than to the under absorption that occurred.

The company produced fewer units than expected and spent less on fixed overheads is incorrect. The company has under absorbed overheads because of lower production levels than expected.

26　A　20,000

Actual overheads　　　= £343,825

Over absorption　　　= £14,025

Absorbed overheads　= Actual overheads + over absorbed overheads

= £343,825 + £14,025

= £357,850

If the absorbed overheads = £357,850 then the budgeted overhead absorption rate = Absorbed overheads/actual labour hours = £357,850/21,050 = £17 per labour hour.

If budgeted overheads for the period were £340,000 and the budgeted overhead absorption rate is £17 per labour hour, then the budgeted labour hours = budgeted overheads/overhead absorption rate = £340,000/£17 = 20,000 hours.

If you selected 20,225 hours you calculated the correct absorption rate but then you divided this into the actual overhead cost. You should have divided it into the budgeted overhead cost.

If you selected 21,700 hours you subtracted the over absorption to derive the absorbed overheads. However, if overheads are over absorbed then the amount of overhead absorbed must be greater than the actual overhead incurred.

27　A　£4,000 under-absorbed

When expenditures are as budgeted, but actual and budgeted production activity levels are different, only fixed overhead can be under or over absorbed.

Under-absorbed overhead = 1,000 hours × £4 = £4,000.

Variable overhead absorbed would be (1,000 × £2.50) = £2,500 less than in the original budget, but variable overhead incurred would be £2,500 less as well, leaving neither under nor over absorbed variable overheads.

28　C　£3,400 under-absorbed

Overhead absorption rate　= £54,500/((1,700 × 2) + (2,500 × 3))

= £5 per machine hour

Overhead absorbed by actual production achieved:

		£
Product A	1,900 units produced × £5 × 2 hours	19,000
Product B	2,200 units produced × £5 × 3 hours	33,000
		52,000
Actual overhead incurred		55,400
Under absorbed overhead		3,400

If you calculated the under or over absorption as £900 you calculated the difference between the budgeted and actual overheads without taking account of overhead absorbed by the units produced.

29　C　A factor which causes the costs of an activity

The cost driver is the factor which causes the costs of an activity to increase or decrease. For example, a cost driver for materials handling costs could be the number of production runs: the higher the number of production runs, the higher will be the cost of material handling.

'A mechanism for accumulating the costs of an activity' is a description of a cost pool.

'An overhead costs that is caused as a direct consequence of an activity' is a description of an overhead cost that is attributable to a particular activity.

'A cost relating to more than one product or service' describes a common cost that must be apportioned.

30 D   Activity based costing (ABC) involves tracing resource consumption and costing final outputs

    E   Just-in-time (JIT) systems are referred to as 'pull' systems because demand from a customer pulls products through the production process

         JIT purchasing requires that materials are delivered by the supplier, in small quantities not large quantities, just as they are needed in the production process.

         ABC is concerned with all types of overhead cost, including the cost of non factory-floor activities such as quality control and customer service. It therefore takes cost accounting beyond its traditional factory floor boundaries.

         ABC does not eliminate the need for arbitrary cost apportionment. Some apportionment may still be required at the pooling stage for items such as rent and rates.

31 B   (1), (2), (3) and (4)

    (1) JIT requires close integration of suppliers with the company's manufacturing process.

    (2) To respond immediately to customer requirements, production must be flexible and in small batch sizes.

    (3) JIT systems attempt to reduce set-up times in order to achieve fast throughput.

    (4) Each component on a production line is produced only when needed for the next stage.

32 A   When target costing is used, the selling price of a product or service determines its target cost

    B   An activity based costing (ABC) system makes some use of volume-related cost drivers

         The target cost is derived by deducting the required profit margin from the selling price.

         An ABC system uses volume-related cost drivers such as machine hours as well as transaction related cost drivers such as the number of quality control checks.

         A JIT system tends to reduce storage costs because lower inventories are held, not increase them.

         Life cycle costing does track costs that are incurred once production has ceased, since it tracks costs over the whole of a product's life cycle.

         A product's target cost is derived from a selling price which is determined by a consideration of external market conditions.

33 C   Lower levels of receivables

         A lower level of receivables is not the result of the adoption of a JIT system and is more to do with credit control procedures.

34 A   Brewing   = Process

    F   Motorway construction = Contract

    H   Plumbing repairs   = Job

    L   Shoe manufacture   = Batch

         Brewing involves a continuous flow of processes.

         Each motorway would be a separately identifiable cost unit of relatively long duration. Therefore contract costing is appropriate.

         Each plumbing repair would be a separately identifiable cost unit of relatively short duration. Therefore job costing is most appropriate.

         In shoe manufacturing a number of identical shoes would be manufactured in separately identifiable batches.

35   A   In process and batch costing the cost per unit of output is found indirectly by dividing total costs by the number of units produced.

      D   The procedures used to calculate unit costs in manufacturing industries can equally be applied to service industries.

It is incorrect to state that in process and job costing the cost per unit of output is found directly by accumulating costs for each unit. This applies only to job costing since it is not possible to identify individual units in a process costing environment.

It is incorrect to state that costing is irrelevant. Both financial accounts and cost accounts use the same basic data. However, the cost accounting analyses the data in a more detailed way and in a manner that is useful for management planning, decision-making and control.

36   A   Actual material cost

      C   Absorbed manufacturing overheads

The actual material cost for a batch can be determined from the material recording system.

Actual manufacturing overheads cannot be determined for a specific batch because of the need for allocation and apportionment of each item of overhead expenditure, and the subsequent calculation of a predetermined overhead absorption rate. Therefore actual manufacturing overheads is incorrect and absorbed manufacturing overheads is correct.

Budgeted labour costs are irrelevant when considering actual batch costs.

37   D   The construction industry

The construction industry would be more likely to use contract costing, not process costing.

The brewing industry, the oil industry and the steel industry would all use process costing.

38   B   (1) and (3) only

Statement (2) is not correct. Contract costing often applies to projects which are based on sites away from the contractor's premises.

39   C   £217,323

	Work in progress (WIP) £
Job A	
£(26,800 + 17,275 + 14,500) + £(14,500/42,600 × 126,000)	101,462
Job C	
£(18,500 + 24,600) + £(24,600/42,600 × 126,000)	115,861
Total WIP cost	217,323

£58,575 is the direct cost of job A, with no addition for overhead. £101,675 is the direct cost of both jobs in progress, but with no addition for overhead.

£227,675 is the result of charging all of the overhead to the jobs in progress, but some of the overhead must be absorbed by the completed job B.

SAMPLE PAPER

40   D   £2,400

Idle time is 10% of the hours to be paid for. Hours to be paid for are therefore

= 270/0.9 = 300 hours

Therefore labour cost   = 300 hours × £8 = £2,400

The answer of 300 is the number of hours to be paid for. This needs to be evaluated at the hourly rate of £8.

If you selected £2,160 you made no allowance for the extra payment for idle time.

The answer of £2,376 is derived by simply adding 10% to the active hours. However, the idle time is calculated as a percentage of the total hours paid for, not as a percentage of the active hours worked.

41   A,F,H

Oil refining involves a continuous manufacturing process of homogeneous output and therefore is ideally suited to process costing.

Clothing would be manufactured using batches of material, for example of a certain texture or colour. Production would be halted before the next batch of items of a particular style is produced. The most appropriate costing method would therefore be batch costing.

Car repair work would be very varied and each repair would be bespoke. Therefore neither process nor batch costing would be appropriate but job/contract costing would be a suitable costing method.

SAMPLE PAPER

Chapter 4: Marginal costing and absorption costing

1   A   £85,355

	£ per unit
Variable materials	9.80
Variable labour	8.70
Variable production overheads	1.35
Variable production cost per unit	19.85

Value of inventory in a marginal costing system   = £19.85 × 4,300 units

= £85,355

If you selected £117,562 you included the variable selling and distribution overheads in the inventory valuation. The inventory should be valued at variable **production** cost.

The value of £125,603 includes fixed production overheads. In a marginal costing system these overheads would be charged against the revenue as a period cost and would not be included in the inventory valuation.

If you selected £172,430 you valued the inventory units at total cost. Selling and distribution overheads should not be included in inventory valuation and fixed production overheads should not be included in a marginal costing inventory valuation.

2   A   £52,000

The value of this inventory using marginal costing would have been £52,000.

Fixed production overhead per unit of product S	= £6.50 × (£60/£12) hours
	= £32.50 per unit
Full production cost per unit of product S	= £(32.50 + 60.00 + 70.00)
	= £162.50
Number of units of product S in inventory	= £65,000/£162.50
	= 400 units
Marginal costing valuation of inventory	= 400 × (£60 + £70)
	= £52,000

You should have been able to eliminate the options of £260,000 and £442,000 since the inventory valuation using marginal costing will always be lower than with absorption costing.

If you selected £53,150 you re-calculated the fixed overhead absorption rate on a per unit basis rather than using a rate per labour hour.

3   B   Contribution: £20,000, Profit £15,000

Contribution = 800 clocks × £(50 − 25) = £20,000

Profit   = £20,000 − £5,000 fixed costs = £15,000

The contribution figures of £25,000 relate to a sales volume of 1,000 clocks but this was the production volume.

The profit figure of £16,000 is the absorption costing profit for September.

4   A   Marginal costing is an alternative method of costing to absorption costing.

    D   Fixed costs are treated as a period cost and are charged in full to the income statement of the accounting period in which they are incurred.

    E   Marginal cost is the cost of a unit which would not be incurred if that unit were not produced.

Contribution is calculated as sales revenue minus **all variable costs** (and not fixed cost of sales). Closing inventories are valued at **marginal** production cost (and not full production cost).

5   A   Such systems value finished goods at the variable cost of production.

    D   Such systems write off fixed overheads to the income statement in the period in which they were incurred.

Under- or over-absorbed overheads cannot arise with marginal costing because fixed overhead is written off in full as it is incurred.

6   D   £113,250

	£
Gross profit (16,000 units × £(24.00 – 8.50 – 2.50))	208,000
Selling costs (16,000 units × £6)	(96,000)
	112,000
Over absorbed fixed production costs	
(16,400 units produced – 15,900 budgeted) × £2.50	1,250
Absorption costing profit	113,250

If you answered £110,750 you deducted the over absorption instead of adding it to the calculated profit. The option of £112,000 makes no allowance for the over absorption and £112,250 is the marginal costing profit for the quarter.

7   D   Profits measured using absorption costing may be the same as, or lower than, or higher than profits measured using marginal costing.

Whether **profits under absorption costing are the same as, lower than or higher than profits under marginal costing** depends entirely on opening and closing inventory figures. For example, if there is no opening or closing inventory, then the two measures of profit will be the same.

8   A   Less operating profit than the absorption costing method

If the number of units in inventory increased then with absorption costing more fixed overhead will be carried forward in inventory to the next period. Thus operating profits will be higher than with the marginal costing method.

9   B   £5,160 higher

Since production exceeded sales the inventory of 200 units carried forward to the next period would include fixed production costs of (200 × (£25,800/1,000)) = £5,160 with absorption costing.

Under marginal costing these fixed costs would be charged against the revenue for the period. Thus the absorption costing profit would be £5,160 higher.

If you selected £24,260 higher or lower you calculated the profit difference as the total production cost of the 200 units in inventory. However, the difference in inventory valuation is caused by the differing treatment of the **fixed** costs only.

10   B   £10,000 lower

The marginal costing profit is lower because with absorption costing some of the fixed production costs would be carried forward in the inventory valuation.

Profit difference = 250 units in inventory × (£30,000 / 750)

                 = £10,000

If you calculated the profit difference as £22,500 you included the fixed selling costs. However, selling costs are not included in the inventory valuation, which should include production costs only.

11   B   £57,500

Sales volume exceeded production volume by 500 units, therefore inventories reduced. The absorption costing profit will be lower than the marginal costing profit because fixed overheads were 'released' from inventory.

Profit difference = inventory reduction in units × fixed overhead per unit

                 = 500 × £5 = £2,500

Absorption costing profit   = £60,000 – £2,500

                          = £57,500

If you selected £47,500 you based your calculation of the profit difference on the closing inventory of 2,500 units. The answer of £59,500 is calculated as £7 profit per unit × 8,500 units sold, however, this takes no account of the actual level of fixed overhead cost.

If you selected £62,500 you calculated the correct profit difference but you added it to the marginal costing profit instead of subtracting it.

12   D   £2,400 loss

Change in inventory   = 200 units reduction.

Profit difference   = 200 units × £7

                          = £1,400

Since inventory reduced the absorption costing profit would be lower than the marginal costing profit. This would increase the loss from £1,000 to £2,400.

If you selected £400 profit you added the difference in inventory value to reduce the loss. However, since fixed overhead is 'released' from inventory with absorption costing, the loss will be greater.

13   D   £9.00

Decrease in inventory levels = 48,500 – 45,500

                              = 3,000 units

Difference in profits   = £315,250 – £288,250

                              = £27,000

Fixed overhead per unit   = £27,000/3,000

                              = £9 per unit

If you selected one of the other options you attempted various divisions of all the data available in the question.

14 B £75,800

Decrease in inventory levels = 760 – 320

= 440 units

Difference in profits = 440 × £5 fixed overhead per unit

= £2,200

Inventories decreased, therefore the absorption costing profit would be lower as overheads are 'released' from inventory.

Absorption costing profit = £78,000 – £2,200

= £75,800

If you selected options A or C you based your calculation of the profit difference on only the opening inventory or closing inventory respectively.

If you selected option D you calculated the correct profit difference, but you added it, instead of subtracting it from the marginal costing profit.

15 D Absorption costing profits will be higher and closing inventory valuations higher than those under marginal costing.

Closing inventory valuations are always higher with absorption costing because of the inclusions of fixed overhead. Therefore the statements that closing inventory valuations are lower are incorrect.

If inventories increase, absorption costing profits are higher because of the fixed overhead being carried forward in inventory.

16 C It is more appropriate for short-term decision-making.

D Fixed costs are treated in accordance with their nature (ie, as period costs).

Marginal costing does not comply with accounting standards for external reporting. It does ensure that the company focuses on producing a positive contribution but that may not be sufficient to cover fixed costs and hence make an overall profit.

In situations of highly fluctuating demand, marginal costing will produce highly fluctuating profits. There is less of a fluctuation under absorption costing and as a result, it can be argued that this costing method is more appropriate when there are strong seasonal variations in sales demand.

17 A Absorption costing profits will be lower and closing inventory valuations higher than those under marginal costing.

Closing inventory valuations are always higher with absorption costing because of the inclusions of fixed overhead. Therefore the statements that closing inventory valuations are lower are incorrect.

If inventories decrease, absorption costing profits are lower because of the fixed overhead being released from inventory.

18 C,D The statement 'Absorption unit cost information is the most reliable as a basis for pricing decisions' is **not true** because short term changes in activity levels can result in unit costs being artificially high or low, because overheads will be absorbed over the unrepresentative number of units. This could make prices set using this cost basis artificially high or low.

The statement 'A product showing a loss under absorption costing will also make a negative contribution under marginal costing' is **not true** because a product could earn a contribution under marginal costing which then becomes a gross loss under absorption costing only because of the increase in cost from absorbing overheads.

The statement 'Marginal unit cost information is normally the most useful for external reporting purposes' is **not true** because external reporting will need to take account of unit costs right across an operation not just unit costs when incremental (marginal) changes in activity levels are made.

The statement 'When closing inventory levels are higher than opening inventory levels and overheads are constant, absorption costing gives a higher profit than marginal costing' is **true** because an increase in inventory levels will mean that with absorption costing more overhead is being carried forward at the end of the period than at the start of the period. This means that overheads charged against profit in the period would be lower than under marginal costing thereby increasing the reported profit.

The statement 'In a multi-product company, smaller volume products may cause a disproportionate amount of set up overhead cost' is **true** because overheads would normally be apportioned based on the time a product spends on the production line. For smaller volume products the time taken to set up the product run becomes a larger proportion of the total time spent in production than for higher volume products. SAMPLE PAPER

19 A £18

Number of hours in Machining are:

		Hours
Pye	4,000 × 0.5 =	2,000
Tan	4,000 × 1.0 =	4,000
		6,000

Total Machining overhead is £120,000 or £120,000/6,000 per hour = £20 per hour

Machining overhead cost of a unit of Pye is £20 × 0.5 = £10

Number of hours in Assembly are:

		Hours
Pye	4,000 × 0.20 =	800
Tan	4,000 × 0.25 =	1,000
		1,800

Total Assembly overhead is £72,000 or £72,000/1,800 per hour = £40 per hour

Assembly overhead cost of a unit of Pye is £40 × 0.2 = £8

Total overhead cost of a unit of Pye is therefore £10 (Machining) + £8 (Assembly) = £18

If you calculated £20 you incorrectly either just used the total Machining overhead per hour or added together the Machining overhead cost of a Pye and the Assembly overhead cost of a Tan.

If you calculated £28 you incorrectly added together the Machining overhead cost of a Tan and the Assembly overhead cost of a Pye.

£24 was just an incorrect answer.

20 B   £19,500

The manufacturing cost per unit, on an absorption costing basis, is:

£6.00 + (£90,000/75,000) =

£6.00 + £1.20 = £7.20

The cost of sales is therefore 70,000 × £7.20 = £504,000

The sales revenue is 70,000 × £8 = £560,000

The profit before selling and administration costs is therefore £560,000 – £504,000 = £56,000

The selling and administration costs are (70,000 × £0.20) + £22,500 = £36,500

The net profit is therefore £56,000 – £36,500 = £19,500

If you calculated the profit as £13,500 then you calculated the net profit using marginal costing. Total variable costs on this basis would be 70,000 × £6.20 = £434,000 and total overheads £90,000 + £22,500 = £112,500. The net profit would therefore (incorrectly) be calculated as £560,000 – £434,000 – £112,500 = £13,500

If you calculated the net profit as £21,000 or £22,500 then you probably followed the right method but made an arithmetical error.   SAMPLE PAPER

1 D £298.60

	Cost centre A £ per unit	Cost centre B £ per unit	Total £ per unit
Direct material	60.00	30.30	90.30
Direct labour	60.00	15.20	75.20
Production overhead	36.72	14.94	51.66
Total production cost			217.16
General overhead 10%			21.72
Total cost			238.88
Profit margin (×20/80)			59.72
Selling price			298.60

If you selected £271.45 you did not add the general overhead to determine the total cost per unit.

If you selected £282.31 you simply added 30% (20% + 10%) to the total production cost in order to determine the selling price. The two percentages should be added separately and the 20% margin should be determined as a percentage of the selling price, not as a percentage of cost.

The option of £286.66 is the price derived using a 20% mark up on a cost, rather than a 20% margin on the selling price.

2 B £51.84

Production overhead absorption rate per direct labour hour is:

£61,200/(4,000 × 2 hours + 6,000 × 1.5 hours) = £3.60

	Product L £ per unit
Materials	6.00
Labour	30.00
Production overhead (2 hours × £3.60)	7.20
Total production cost	43.20
Profit mark up (20% × £43.20)	8.64
Selling price	51.84

If you selected £47.52 you calculated the correct production overhead absorption rate per hour but you forgot to multiply this by 2 to derive the overhead to be absorbed by product L.

If you selected £54.00 you added a margin of 20% based on the selling price, rather than a mark up of 20% based on the cost.

If you selected £61.56 you calculated the production overhead absorption rate based only on the output of product L. However, some of the production overhead will be absorbed by product T.

3　C　£201.60

Since employees are paid on a per unit basis the wage cost is a variable cost, which will increase in line with the number of binders.

The machine set-up cost and design costs are fixed costs for each batch, which will not be affected by the number of binders in the batch.

For a batch of 300 binders:

	£
Variable materials (£30 × 3)	90.00
Variable wages (£10 × 3)	30.00
Machine set up	3.00
Design and artwork	15.00
Production overhead (£30 × 20%)	6.00
Total production cost	144.00
Selling, distribution and administration overhead (£144 × 5%)	7.20
Total cost	151.20
Profit margin (£151.20 × 25/75)	50.40
Selling price for a batch of 300	201.60

If you selected £189.00 you calculated the cost correctly, but added a profit mark up of 25% of cost, instead of a margin of 25% of selling price.

If you selected £193.20 you failed to absorb the appropriate amount of fixed overhead. If you selected £252.00 you treated all of the costs as variable costs, even though the machine set up and design costs are fixed regardless of batch size.

4　C　£84,963

	£
Opening work in progress	42,790
Labour for period	3,500
Overheads (£3,500/£42,600) × £126,000	10,352
Total cost	56,642
Profit (33$\frac{1}{3}$% on sales)	28,321
	84,963

If you selected £69,435 you forgot to add on overhead cost.

If you selected £75,523 you calculated the profit as 33$\frac{1}{3}$% on cost, instead of 33$\frac{1}{3}$% on sales.

If you selected £258,435 you charged all of the overhead to job B, but some of the overhead should be absorbed by the other two jobs (based on labour cost).

5　D　£505

	£
Direct materials (5 × £20)	100
Direct labour (14 × £8)	112
Variable overhead (14 × £3)	42
Fixed overhead (14 × £5*)	70
Other overhead (fixed per job)	80
Total cost of job 173	404
Profit margin (× 20/80)	101
Selling price	505

*Fixed production overhead absorption rate = £200,000/40,000 = £5 per direct labour hour

£404 is the total cost, but a profit margin should be added to this to determine the selling price. If you selected £424 you added only £5 for fixed production overhead but this is the **hourly rate**, which must be multiplied by the number of direct labour hours. If you selected £485 you calculated 20% of cost to determine the profit but the data states that profit is calculated as 20% of the sales value.

6   B   £60.96

Selling price	= £90.68
	= 119% of pre-tax price
∴ Selling price excluding tax	= 100/119 × £90.68
	= £76.20
∴ New price after 20% reduction	= (100% − 20%) × £76.20
	= £60.96

If you selected £58.76 you calculated the sales tax as 19% of the current selling price, but the price already includes the 19% tax which is based on the pre-tax price.

If you selected £72.54 you calculated the correct pre-tax price but then you added 19% sales tax, which was not required.

If you selected £76.20 you calculated the correct old pre-tax price but forgot to reduce the price by 20%.

7   C   3.0% decrease.

Selling price at end of year 2	= £27.50 × 1.05 × 1.06
	= £30.61

Change in selling price in year 3 is therefore £(30.61 − 29.69) = £0.92 (reduction)

Percentage change in year 3 was therefore (−0.92/30.61) × 100% = −3%

If you selected a 2.7% decrease you calculated the price at the end of year 2 as being 11% of the initial price. You should have compounded the two increases at 6% and 5%, rather than simply adding them together.

If you calculated the year three price change to be a 3.4% decrease you calculated the correct absolute value of the price change. However, you then expressed this as a percentage of the original price, rather than as a percentage of the price at the beginning of year 3.

8   C   £88.13

Let x	= price of article before sales tax
Then 1.12 x	= £84
Therefore: x	= £84/1.12
	= £75
New selling price	= 1.175 × £75
	= £88.13

If you selected £75 you calculated the correct pre-tax price but then forgot to add the revised sales tax.

If you selected a price of £86.86 you calculated the sales tax as 12% of the current selling price, but this price includes the tax which is based on the pre-tax price.

If you calculated a price of £88.62 you simply added an extra 5.5% tax to the current selling price. However, the total sales tax is based on the pre-tax price. Therefore, the current level of tax must first be deducted to derive the basis on which to calculate the new 17.5% tax.

9　C　20%

　　25kg costs £9.00

　　∴ 1 kg costs 　　　　　= £9.00/25

　　　　　　　　　　　　= £0.36

　　∴ Percentage saving 　= (0.45 − 0.36)/0.45 × 100%

　　　　　　　　　　　　= 20%

9% is incorrect since it represents a saving in pence ie, £0.45 − £0.36 = £0.09 and not a **percentage saving**.

11.25% represents 25kg × £0.45 = £11.25 which is incorrect.

If you selected 25%, you used £0.36 as the denominator instead of £0.45.

10　B　£16.67

　　Cost 　　　　　　　　= 75% of selling price

　　And cost 　　　　　　= £50

　　Therefore selling price = £50/75 × 100

　　　　　　　　　　　　= £66.67

　　Profit 　　　　　　　= (£66.67 − £50.00)

　　　　　　　　　　　　= £16.67

If you selected £12.50 you calculated the profit as 25% of the cost rather than 25% of the selling price.

If you selected £62.50 you calculated a profit markup of 25% of the cost and then added the profit to the cost to derive the (incorrect) selling price.

The option of £66.67 is the correct selling price but this was not the requirement of the question.

11　A　£40

Cost + mark up = sales price

Assume cost = £100, then mark up is £20 and sales price = £120 (100 + 20 = 120)

Actual selling price = £240

The profit (mark up) is therefore £240/120 × 20 = £40

If you selected £48 you calculated the profit margin of 20% of the selling price. The **mark-up** is expressed as a percentage of cost.

12　B　£606

	£
Selling price of job	1,690
Less profit mark up (30/130)	390
Total cost of job	1,300
Less overhead	694
Prime cost	606

If you selected £489 you deducted 30% from the selling price to derive the total cost of the job.

£996 is the result of deducting the overhead from the selling price, but omitting to deduct the profit margin.

£1,300 is the total cost of the job; you needed to deduct the overhead to derive the prime cost.

13   D   68.2%

Revised mark up in £	= £(7.99 − 4.75)
	= £3.24
Revised mark up percentage	= (£3.24/£4.75) × 100%
	= 68.2%

If you selected 1.1% you calculated the percentage change required in the selling price rather than the change required in the mark-up percentage.

If you selected 1.8% you calculated the change in the mark up percentage.

The option of 40.6% is the margin as a percentage of the selling price rather than the mark up as a percentage of cost.

14   A   16.7%

Cost of goods sold	= purchases + opening inventory − closing inventory
	= £40,000 + £12,000 − £2,000
	= £50,000
Profit for period	= £60,000 − £50,000
	= £10,000
Percentage margin	= (£10,000/£60,000) × 100%
	= 16.7%

If you selected 20.0% you calculated the percentage mark up on cost rather than the percentage margin on the selling price.

If you selected 33.3% or 50.0% you calculated the margin and the mark up respectively, using the purchases figure as the cost of goods sold, without adjusting for the change in inventory.

15   C   £163.79

	£ per unit
Material	15.00
Labour	52.05
Production overhead (£9.44 × 7 hours)	66.08
Total production cost	133.13
General overhead (£133.13 × 8%)	10.65
Total cost	143.78
Required return from the Super per unit (£136,200 × 0.14)/953	20.01
Required selling price	163.79

If you selected £102.62 you included only £9.44 for production overhead. This hourly rate should have been multiplied by the number of machine hours to determine the total overhead absorbed.

If you selected £153.14 you forgot to include general overhead when you calculated the total cost.

If you selected £163.91 you added a mark up of 14% to the total cost, instead of determining a profit per unit based on the 14% required return on the capital invested.

16 D 233%

	%
Marginal cost	60
Fixed cost	100
Full/total cost	160
Margin (160 × 20/80)	40
Selling price	200

Percentage mark up on marginal costs $= 140/60 \times 100\%$

$= 233\%$

If you selected 67% you calculated the mark up as (40/60) and did not allow for the additional mark up to cover the fixed costs.

If you selected 108% you misread the marginal costs to be 60% of total costs, rather than 60% of fixed costs.

If you selected 220% you calculated the selling price structure based on a 20% mark up on full cost, rather than a 20% margin on the selling price. Mark up on marginal costs is (£200 – £60) = £140.

17 C The total revenue will decrease and the total contribution will increase

Let the current selling price be £P and the current sales volume be V units.

Since the mark up is 100% of variable costs,

Current contribution per unit	= £0.5P
Current revenue	= £VP
Current total contribution	= £0.5VP

After the change in pricing policy, the sales volume will be 0.6V and the revised selling price will be £1.5P. The variable cost per unit remains at £0.5P.

Revised revenue = volume sold × revised selling price

$= 0.6V \times £1.5P$

$= £0.9VP$

Therefore the revenue will decrease.

Revised total contribution $= 0.6V (£1.5P - £0.5P)$

$= £0.6VP$

Therefore the total contribution will increase.

18   C   £12.50

Profit = contribution – fixed costs

Therefore contribution = £10,000 + £160,000 = £170,000

If a 2% increase in selling price is   £5,000 then the sales revenue before the increase was:

£5,000/0.02 = £250,000

The variable costs are sales revenue less contribution, ie

£250,000 – £170,000

= £80,000

Number of units sold   = £80,000/(variable cost per unit = £4)

= 20,000

Current selling price per unit is therefore:

£250,000/20,000 = £12.50

If you selected £0.08 you made a mistake at the last step and performed the final division 'upside down'.

If you selected £10.00 you deducted the profit from the fixed costs to determine the contribution, instead of adding it.

The option of £12.75 is the revised selling price, including the 2% increase.

19   A   The supplier and the buyer will each bear some of the inflation risk but not necessarily equally

The supplier will bear the inflation risk during the credit period, since the price is fixed during that time.

The buyer will bear the inflation risk during the time that the contract is being completed, since the actual costs incurred are to be passed to the buyer.

Despite the fact that both intervals are four weeks the buyer and seller do not bear the inflation risk equally because the risk applies to two different time periods.

20   C   The percentage mark up with full cost plus pricing will always be smaller than the percentage mark up with marginal cost-plus pricing

The percentage mark up with marginal cost-plus pricing must be large enough to cover the fixed costs as well as to earn the required profit.

A cost-plus pricing method does not enable a company to maximise its profits because it fails to recognise that since price may be determining demand, there will be a profit-maximising combination of price and demand.

A selling price in excess of full cost will not always ensure that an organisation will cover all of its costs. The full cost includes fixed costs per unit which have been derived based on estimated or budgeted volume. If this volume is not achieved then the actual fixed cost per unit will be higher and the selling price might be lower than the actual cost per unit.

A full cost-plus pricing method does not take account of the effect of price on the quantity demanded. The quantity is established as a basis for determining the price.

21   B   £30,000 decrease

The company will be buying 5,000 units at £18 each from the external supplier, rather than making the units for £12 each in division X. Profit will therefore fall by 5,000 × £(18 – 12) = £30,000.

If you calculated a change in profit of £10,000 you calculated the difference of £2 between the transfer price of £20 and the external price of £18 and interpreted this as a saving for the company as a whole. However the transfer price of £20 is not an actual cost to the company. It is an external charge made for goods or services supplied between divisions.

22 B   Should encourage output at an organisation-wide profit-maximising level

   E   Should enable the realistic measurement of divisional profit

An effective transfer pricing system should discourage dysfunctional decision-making and should not encourage divisions to act in their own self interest. Instead it should encourage goal congruence where divisions do not make entirely autonomous decisions and there is an alignment between divisional goals and corporate goals.

By providing the supplying division with a realistic profit and the receiving division with a realistic cost, it is possible to measure the divisional profit and to encourage output at an organisation-wide profit-maximising level.

23 C   The receiving division is charged with the standard variable cost of transfers made and the supplying division is credited with the market value

The use of standard cost ensures that efficiencies and inefficiencies are not transferred to the receiving division. The use of variable cost avoids the situation where the receiving division perceives the supplying division's fixed costs to be variable costs of the organisation as a whole. This could lead to sub-optimal decisions.

Crediting the supplying division with the market value reduces the likelihood of sub-optimal decision-making and improves goal congruence.

24 A   Division A   £900 profit

       Division B   £360 profit

	Division A		Division B	
	£		£	£
External sales (180 × £14)	2,520	(90 × £20)		1,800
Transfer sales (90 × £(10 + 20%)	1,080			
	3,600			1,800
Transfer costs			1,080	
Own costs (270 × 10)	(2,700)	(90 × £4)	360	
				(1,440)
Profit	900			360

If you calculated a £720 profit for division B you forgot to include the division's own costs in the calculation.

If you calculated a £1,440 profit for division B you forgot to include the transfer cost in the division's total costs.

If you selected the profit of £1,332 for division A and a loss for division B you calculated the transfer price as £16.80 (£14 + 20%) per unit instead of £12 (£10 + 20%) per unit.

25 C (1) Full production cost plus 40%   £21.00

(2) Two-part tariff   £9

		£
Variable cost per unit		
Direct material cost per unit		3.00
Direct labour cost per unit		4.00
Variable overhead cost per unit		2.00
		9.00
Fixed production overhead absorbed per unit		6.00
		15.00
Add: 40% of full production cost (£15 × 40%)		6.00
Total cost plus		21.00

If you calculated a full production cost-plus transfer price of £12.60 you did not include any absorbed fixed production overhead.

If you selected a two-part tariff price of £19 you added £10 per unit for fixed overhead, based on the fixed fee of £200,000 divided by the expected number of 20,000 units to be transferred.

However the fixed fee is not unitised in a two-part tariff system. The charge of £200,000 is made regardless of the number of units actually transferred.

26 A The offer is not acceptable from the point of view of company C and the manager of Division B will make a sub-optimal decision

The manager of division B accepts the offer, the company as a whole pays £330 per unit but saves only £300 per unit, which are the variable costs of division A. Thus overall the company's costs increase by £30 per unit and the offer is not acceptable.

Division B will pay £330 per unit but saves £410 per unit and so will decide to accept the offer. Thus the manager of Division B will make a sub-optimal decision from the point of view of the company as a whole.

27 B £55.50

The total demand for product K exceeds the capacity of division J therefore internal transfers will displace external sales.

Optimum transfer price = external market price – cost savings with internal transfer.

Cost savings with internal transfer	= 5% × total variable cost
	= 5% × (100/190 × £57)
	= £1.50
Optimum transfer price per unit	= £57 – £1.50
	= £55.50

If you selected £54.50 per unit you calculated the cost savings on internal transfers as 5% of the total cost of £50, rather than as 5% of the total variable cost.

If you selected £56.72 per unit you calculated the variable costs as 10% of the selling price of £57. This misinterprets the meaning of the 90% mark up on marginal cost.

If you selected £57.00 per unit you simply opted for a transfer price equal to the external market price. However this makes no allowance for the cost savings which arise on internal transfers.

28　C　Because the selling price is agreed to be the actual costs incurred by the supplier plus a profit mark-up using a fixed percentage then any inflation adjustment to costs would also affect the selling price. The supplier can pass on all inflation increases to the buyer and will also earn a mark-up on the cost increase.

In this case:

The statement 'The supplier and the buyer will each bear some of the inflation risk' is incorrect as the supplier bears no risk.

The statement 'Only the supplier will bear the inflation risk' is incorrect, as the supplier bears no risk.

The statement 'The supplier and the buyer will each bear equal amounts of the inflation risk' is also incorrect for the same reason.　　　　SAMPLE PAPER

29　B　Because the demand for Rex is more than sufficient for division F to manufacture to capacity, the price that the product should be transferred to division G should represent the same profit margin as if the product were sold externally. The external selling price is £64 but if an external sale is made then additional selling overhead of £8 would be incurred. The net transfer price is therefore £56.

The £64 price doesn't reflect the saving in selling costs. £40 and £48 give lower profit margins for the producing division F, hence they would want to sell outside.　　　　SAMPLE PAPER

30　B　If it is assumed that the direct cost of the product is £100, then the indirect costs would be £40 and the total cost £140. The selling price is set to recover the full cost (£140) plus 50%, ie, plus £70. This makes the selling price £210 (£140 + £70).

The mark-up on direct costs is therefore £210 (selling price) less £100 (direct cost) = £110.

The percentage mark-up is therefore £110/£100 = 110%

If you calculated the mark-up as 210% you probably calculated the selling price (£210) as a percentage of the direct cost in error.

If you calculated the mark-up as 190% or 110% you probably made calculation errors.

31　C　The total sales will use 25,000 tonnes of material, at a cost of:

$(18,000 \times £10) + (7,000 \times £10 \times 95\%)$

$= (£180,000) + (£70,000 \times 95\%)$

$= £246,500$

The variable labour and overhead cost for this level of production would increase to:

$(£96,000 + £48,000) \times 125\% = £144,000 \times 125\% = £180,000$

The fixed costs remain at £72,000

Total costs are therefore $(£246,500 + £180,000 + £72,000) = £498,500$

The requirement is to earn the same budget profit of £64,000. This means the total required sales income will be $(£498,500 + £64,000) = £562,500.$

The sales revenue without the extra order is £480,000 and therefore the revenue to be generated from the extra order is $(£562,500 - £480,000) = £82,500.$

If you calculated the answer as £100,500 then you probably incorrectly increased the fixed costs by 25% as well, from £72,000 to £90,000, meaning an extra £18,000 would need to be recovered through the selling price.

If you calculated the answer as either £83,500 or £101,500 then you either followed the correct logic or the incorrect logic set out above, and also made an arithmetical error.　　　　SAMPLE PAPER

32   D   The contribution is selling price less variable costs only. The variable costs are £9 + £2 = £11

The contribution is therefore £30 (selling price) – £11 = £19

The percentage mark-up on total cost is the profit as a percentage of total costs. The total costs per unit are £9 + £6 + £2 + £3 = £20. The profit is therefore £30 – £20 = £10 and the mark up % is £10/£20 = 50%.

If you incorrectly calculated the contribution as £21 then you ignored the variable advertising costs in error.

If you incorrectly calculated the contribution as £10 then you deducted all costs from the selling price rather than just the variable costs.

If you correctly calculated the contribution as £19 but incorrectly calculated the mark up % as 100% then you incorrectly used the cost value of £20 as the numerator, rather than the profit of £10.

33   A   Contribution is defined as sales revenue less variable costs. The current contribution ratio is therefore (600,000 – 216,000 – 132,000)/600,000 = 42%.

The variable manufacturing cost is expected to increase by 10% to £237,600 and therefore total variable costs will be (£237,600 + £132,000) = £369,600. If the contribution ratio is maintained at 42% then these costs would represent 58% of sales revenue. Sales revenue is therefore £369,600/0.58 = £637,241.

As the sales volume remains at 1,200 units the unit selling price must be £637,241/1,200 = £531.

If you incorrectly calculated the selling price as £550 then you either calculated the contribution as sales revenue less manufacturing variable costs only (64%) and incorrectly ignored variable selling costs or alternatively increased both manufacturing and selling variable costs by 10%.

If you incorrectly calculated the selling price as £518 then you probably calculated the current contribution correctly but then inflated the selling variable costs by 10% rather than the manufacturing variable overheads.

34   D   Delta loses a contribution of £(176 – 140) = £36/unit so its profits fall. The company is paying £152 for a unit which costs £140 to make internally (fixed costs are fixed) so its profits fall.

Gamma's profit would increase (paying £152 not £176). If you selected an increase in the company's profits then you forgot that fixed costs are fixed and the relevant cost per unit in Delta is £140 not £160.

35   C   For every Y not sold internally, Delta would sell an equally profitable X externally, so there would be no change in its profits. For the company, it gains £(176 – 140) = £36/unit on an X and pays £(152 – 140) = £12/unit more on a Y so gains overall (fixed costs are fixed).

Gamma's profits would increase as it pays less per unit for Y. If you thought the company profits would fall then you probably allowed for the extra cost of a Y but not the gain from an X.

36   A   To find variable costs per unit, 1.25VC = 10, VC = 8

Profit = £(10 – 8) 100,000 – 80,000 = £120,000
240,000 = TR – 800,000 – 80,000, so TR = £1,120,000
Unit price = £1,120,000/100,000 = £11.20 ie 12% increase.

If you got 17% then you found VC by 0.75 × £10 = £7.50
If you got 20% you doubled contribution, not profit
If you got 25% you had VC = £7.50 and doubled contribution.

Chapter 6: Budgeting

1 B Expansion

Although plans to expand may underlie the framework within which an organisation's budget is set, expansion is not itself an objective of the budgetary planning process. In fact, some organisations may include a reduction in activity in their budgetary plans.

In many budget systems, expenditure that is included in the budget is automatically approved as expenditure which may be incurred by the budget holder, without further approval being sought. The budget acts as an authorisation mechanism and therefore authorisation is an objective of budgeting.

Budgets ensure that the organisation sets out in the right direction for the forthcoming period. It is comparison of the actual results with the budget which ensures that the organisation continues in the right direction, however. An objective of the budget is therefore to provide a basis for performance evaluation.

Most organisations work with limited resources. By considering carefully the demands on those resources from each budget centre, an objective of the budgeting process is to ensure that these resources are used in the most effective way.

2 C To inform shareholders of performance in meeting targets

Budgets are prepared for **internal** use and are not usually communicated to shareholders.

3 B The budget committee coordinates the preparation and administration of budgets

   D A budget manual will contain instructions governing the preparation of budgets

A budget is set within the framework of the long term or strategic plan but is not itself used for strategic planning. It acts as one step towards the achievement of the long term or strategic plan.

The budget committee is responsible for coordinating the preparation and administration of budgets but not for actually preparing the individual functional budgets.

Shareholders (unless also managers) would not usually be involved in budget preparation.

4 B Establish the organisation's long-term objectives

Since each budget is set within the framework of the long-term plan, the long-term plan must be established before any of the other budget tasks can be undertaken. The (usually annual) budget acts as the first step towards the achievement of the organisation's long-term plans.

Calculation of the overhead absorption rate is unlikely to be the first task undertaken. It will depend on other budgets being prepared first, for example the production budget and the production overheads budget.

The principal budget factor is important because it is the limiting factor which must be identified before the other budgets can be prepared. The limiting factor may be affected by the organisation's long-term objectives, however, and so its identification is not the first task to be undertaken.

The sales budget may be the first budget to be prepared, if sales are the principal budget factor. The establishment of the long-term plans and identification of the principal budget factor must come first, however.

5   B   Identify the principal budget factor

      C   Prepare a budgeted income statement

      D   Budget the resources for production

A visit to the bank manager may be necessary but is not normally a step in the preparation of a budget.

The budget would normally be prepared before the start of the finanical year to which it relates, meaning that the audit of the prior year's results would not be complete.

6   B   A factor which limits the activities of an undertaking

The factor which limits the activities of an undertaking will drive the budget and is called the principal budget factor.

The highest value item of cost will not drive the budget unless they are limited in some way.

Both a factor common to all budget centres and a factor controllable by the manager of the budget centre are incorrect. These factors will not drive the budget unless it is limited in some way.

7   B   (1), (2), (3) and (4)

Sales demand is usually the principal budget factor. However the identification of a principal budget factor depends on what factor limits the organisation's activities and so is the limiting factor.

All of the factors listed could therefore be the principal budget factor in certain circumstances.

8   B   Cash budget

The cash budget is not a functional budget but part of the overall master budget.

9   B   Sales budget, Finished goods inventory budget, Production budget, then Materials usage budget

Sales would be the principal budget factor (as there are no production resource limitations) and so this is the first budget to be prepared.

Inventory adjustments in the finished goods inventory budget indicate the production requirements for the production budget. Once the level of production is known, the materials usage budget can be prepared.

10   A   Will include a budgeted balance sheet and a budgeted income statement prepared on the accruals basis

      B   Will include a cash budget

The master budget consists of a budgeted balance sheet, a budgeted income statement and a cash budget. It is prepared from the information in the functional budgets, and is therefore the last to be prepared.

Instructions for the preparation of the budgets will be contained in the budget manual.

A budget timetable is drawn up at the start of the budgetary process, and is not included in the master budget.

11   C   Closing inventory + sales – opening inventory = production (in units)

The units in opening inventory plus those produced will either be sold or become closing inventory.

12   B   1,488

	Units
Budgeted sales	1,500
Less inventory reduction (120 × 10%)	(12)
Budgeted production	1,488

If you selected 1,392 units you deducted the budgeted opening inventory from the budgeted sales volume and then added the budgeted reduction in inventory. This is double-counting.

The option of 1,500 units is the budgeted sales volume. This would only be the correct answer if there was no budgeted change in inventory. Because a reduction in inventory is budgeted it is possible to produce fewer units in order to satisfy the sales demand.

If you selected 1,512 units you added the inventory reduction instead of deducting it. As mentioned earlier, a budgeted reduction in inventory means that it is possible to produce **fewer** units in order to satisfy the sales demand.

13   D   43,300 litres

	Dec Litres	Jan Litres	Feb Litres
Closing inventory of refined [30% of next month's sales]	12,000	15,000	9,000
Sales for the month		40,000	50,000
Less opening inventory of refined		(12,000)	(15,000)
Required refined chemical		43,000	44,000
Closing inventory of unrefined [30% of next month's requirements of refined]	12,900	13,200	
Total production requirement		56,200	
Less opening inventory		(12,900)	
Budgeted purchases		43,300	

14   B   Materials required for production – opening inventory of materials + closing inventory of materials

It may help if you think in terms of the inputs to a material purchases budget (opening inventory plus purchases) and the outputs (closing inventory and the quantity used in production). Inputs should equal outputs. You can then manipulate the inputs and outputs to calculate whichever input or output you need to determine.

15   C   £93,100

	Material Z kg	Material Y kg
Vip 2,000 × 2 kg of Z	4,000	
Vip 2,000 × 1 kg of Y		2,000
Bip 2,000 × 3 kg of Z	6,000	
Bip 2,000 × 4 kg of Y		8,000
Total usage	10,000	10,000
Increase in inventory	400	300
Materials purchases budget	10,400	10,300
Cost per kg	£4	£5
Cost of material purchases	£41,600	£51,500

Total materials purchases = £93,100 = £(41,600 + 51,500)

If you selected £86,900 you deducted the inventory increase instead of adding it. If inventories are budgeted to increase then more material must be purchased.

If you selected £90,000 you calculated the material usage correctly but did not then add on the additional material purchases required to increase the inventory.

If you selected £96,400 you missed the information about the materials inventory of Z and Y and interpreted that it would increase by 600 kg and 800 kg respectively.

16   C   £19,250

	£
Cost of sales for June (£25,000 × 0.75)	18,750
Increase in inventory (£5,000 × 0.10)	500
Budgeted inventory purchases	19,250

If you selected £18,250 you deducted the inventory increase instead of adding it. A budgeted increase in inventory means that a higher level of purchases are required to satisfy the sales demand as well as leaving sufficient inventory for the forthcoming period.

If you selected £19,125 you deducted a profit margin from the £5,000 value of the inventory. This is incorrect because inventory is valued at cost.

If you selected £25,500 you did not deduct the profit margin from the sales revenue figure for June. This is incorrect because purchases are valued at cost.

17   D   16,000

	Units
Budgeted sales	18,000
Budgeted reduction in finished goods	(3,600)
Budgeted production of completed units	14,400
Allowance for defective units (10% of output = 1/9 of input)	1,600
Production budget	16,000

If you selected 12,960 you deducted a 10% allowance for defective units, instead of adding it.

If you selected 14,400 then this makes no allowance for defective units at all.

If you selected 15,840 then you added 10% to the required completed units to allow for the defective units, but then 10% **should be based on the total number of units output**, ie 10% of 16,000 = 1,600 units

18   C   Raw materials inventories are budgeted to increase

Once the material usage budget has been prepared, based on the budgeted production volume, the usage is adjusted for the budgeted change in materials inventories in order to determine the required budgeted purchases. If purchases exceed production requirements this means that raw material inventories are being increased.

The first statement is incorrect because wastage would have been allowed for in determining the material usage budget. A budgeted increase in finished goods inventory would have been allowed for in determining the production budget and hence the material usage budget.

19   B   £3,700

	£	£
Sales (3,000 + (2 × 4,500) + (3 × 5,000))		27,000
Cost of sales (2/3 × £27,000)		18,000
Gross profit		9,000
Running expenses (6 × £800)	4,800	
Depreciation (£5,000 × 20% × 6/12)	500	
		5,300
Net profit		3,700

If you selected £3,200 you charged a full year's deprecation on the non-current assets, instead of only six months.

If you selected £3,950 you charged depreciation only from the date that the non-current assets are paid for. However, depreciation should have been charged for all of the six months that the assets were in use.

If you selected £8,200 you calculated the gross profit as 50% of the selling price, instead of one third.

20 B £77,800

	£
23% of opening receivables	13,800
40% of March sales	64,000
	77,800

Note that an adjustment does not have to be made for the settlement discount in this case as the question states that 60% of the sales will be settled, rather than that 60% of the gross invoice value will be received.

21 B £51,592

Payables balance at end of March = February and March purchases

The purchases for each month are equal to the sales requirement for the following month.

∴ Payables balance at end of March = March and April cost of sales

$$= £(33,800 + 30,690) \times 0.8$$

$$= £51,592$$

If you selected £64,490 you calculated the sales value for March and April, rather than the cost of sales for which credit is obtained.

22 B £6,975

	£	£
Sales revenue £120,000 × 0.98 × 0.95		111,720
Variable materials cost £24,000 × 0.9 × 0.95	20,520	
Variable labour cost £32,500 × 0.95	30,875	
Variable overhead £13,000 × 0.95	12,350	
Fixed overhead	41,000	
		104,745
Budgeted net profit		6,975

If you selected £3,620 you made the common mistake of failing to reduce all of the variable costs by 5% in line with the reduction in sales volume.

If you selected £9,025 you reduced the budgeted fixed costs by 5%. The fixed costs do not alter when activity levels change.

If you selected £9,375 you did not take account of the reduction in the selling price.

23 B A budget must be quantified if it is to be useful for planning and control purposes

E An organisation's long term plan provides the framework within which an annual budget is set

If a budget is not quantified then it is merely a general statement of intention rather than a quantified plan of action that the organisation will aim to achieve.

The long term plan does provide the framework for the annual budget. Each budget is a step towards the achievement of the long term plan.

A forecast and a budget are not the same thing. A forecast is a prediction of what might happen given a certain set of circumstances. A budget is a quantified plan that the organisation will aim to achieve. A budget is often based on a forecast.

Standard costs provide the basic unit rates to be used in the preparation of a number of functional budgets, rather than the other way round.

The first budget to be prepared is the budget for the principal budget factor, ie, the factor which limits the organisation's activities. Often this is sales demand but it will not always be so. There may be a limitation on some other factor such as machine capacity. In this case the production budget will be prepared before the sales budget.

24 B Total cost = 65,000 + (3 × quantity)

		£
Highest production	3,000 units	74,000
Lowest production	1,500 units	69,500
	1,500	4,500

Variable cost per unit = £4,500/1,500 = £3 per unit

Total cost	= fixed cost + (£3 × quantity)
£74,000	= fixed cost + (£3 × 3,000)
Fixed cost	= £74,000 – £9,000
	= £65,000

SAMPLE PAPER

25 B £18,700

	Units	£
Highest output	1,090	19,540
Less lowest output	700	17,200
	390	2,340

Variable cost per unit = £2,340/390 = £6

Fixed cost at a production level of 1,090 units = £19,540 – (1,090 × £6) = £13,000

(Note that the fixed cost will be the same if calculated at the lowest production level, but not if production levels other than the ones used in the calculation of variable cost are used.)

Total cost of producing 950 units:

	£
Variable cost (950 × £6)	5,700
Fixed cost	13,000
	18,700

Be careful when you begin these calculations to ensure that you base them on the highest and lowest production/output, and not the highest and lowest costs. This could lead to a different answer, as the highest and lowest outputs do not necessarily correspond to the highest and lowest costs.

26 C £41,250

	Production costs £	Sales etc costs £
Total costs of 60,000 units (fixed plus variable)	510,000	150,000
Total cost of 36,000 units (fixed plus variable)	366,000	126,000
Difference = variable costs of 24,000 units	144,000	24,000
Variable costs per unit	£6	£1

	Production costs £	Sales etc costs £
Total costs of 60,000 units	510,000	150,000
Variable costs of 60,000 units	360,000	60,000
Fixed costs	150,000	90,000

The **rate of absorption** of fixed production overheads will therefore be £150,000/60,000 = £2.50 per unit

The fixed production overhead absorbed by the product would be 16,500 units produced × £2.50 = £41,250

If you selected £33,750 you based the overhead absorption on the number of units sold, rather than on the number of units produced.

If you selected £37,500 you calculated the correct value of the fixed production overhead incurred during the quarter, but this is not the same as the overhead absorbed.

If you selected £66,000 you absorbed the fixed sales, distribution and administration costs in addition to the fixed production costs.

27 D

				£
Total fixed cost		= £7,600		
Variable cost per unit		= £9.90		

Department 1

	Units		£
Total production overhead cost for	1,000	= 1,000 × £6 =	6,000
Total production overhead cost for	2,000	= 2,000 × £4.20 =	8,400
Increase	1,000		2,400

Variable overhead cost per unit = £2.40

Fixed overhead cost = £6,000 – (1,000 × £2.40)

  = £3,600

Department 2

	Units		£
Total production overhead cost for	1,000	= 1,000 × £4 =	4,000
Total production overhead cost for	2,000	= 2,000 × £2 =	4,000

The production overhead cost in department 2 is wholly fixed.

Summary

	Total fixed cost £	Variable cost per unit £
Variable materials		4.00
Variable labour		3.50
Production overhead – 1	3,600	2.40
Production overhead – 2	4,000	
	7,600	9.90

If you selected £3,600 and £9.90 you omitted the fixed cost for department 2.

The combination of £4,000 and £11.70 treats the unit rate for 2,000 in department 1 as wholly variable, but it is a semi-variable cost.

If you selected £7,600 and £7.50 you forgot to include the variable cost per unit for department 1.

28 C All of the stated factors can affect the accuracy of any forecast

29 C A perfect linear relationship between the two variables

Two variables may have a perfect linear relationship (r = +1 or r = -1) but this is not necessary for forecasting purposes.

30 A Fixed costs are £100. Variable costs per unit are £20

If C = 100 + 20P, then fixed costs are the constant, £100, and variable costs are £20 per unit.

31 A Positive correlation means that low values of one variable are associated with low values of the other, and high values of one variable are associated with high values of the other.

**   D** Negative correlation means that low values of one variable are associated with high values of the other, and high values of one variable are associated with low values of the other.

Positive correlation means that both variables move together from low to high. Negative correlation means that as one variable increases, the other decreases.

32 C Diagram (a) represents perfect negative correlation; diagram (b) represents imperfect positive correlation.

Diagram (a) shows perfect correlation because all the points lie on the line. The correlation is negative because as X increases, Y decreases.

Diagram (b) shows imperfect correlation because not all the points lie on the line. The correlation is positive because as X increases, Y increases.

33 A 0.52

The coefficient of determination, r^2, measures the proportion of the total variation in the value of one variable that can be explained by variations in the value of the other variable.

$r^2 = 0.72^2 = 0.52$

Therefore, only just over half of the variation in one variable can be explained by variation in the other.

If you selected 0.85 you calculated the square root of 0.72, rather than squaring it to derive the coefficient of determination.

If you selected 1.44, you multiplied 0.72 by 2 instead of squaring it.

34 A The coefficient of determination must always fall between 0 and +1

B The correlation coefficient must always fall between –1 and +1

The correlation coefficient (r) can take any value from –1 (perfect negative correlation) to +1 (perfect positive correlation).

The coefficient of determination (r^2) must therefore lie between 0 and +1.

A major disadvantage of the high-low method is that it does not take into account the full range of available data. Only two pairs of historical cost data are used in the cost estimation.

A cost estimate produced using the high-low method cannot be used to reliably predict the cost for any level of activity. It can reasonably be used to **estimate** a cost within the range of activity covered by the data available. Although managers are often forced to use this data as a basis for prediction outside this range, the results will be unreliable.

35 C 72% of the variation in sales revenue can be explained by the corresponding variation in advertising expenditure

Correlation coefficient, r = 0.85

Coefficient of determination, $r^2 = 0.85^2 = 0.72$

The coefficient of determination tells us that 72% of the variation in sales revenue can be explained by the corresponding variation in advertising expenditure.

36 B When nothing is spent on advertising the average level of sales is £50,000

C For every £1,000 spent on advertising, sales revenue increases by £20,000 on average

When nothing is spent on advertising, X = 0.

$\therefore Y = 5 + (2 \times 0) = 5$

Therefore sales revenue is £5 × 10,000 = £50,000 on average.

If £1,000 extra is spent on advertising, then sales increase by 20 × £1,000.

Therefore the increase in sales revenue when an extra £1,000 is spent on advertising is £20,000 (2 × £10,000)

37 B Top management prepare a budget with little or no input from operating personnel.

A 'top down' budgeting process is an imposed style of budgeting. This style of budgeting has its advantages but it can cause motivational problems.

38 A Increase operational managers' commitment to organisational objectives

D Based on information from employees most familiar with day to day activities

A 'bottom-up' style of budgeting is a participative approach where lower-level managers are involved in preparing their own budgets. This tends to increase their commitment to the budget and to the overall objectives. It also means that budgets are likely to be more accurate and realistic because managers who are undertaking tasks on a daily basis will have greater knowledge about what is achievable.

Since each division is preparing its own budget, a participative process can be more time consuming and it can be more difficult to coordinate the divisions' activities than if centrally-prepared budgets are imposed on the divisions.

Budgetary slack is unnecessary expenditure built into the budget. If managers are involved in preparing their own budgets they may be tempted to build in slack to give some protection against underperformance.

39 A It is time consuming because it involves starting each budget from scratch.

Starting each budget from scratch is not a criticism of incremental budgeting as this is a feature of zero-based budgeting.

40 C The budget for each period is based on the current year's results, modified for changes in activity levels.

Increments of expenditure are compared with the expected benefits to be received in a zero-based budgeting system, not in an incremental budgeting system.

The regular updating of the budget by adding the budget for a further accounting period occurs with a system of rolling budgets.

41 B A new accounting period, such as a month or a quarter, is added as each old one expires.

C The budget is more realistic and certain as there is a short period between the preparation of budgets.

The other characteristics relate to annual budgets and zero based budgets (where each item of expenditure has to be justified from scratch).

42 B A method of budgeting whereby all activities are re-evaluated each time a budget is formulated.

Zero-based budgeting builds up a budget from scratch. It rejects the assumption that this year's activities will continue at the same level next year.

43 C Company C: Product based budget

E Company B: Responsibility based budget

G Company A: Activity based budget

The use of an activity based budget by company A will ensure that the non-production costs are planned and controlled more accurately through the identification of appropriate cost drivers. The use of non-volume related cost-drivers should also help with more accurate planning and control of production costs, where low volume products might cause a disproportionate amount of cost.

Within company B each specialist manager will have their own budget and will be responsible for the achievement of that budget.

A product based budget is most appropriate for company C because a separate budget would be prepared for each of the diverse products.

44 A,B A forecast is a prediction by management of the expected outcome whereas a budget represents a set of targets of what management intend to happen. A budget is usually set just once a year whereas forecasts and re-forecasts can be carried out much more frequently.

The statement 'All budgets are prepared in financial terms' is incorrect as often a budget could include, for example, tonnage of raw material needed or quantity (in units) of finished product.

The statement 'The master budget consists of a budgeted income statement and a budgeted balance sheet' is incorrect as a master budget would also contain a cash flow budget.

The statement 'A flexible budget adjusts both fixed and variable costs for the level of activity' is incorrect as a flexible budget adjusts just variable costs for the level of activity and not fixed costs.
SAMPLE PAPER

45 A Zero-based budgeting, by its very definition, starts from zero and is built upwards

The statement 'a zero variance between budgeted and actual overhead' is incorrect as this merely refers to the comparison of actual performance with budgeted performance.

The statement 'an assumed sales level of zero as the starting point for budgeting the coming year's overheads' is a meaningless statement as an overhead budget would be based on budgeted sales not zero sales.

The statement 'an overhead budget of zero' is incorrect.
SAMPLE PAPER

46 A The high-low method of cost estimation is a method of linear extrapolation or interpolation between two actual data points. It is a method for flexing a budget by calculating the budgeted cost for the actual activity.

The high-low method uses the highest and lowest costs in the budget period for the extrapolation process itself.

The measurement of actual cost for the budgeted activity is irrelevant.

The high-low method estimates a single cost at a certain level of activity and not a range of costs.
SAMPLE PAPER

47 A Month 4 materials cost included within cost of sales is £116,000 × 40% = £46,400. Inventory of materials are budgeted to reduce from £22,000 to £12,000 and therefore budgeted materials purchased in the month would be (£46,400 + £12,000 – £22,000) = £36,400.

£46,400 (see above) represents the materials cost of sales rather than purchases. £46,400 - £12,000 + £22,000 = £56,400 incorrectly deducts closing inventory and adds the opening. 40% (£116,000 + £12,000 - £22,000) = £42,400 incorrectly applies the 40% adjustment to the materials inventory figures.
SAMPLE PAPER

48 B As sales are increasing at 20% per month the expected sales for February are £120,000 × 120% = £144,000. As the gross margin is 30% on sales the cost of sales for February is expected to be £144,000 × 70% = £100,800.

The company policy is to maintain closing inventory at 10% of the expected next month's sales. The closing inventory for January is therefore £10,080. The cost of a unit is £2 × 70% = £1.40, meaning the closing inventory for January is £10,080/£1.40 = 7,200 units.

The budgeted cost of production for January would therefore need to cover January sales (£120,000/£2 per unit = 60,000 units) plus an increase in inventory from 6,000 to 7,200 units, ie, a total of 61,200 units. This is a cost of 61,200 × £1.40 = £85,680.

If you incorrectly calculated the cost of production as £84,000 then you calculated the production volume as 60,000 units (the number sold in January) and did not allow for an increase in inventory levels.

If you incorrectly calculated the cost of production as £120,000 then you again calculated the production volume as 60,000 units in error and made a further error in valuing this volume at the selling price of £2 per unit rather than the cost price.

If you incorrectly calculated the cost of production as £122,400 then you correctly calculated the production volume as 61,200 units but in error valued this volume at the selling price of £2 per unit rather than the cost price.
SAMPLE PAPER

Chapter 7: Working capital

1   B   Depreciation of the new rolling mill

This is a non-cash item and should therefore be excluded.

2   D   £18,250

	January £	February £	March £
Receipts			
Credit sales	10,000	11,000	12,500
Cash sales	5,000	4,500	6,000
	15,000	15,500	18,500
Payments			
Suppliers	6,500	4,200	7,800
Wages	2,300	2,300	3,000
Overheads	1,500	1,750	1,900
	10,300	8,250	12,700
Opening cash	500	5,200	12,450
Net cash receipts	4,700	7,250	5,800
Closing cash	5,200	12,450	18,250

3   C   £17,600 inflow

Depreciation and profits and losses on sales are accounting entries only. The only amount that will appear in the cash budget is the receipt of the £17,600 sale proceeds.

4   B   £20,000

July receipts

(Ignore the discounts: the percentages add to 100 so discounts have already been accounted for)

20% July sales   = £5,000

60% June sales   = £12,000

10% May sales   = £3,000

Total   = £20,000

5   A   £338,025

Receipts for March:

	£
50% × March sales for cash (50% × £215,000)	107,500
80% × February credit sales less 4% discount	
(50% × 80% × £580,500 × 96%)	222,912
15% January credit sales (50% × 15% × £101,500)	7,613
	338,025

If you selected £347,313 you forgot that receivables who pay in the month after sale are entitled to a 4% discount.

If you selected £568,550 you calculated the amount to be received from credit customers as 80% and 15% respectively of total sales, rather than of the credit sales.

The option of £587,125 combines both of the errors discussed.

6   B   43%

Suppose the total gross invoiced sales is £100.

Cash received 45%.

But these customers have taken a 10% discount before paying, hence the gross value of bills settled is 45/0.9   = £50

Bad debts 7%   = £7

Balancing figure ie, received in month two = £43

Total   = £100

If you selected 38% or 58% you did not deal correctly with the early settlement discount. If you selected 48% you made no allowance at all for the discount.

7   A   £211,475

(£175,000 × 0.6 × 0.96 from March sales)	=	£100,800
(£332,000 × 0.3 from February sales)	=	£99,600
(£221,500 × 0.05 from January sales)	=	£11,075
April receipts	=	£211,475

If you selected £215,675 you forgot to allow for the 4% settlement discount.

The option of £290,284 calculates the receipts on the assumption that the first customers pay in the month of sale rather than in the month after sale.

If you selected £299,500 you combined both errors.

8   B   £25,500

Production of Z	Units
Sales requirement	10,000
Closing inventory	15,000
	25,000
Opening inventory	(14,000)
Budgeted production	11,000

Purchases of W	Litres
Purchase requirement (11,000 units × 2 litres)	22,000
Closing inventory	15,000
	37,000
Opening inventory	(20,000)
	17,000
Cost at £1.50 per litre	£25,500

If you selected £17,000 you forgot to value your answer in litres at a cost of £1.50 per litre.

If you selected £33,000 you made no allowance for the reduction in materials inventory.

If you selected £34,500 you reversed both the adjustments for changes in inventory.

9 D £24,060

April cost of sales	= 60% × £48,500	= £29,100
Closing payables balance for April	= £29,100 × 30%	= £8,730
May cost of sales	= 60% × £36,500	= £21,900
Closing payables balance for May	= £21,900 × 30%	= £6,570
Reduction in payables balance in May		= £2,160
Cost of sales for May		= £21,900
Supplier Payments in May		= £24,060

If you selected £19,740 you deducted the change in payables balance from the cost of sales. The reduction in the payables balance should have been added, since this means that higher payments were made to suppliers to reduce the balance owed.

The option of £21,900 is the cost of sales, which takes no account of the change in the payables balance.

If you selected £23,340 you took the cost of sales to be 40% of the sales value, instead of 60%.

10 B £62,143

Bendy will pay for March's purchases in May.

In March, he will top up inventories by those required for June's sales.

Cost of goods sold in June = £87,000 × 100/(100 + 40) = £62,143

The more traditional approach to calculating this would be:

March opening inventory	= (84,000 + 90,000 + 90,000) × 100 /140	= (£188,571)
March closing inventory	= (90,000 + 90,000 + 87,000) × 100 /140	= £190,714
March cost of sales	= 84,000 × 100/140	= £60,000
		£62,143

If you selected £52,200 you deducted a profit **margin** of 40% to determine the cost of goods sold, instead of deducting a 40% **mark-up**.

If you selected £64,286 you misinterpreted the timings of purchases and calculated the payments as being the cost of goods sold in May.

If you selected £87,000 you interpreted the timings of purchases correctly but then you forgot to deduct the profit mark up.

11 A £327,000

	£'000
Cost of sales for month = £520,000 × 70%	364
Increase in trade payables	(15)
Decrease in inventory	(22)
Budgeted payment to trade payables	327

If you selected an incorrect option you did not deal correctly with the change in trade payables and inventory balances.

An increase in trade payables will reduce the amount paid to suppliers, since more credit is being taken. A decrease in inventory will also reduce the amount paid to suppliers because required purchases will be lower.

12   B   £9,400

Month	1 Units	2 Units	3 Units	4 Units
Sales	2,000	2,200	2,500	2,600
Closing inventory	1,100	1,250	1,300	
Opening inventory	(1,000)	(1,100)	(1,250)	(1,300)
Purchases	2,100	2,350	2,550	
Payments (£)		8,400	9,400	10,200

If you selected £8,200 you reversed the opening and closing inventory figures for month 2.

The cost of sales of £10,000 for month 3 is the incorrect figure.

If you selected £10,200 you have calculated the purchases figure for month 3. However, the question asks for the budgeted **payment** for month 3, which represents month 2 purchases.

13   C   £50,200

Payments in June will be in respect of May purchases.

	May
Production requirements (8,400 units × 3kg)	25,200 kg
Closing inventory	4,100 kg
	29,300 kg
Less opening inventory	4,200 kg
Purchase budget	25,100 kg
25,100 kg × £2 per kg = payment for purchases in June	£50,200

If you selected £25,100 this is the figure for quantity of material to be paid for, not its value.

The option of £48,800 is the value of June purchases, which will be paid for in July.

If you selected £50,600 your adjustments for opening and closing material inventories were the wrong way round.

14   B   £231,000

	£
75% × May wages cost = 75% × 8,400 × £7 × 4 hours	176,400
25% × April wages cost = 25% × 7,800 × £7 × 4 hours	54,600
Wage payments for May	231,000

If you selected £222,600 you calculated the payment the wrong way round as 25% of May wages cost and 75% of April wages cost.

If you selected £233,800 you calculated the payment as 75% to be paid in the month and 25% in advance for the following month.

The option of £235,200 is the labour cost for May, which makes no allowance for the timing of cost payments.

15 D £143,000

	£
Average receivables after change in policy 90/360 × £960,000 × 120%	288,000
Less: current average receivables 60/360 × £960,000	(160,000)
Increase in receivables	128,000
Increase in inventories	30,000
Increase in payables	(15,000)
Net increase in working capital investment	143,000

If you selected £31,000 you calculated the effect of the 30 days increase in the collection period based on only the increase in the sales revenue, rather than on all of the sales revenue.

If you selected £95,000 you took no account at all of the increase in sales revenue and if you selected £113,000 you reversed the adjustments for the changes in inventories and trade payables. An increase in inventories means that more money will be invested in working capital and the reverse applies for payables.

16 B,D,E

In order to improve cashflow, a business needs to decrease receivables, decrease inventory and increase the credit period taken from suppliers.

17 C Arrange an overdraft

D Implement better credit control procedures

Arranging short-term finance in the form of an overdraft, and encouraging receivables to pay sooner will alleviate the short-term cash deficit problem.

Paying payables early would exacerbate the situation and issuing shares is most appropriate for long-term finance.

Replacing non-current assets would not provide any extra cash with immediate effect, thereby making the situation worse in the short term.

18 D Maximum £12,000

End of June £8,000

	Jan £'000	Feb £'000	Mar £'000	Apr £'000	May £'000	Jun £'000
Payments to suppliers						
Current month 50%*	3	4	6	5	4	4
Following month 50%	–	3	4	6	5	4
Revised payments	3	7	10	11	9	8
Payments in original budget	6	8	12	10	8	4
Change in cash flow	3	1	2	(1)	(1)	(4)
Previous inflow/(outflow)	(5)	(9)	(5)	–	2	7
Revised cash flow	(2)	(8)	(3)	(1)	1	3
Balance b/f	2	–	(8)	(11)	(12)	(11)
Revised balance c/f	–	(8)	(11)	(12)	(11)	(8)

* 50% Jan – May, 100% Jun

If you calculated the maximum overdraft to be £18,000 you simply added the change in cash flow for each month to the previous budgeted closing balances. However, the cash flow change is cumulative and delaying the payment of suppliers must improve the overdraft balance from its current level.

If you selected £6,000 as the overdraft balance for June you budgeted for the delayed payment of suppliers in all six months, rather than in only the first five months.

19   A   £82,500

Gross profit = 10% sales, and cost of sales = 90% sales

Annual cost of sales = 90% × £1.1m = £990,000

As inventories remain constant, this is also the annual purchase cost, which is spread evenly over the year.

Thus one month's purchases = £990,000/12 = £82,500

This is the value of one month's extra trade credit, ie, the cash benefit to be derived from delaying payment by one month.

If you selected £83,333 you interpreted the 10% gross profit as a mark up on cost, rather than as a margin based on the sales revenue.

The option of £91,667 is the sales revenue for one month. However, the cash saved in delayed payments to suppliers must be based on the **cost** of sales, after deducting the 10% margin.

20   B   Buy back the company's shares

     C   Increase payables by delaying payments to suppliers

Buying back the company's shares would be a suitable use of a long-term surplus (but not short-term), by returning surplus cash to the shareholders.

Increasing payables would increase the surplus still further because additional credit would be taken from suppliers.   SAMPLE PAPER

21   B   £403,000

		£
Inventories	60/365 × 40% of £3m	197,260
Receivables	35/365 × £3m	287,671
		484,931
Trade payables	25/365 × 40% of £3m	(82,192)
		402,739

If you selected £280,000 or £699,000 you valued the trade payables and the inventories respectively at sales value. However, as far as the company's working capital is concerned, their investment amounts to the cost value of these elements.

If you selected £567,000 you added the trade payables figure, but the availability of trade credit reduces the required investment in working capital.

22   C   17 weeks

	Weeks
Raw materials	3
Payables	(6)
Production	2
Finished goods	7
Receivables	11
	17

If you selected 29 weeks you added the payables period instead of deducting it. However, the availability of credit from suppliers reduces the cash operating cycle.

23　B　182 days

	Days
Raw material inventory turnover (250/1,070 × 365 days)	85.3
Less payables: average payment period (162/1,070 × 365)	(55.3)
	30.0
Production cycle (WIP turnover) (115/1,458 × 365)	28.8
Finished goods inventory turnover (186/1,458 × 365)	46.6
Debt collection period (345/1,636 × 365)	77.0
Full operating cycle	182.4

If you calculated the operating cycle to be 174 days you made the common mistake of basing the calculation for raw materials inventory and payables on the figure for cost of goods sold. If the purchases figure is not available then this might be acceptable but the use of the purchases figure is more accurate.

24　A　Lower net operating cash inflow

　　D　Slower inventory turnover

When the cash cycle lengthens, there will be a slow-down in operating cash inflows, and net cash inflow will be lower. The reasons for a longer cash cycle could be a slower inventory turnover, a lengthening of the average credit period taken by customers and/or paying suppliers sooner. Net assets will be either increased or remain the same, depending on how the extra working capital is financed. Net assets should not decrease, however, and so net asset turnover should not rise.

25　B　66 days

Average inventory	= £170,000	
Inventory period	= (170 / 2,000) × 365 =	31.03 days
Sales value	= £2,000,000 × 100/80 =	£2,500,000
Credit sales	= £1,250,000	
Average receivables	= £210,000	
Receivables period	= (210 / 1,250) × 365 =	61.32 days
Purchases	= cost of goods sold + inventory increase	
	= £2,000,000 + £100,000	
	= £2,100,000	
Average payables	= £150,000	
Payables period	= (150 / 2,100) × 365 =	(26.07) days
Cash operating cycle	=	66.28 days

If you selected 65 days you based your payables calculation on the cost of goods sold. Since credit is received on the **purchases** for the year, this should be the basis of the calculation.

If you selected 68 days you miscalculated the sales revenue using a 20% mark up rather than a 20% margin.

If you selected 118 days you added together the days for each element of working capital. However, the payables period, during which the company takes credit from suppliers, reduces the length of the cycle and hence should be deducted.

26　A　Cash operating cycle decreases, Liquidity ratio decreases

The reduction in the amount of time taken for customers to pay their bills would reduce the cash operating cycle.

The reduction in receivables and in the overdraft mean that the numerator and denominator of the liquidity ratio would both reduce by the same amount. Therefore the ratio would decrease.

27 B 0.91

Quick ratio = Current assets excluding inventories/current liabilities

$$= (2.8 + 0.3)/(2.6 + 0.8)$$

$$= 0.91$$

If you selected 0.31 you included the loan repayable in five years in the denominator. Since the ratio is concerned with short-term liquidity this long-term loan should have been excluded.

If you selected 1.80 you included non-current assets, inventories and the long-term loan in your calculation. All of these should be excluded for the same reason as stated above.

If you selected 2.15 you included inventory in the numerator. This would have been the correct calculation for the current ratio, but not the quick ratio.

28 B Proposal 1   Decrease

    D Proposal 2   Increase

Let receivables	= 100
Cash	= 50
Therefore payables	= 300

Proposal 1

Receivables	= 0
Cash	= 50 + 98 (100 less 2%) = 148
Therefore current ratio	= 148/300
	= 0.493

Proposal 2

Cash and payables will both rise at same rate, say, by 50

Therefore current ratio	= 200/350
	= 0.57

29 B The quick (liquidity) ratio is current assets (excluding inventory) divided by current liabilities. As inventory is excluded from the ratio any change in inventory levels would have no effect on the ratio unless either other current assets (such as cash at bank) or current liabilities are also affected. If inventory levels are financed by an increase in the bank overdraft then the denominator of the ratio would increase, reducing the ratio itself. This will always be the case regardless of the relative values of current assets and current liabilities.

It is worth noting that if inventory levels are increased by reducing the cash at bank balance then the quick ratio would again decrease.

30 A,E Current ratio increases, quick ratio decreases

The current ratio is current assets divided by current liabilities. If cash is used to reduce trade payables then both the numerator and denominator will reduce. As the current ratio is greater than 1:1 the numerator is larger than the denominator. This means that the same absolute change to the numerator would represent a larger proportionate change to the denominator than the numerator, thereby increasing the ratio.

The quick ratio is current assets (excluding inventory) divided by current liabilities. If cash is used to reduce trade payables then both the numerator and denominator will reduce. As the quick ratio is less than 1:1 the denominator is larger than the numerator. This means that the same absolute change to the numerator would represent a smaller proportionate change to the denominator than the numerator, thereby reducing the ratio.

31 A The inventory value is £2,100. The rate of inventory turnover is 10 times p.a., therefore the annual cost of sales is £21,000 (we are told opening inventory equals closing inventory). The gross profit margin is 30% which means annual sales are £21,000/0.7 = £30,000.

The receivables collection period is 1 month, which means closing receivables are £30,000/12 = £2,500.

The payables payment period is 1.6 months, which means closing payables are £21,000/12 × 1.6 = £2,800.

The quick ratio is 2:1 which means current assets (excluding inventory) are £2,800 × 2 = £5,600. As receivables are £2,500 the cash balance must be (£5,600 – £2,500) = £3,100.

If you calculated incorrectly the cash balance as £1,000 then you probably incorrectly calculated closing payables as £21,000/12 = £1,750 which would mean current assets (excluding inventory) of £3,500 and cash of (£3,500 – £2,500) = £1,000.

If you calculated incorrectly the cash balance as £100 then you probably incorrectly calculated closing receivables as £2,100/12/0.7 = £250 and closing payables as £2,100/12 = £175 and therefore current assets (excluding inventory) of £350.   SAMPLE PAPER

32 B January sales are £350,000 × 12% = £42,000. Sales in each of the other months are (£350,000 – £42,000)/11 = £28,000.

March cash collections will be:

50% of March sales   =   £28,000 × 50% = £14,000

45% of February sales =   £28,000 × 45% = £12,600

Total = (£14,000 + £12,600) = £26,600

If you incorrectly calculated the cash collections in March as £28,000 then you probably calculated collections using 50% on both March and February sales.

If you incorrectly calculated the cash collections in March as £32,900 then you probably used January sales of £42,000 × 45% and February sales of £28,000 × 50% in error.

33 C The company's cash operating cycle is calculated as:

(Inventory days + receivables days – payables days)

Inventory days = £490,000/£4,500,000 × 365 = 39.7 days

Receivables days = £610,000/(£4,500,000/0.68) × 365 = 33.6 days

Payables days = £340,000/£4,660,000 × 365 = 26.6 days

Note: The cost of sales value is used for the inventory days and also to calculate sales (using the gross margin of 32%). However, the purchases figure is used to calculate the payables days.

The answer is therefore (39.7 + 33.6 – 26.6) days = 46.7 days (rounded to 47).

If you incorrectly calculated the answer as 34 days then you probably rounded up the inventory days to 40 days, added the payables days in error (also rounded up at 27 days) and then deducted the receivables days (rounded down to 33 days).

If you incorrectly calculated the answer as 44 days then you probably used the purchases figure of £4,660,000 in the calculations for inventory days and receivables days rather than the cost of sales figure.

If you incorrectly calculated the answer as 51 days you probably calculated the inventory days and payables days correctly but used the wrong gross margin to calculate the sales figure in the receivables days formula (using 22% margin rather than 32%).   SAMPLE PAPER

34 C

	Months
The average time the raw materials are in inventory	1.0
Less the time taken to pay suppliers	(2.5)
Time taken to produce the goods	2.0
Time taken by customers to pay for the goods	1.5
Total	2.0

35 D The purchase of goods increases inventory (current assets) while the taking of credit in respect of the purchase increases payables (current liabilities).

36 A,E,I

	20X4	20X5	20X6
Inventory turnover	23 days	25 days	29 days
Plus receivables collection	49 days	38 days	35 days
Less payables payment	(51 days)	(35 days)	(30 days)
Cash operating cycle	21 days	28 days	34 days

37 A All businesses face a trade-off between being profitable and being liquid. Less liquidity may yield greater profitability, but less liquidity equals greater risk (A). Liquidity and risk (B) are not the trade-off – they are on the same side of the trade-off. The equity and debt (C) trade-off is concerned with long-term capital structure rather than current assets and the short-term versus long-term borrowing trade-off (D) is a financing decision unrelated to current assets.

38 A The transactions motive means that a business holds cash to meet its current day-to-day financial obligations.

39 A,C,D

A business suffering from liquidity problems might consider:

Reducing the production period – not easy to do but it might be worth investigating different machinery or different working methods.

Reducing the credit period extended to receivables.

Extending the period of credit taken from suppliers.

The business would not want pay its payables quicker (B) or to hold inventory for longer (E).

40 A An aggressive policy implies financing long-term needs with short-term funds which would reduce liquidity but increase profitability (A) due to the cheaper short-term debt relative to long-term debt: decreased liquidity = increased risk.

41 A,D There is no reason to believe that the current ratio would increase (C) – there could be a rapid increase in current assets (particularly receivables) but this would be often more than matched by a commensurate increase in current liabilities (payables and bank overdraft). A lengthening cash operating cycle (A) and a rapid increase in sales (D) are the classic signs of overtrading.

42 B,C Holding costs include insurance (B) and the opportunity cost of capital tied up (C). (D) and (E) are production costs, while clerical and administrative expenses are overheads.

43 C If we order inventory more frequently we can expect higher order costs but lower average levels of inventory.

44 A **c** is the cost of placing one order and **d** is the estimated usage of the inventory item over the period.

45 C EOQ = 1,600 boxes and the re-order interval = 40 days

Annual demand = 40 × 250 = 10,000 boxes = d

Order cost = £64 = c

Holding cost per year per unit = 25% of £2 = £0.50 = h

$$EOQ = \sqrt{\frac{2cd}{h}} = \sqrt{\frac{2 \times 64 \times 10,000}{0.5}} = 1,600 \text{ boxes}$$

46   C   The ABC system is the most suitable. It aims to reduce the work involved in inventory control in a business which may have several thousand types of inventory items. It is a technique which divides inventory into sub-classifications based on their annual usage and involves using different control systems for each classification.

47   D   All businesses face a trade-off between being profitable (providing a return) and being liquid (staying in business).

48   A,C,F

Credit control – Yes

Short-term investment – Yes

Capital investment appraisal – No

Treasury management involves managing cash surpluses and deficits by making short-term investments, and also managing working capital from day to day so as to optimise cash flow, including inventory, receivables (credit control) and payables management. Credit control in many businesses is managed jointly by the treasury management and recording transactions (receivables ledger) departments, via a separate credit control department. Management accounting will attend to capital investment appraisal.

49   A,C,F

Cost per order (£180) – Included

Carrying cost per unit per month (£2) – Included

Purchase price per unit (£4) – Not included

In the formula, c = the cost of placing one order; d = the estimated usage of an inventory item over a particular period; and h = the cost of holding one unit of inventory for that period. The purchase price per unit is not a constituent part of the formula.   SAMPLE PAPER

50   D   If the company is offering a 10% discount for settling within the first month, then if it receives 45% of gross sales value that must equate to 45 × 100/90 = 50% of invoices settling within that first month. With bad debts of 20%, that leaves 30% to be collected in the second month.

51   B   The closing receivables of £72,000 represent the customers who did not take advantage of the discount available in December; the total invoicing on 30 November must therefore have been £72,000 × 2 = £144,000. This means that from January to October invoicing was £276,000 – £144,000 = £132,000.

	Cash received £	Discount allowed £
Opening receivables taking discount (£56,000 × 0.5 × 0.9)	25,200	2,800
Opening receivables not taking discount (£56,000 × 0.5)	28,000	–
Sales in year taking discount (£132,000 × 0.5 × 0.9)	59,400	6,600
Sales in year not taking discount (£132,000 × 0.5)	66,000	
November invoicing taking discount (£144,000 × 0.5 × 0.9)	64,800	7,200
	243,400	16,600

Chapter 8: Performance management

1   D   Budgets and standards

To exercise control, managers must compare actual performance with budgets and standards.

The term 'feedback' describes the whole process of reporting control information to management and might also refer to the control information itself.

Information about fixed costs and activity levels might be included with the control information but they are not a separate element of the control cycle itself.

SAMPLE PAPER

2   C   Distributed to as many managers as possible

Reports should be communicated to the manager who has responsibility and authority to act on the information. There is no point in distributing reports to managers who cannot act on the information contained therein.

In this situation managers could suffer from information overload where they are supplied with so much information that their attention is not drawn clearly to that which is specifically relevant to them. Important information could be overlooked or simply ignored.

SAMPLE PAPER

3   C   Reporting only of variances which exceed a certain value

When reports are prepared using the exception principle, areas that are conforming to plan are given less prominence in control reports, allowing managers to focus on areas requiring attention.

4   B   Reports should be clear and comprehensive

     D   Based on the information contained in reports, managers may decide to do nothing

Management reports should be sufficiently accurate for the purpose intended. Complete accuracy might not be possible, or might take so long to attain that the value of the information is diminished by its late arrival.

Although reports should distinguish between controllable and uncontrollable items it is incorrect to say that uncontrollable items should not be included. Uncontrollable items might be included for information rather than for action.

5   B   A manager's advertising budget is disproportionately large in comparison with the budgeted revenue to be generated.

As long as the advertising budget is a realistic plan of the expenditure necessary to achieve the company's objectives, the disproportionate amount of expenditure is not an example of budget bias. The manager might perhaps be responsible for a new product or service and the company is budgeting to spend heavily on advertising to increase consumer awareness.

The other three examples are all incidences of budget bias, ie, the manipulation of budgetary plans in a way which distorts the planning and control process.

6   D   Management control activity might involve a comparison of the latest forecast results with the original budget.

This form of control is known as feed forward control. If necessary, management can take control action now to attempt to bring forecast results back into line with the original budget.

Although management accounts are prepared for a different purpose from that of external financial reports, ensuring continual convergence between the two systems is an important aspect of integrating performance and compliance measures into general systems of control.

The setting of appropriate performance measures will not on its own ensure that an organisation's performance management is effective. Continual monitoring of the measures and the instigation of appropriate control action is another important aspect of integrating performance and compliance measures into general systems of control.

The board of directors does require management reports to monitor progress.

7   C   Revenue focused

Although managers might focus on the achievement of revenues in the context of a budget constrained or profit conscious style of evaluation, 'revenue focused' is not a specific style identified by Hopwood.

8   A,F,G

With a budget constrained style of evaluation the focus is on meeting the budget on a short-term basis. Compared with the other styles of evaluation this is more likely to lead to job-related tension and budget bias.

With a non-accounting style of evaluation the budgetary information is not as important in the evaluation of a manager's performance. Compared with the other styles of evaluation there will be less focus on cost control.

9   C   Improve gross profit

A new budgetary planning and control system is not designed to improve actual performance levels.

It is designed to improve the control of actual performance, the coordination of activities, and the communication of ideas and plans.

10   B   Rapid management response to changes in the trading environment.

One of the advantages of decentralisation is the opportunity for a speeder response to problems and situations as a result of divisional managers' more detailed and 'local' knowledge.

Improved goal congruence is not an advantage of decentralisation. Once an organisation is decentralised it might effectively divide into a number of self-interested segments.

The availability of objective performance measures is not an advantage of decentralisation. There are often difficulties in setting suitable measures of performance in decentralised organisations.

Improved communication is not an advantage of decentralisation. There are often difficulties with communication between managers in a decentralised organisation.

11   B   (1), (2) and (3) only

Apportioned head office costs are not controllable by the manager of an investment centre. Discretionary fixed costs (those which do not have to be incurred in the short term, such as advertising and training) are within the manager's control since they can be increased or reduced at fairly short notice.

The level of inventory in the division is a part of the capital invested in the division, which is usually controllable by the manager of an investment centre. The manager also has control over the revenue from sales within the organisation (transfer prices).

12 B $[C - F] - [(N + D + I + B) \times R]$

The fixed costs are labelled as controllable therefore they should be deducted from the contribution but the head office charges should not. The divisional manager cannot exercise control over the latter costs and therefore should not be held responsible for them.

The divisional manager is responsible for the non-current assets and all of the current assets. Although inventories of goods for sale are kept in central stores, the division calls off its requirements on a monthly basis. The divisional manager is therefore responsible for the amount of inventory held.

13 A ROI Manager would wish to act in the interest of Distan Ltd.

    C RI Manager would wish to act in the interest of Distan Ltd.

The project is acceptable to the company as a whole because the RI is positive and the ROI exceeds the target return of 10%.

The manager of divison D will be willing to undertake the project whichever performance measure is used, since both the ROI and the RI will increase. Therefore both measures will motivate the divisional manager to act in the interest of the company as a whole.

14 B The revised divisional ROI will be above 20% and the manager will not make a goal congruent decision.

Revised profit	£m
Current projection	4.5
Profit on sale of houses (£14m – £12m)	2.0
	6.5

Revised divisional investment	£m
Current level	25
Cash from sales of houses	14
Less book value of houses	(12)
	27

Revised ROI = (6.5 / 27) × 100% = 24.1%

The manager would wish to undertake the transaction since the projected ROI of (4.5/25) 18% would otherwise not satisfy the target ROI of 20%. However this is not a goal congruent decision since the houses would be sold for £2m below their market value of £16m.

15 B 19.3%

	£
Original profits £300,000 × 18%	54,000
Profit on sale	5,000
Revised profit	59,000

	£
Original net asset value	300,000
Less carrying amount of asset sold	(15,000)
Plus cash received from sale of asset	20,000
	305,000

Revised ROI after sale of asset = (£59,000/£305,000) × 100%

                                             = 19.3%

If you answered 17.7% you omitted to include the sale of the asset in the numerator.

If you selected 20.7% you made the common error of omitting the cash received from the sale in the revised figure for the divisional investment.

16   C   Supplier

The supplier perspective is not one of the four perspectives of the balanced scorecard. Aspects of a supplier relationship would be monitored, if appropriate, within the internal business perspective.

17   B   (2) only

(1)   is false as the ROI and residual income might be used as one of the measures within the financial perspective.

(2)   is true as the residual income will increase because the additional imputed interest charge will be lower than the additional profit generated.

(3)   is false as the internal business perspective monitors what the business must be good at in order to succeed, for example, the average set-up time or the speed with which inter-departmental queries are handled.

(4)   is false as a disadvantage of residual income (RI) is that it does not facilitate comparisons between investment centres. The same absolute value of RI might be earned by two investment centres but it is much easier for a larger investment centre to generate a given level of RI than it is for a smaller investment centre.

18   C   A budget which shows the costs and revenues at different levels of activity.

A flexible budget **recognises different cost behaviour patterns** and is designed to change as the volume of activity changes.

A flexible budget includes both fixed and variable costs, and identifies them separately. Therefore the first statement is not correct. Any budget can be prepared using a spreadsheet model therefore the last statement is not correct.

19   D   (2) only

Statement (1) is not correct. A fixed budget may be useful for control purposes **where activity levels are not prone to change**, or **where a significant proportion of costs is fixed**, so that alterations in activity levels do not affect the costs incurred.

Statement (2) is correct. **Fixed and variable costs must be separately identified** so that the allowance for variable costs may be flexed according to the actual activity level.

Statement (3) is not correct. Budgetary control procedures can be used to monitor and control **income** as well as **expenditure**.

20   B   £370,300

		£
Variable material cost per 1% activity =		£2,000
Variable labour cost per 1% activity =		£1,500

Production overhead		£
At	60% activity	54,000
At	80% activity	62,000
Change	20%	8,000

Variable cost per 1% change in activity is (£8,000 / 20) = £400

Substituting in 80% activity	£
Variable cost = 80 × £400	32,000
Total cost	62,000
Therefore fixed cost	30,000

Other overhead is a wholly fixed cost.

Budget flexed at 77% level of activity

	£'000
Variable material 77 × £2,000	154.0
Variable labour 77 × £1,500	115.5
Production overhead	
Variable 77 × £400	30.8
Fixed	30.0
Other overhead	40.0
	370.3

If you selected £330,300 you did not include a fixed cost allowance for the other overhead. The option of £373,300 ignores the fact that production overhead is a semi-variable cost and the option of £377,300 simply multiplies the total cost for 70% activity by a factor of 1.1. This makes no allowance for the fact that there is an element of fixed costs within production overhead, and other overhead is wholly fixed.   SAMPLE PAPER

21   B   Cost centres have the lowest degree of autonomy with managers only able to control costs. Profit centres have a higher degree of autonomy as managers can not only control costs but can also control sales prices and revenue. Investment centres have the highest degree of autonomy as managers can not only control costs and revenues but can also make investment decisions not open to managers in either of the other two centres.   SAMPLE PAPER

22   A   Controllable residual income is defined as controllable profit less the 'cost of capital' used in the business, to the extent that capital is controllable.

Controllable profit is not N (as management cannot control the head office management charges) but is P.

The cost of capital will be R multiplied by the controllable capital. As head office collects cash from receivables and pays suppliers then D and L do not form part of controllable capital. The division has complete control over non-current assets (F) and inventory (S) and therefore controllable capital is (F + S). The 'cost of capital' is therefore (F + S) × R.

The controllable residual income is therefore P – [(F + S) × R]

If you selected the formula N – [(F + S) × R] then you correctly excluded the non-controllable receivables and payables balances but you included the non-controllable head office management charges.

If you selected the formula P – (Z × R) then you incorrectly included the non-controllable receivables and payables balances.

If you selected the formula N – (Z × R) then as well as incorrectly including the non-controllable receivables and payables balances you included the non-controllable head office management charges.   SAMPLE PAPER

23   A   Under a responsibility accounting system it is imperative that each manager knows what is expected of them. The criteria used for evaluation of their performance must therefore be known.

The statement 'The details on the performance reports for individual managers should add up to the totals on the report of their superior' is not necessarily true and is certainly not required for a responsibility accounting system.

The statement 'Each employee should receive a separate performance report' represents best practice but this is not a feature of a responsibility accounting system.

The statement 'Service department costs should be apportioned to the operating departments that use the service' is true but relates to a method of cost apportionment and is irrelevant when considering a responsibility accounting system.

24 C Residual income is calculated by comparing the actual return with the target return using the cost of capital. The ranking of the three divisions based on return on investment is:

P   Third

Q   Second

R   First

To establish the ranking using residual income the following table is produced:

	Actual return using ROI	Cost of capital At 11.9%	At 13.9%	At 17.9%	At 23.9%
P	£132k	£130.9k	£152.9k	£196.9k	£262.9k
Q	£156k	£142.8k	£166.8k	£214.8k	£286.8k
R	£210k	£178.5k	£208.5k	£268.5k	£358.5k

The residual income at each cost of capital is calculated by subtracting the cost of capital from the actual return:

	Residual income At 11.9%	At 13.9%	At 17.9%	At 23.9%
P	£1.1k	-£20.9k	-£64.9k	-£130.9k
Q	£13.2k	-£10.8k	-£58.8k	-£130.8k
R	£31.5k	£1.5k	-£58.5k	-£148.5k

The ranking of the divisional projects is therefore:

	Residual income At 11.9%	At 13.9%	At 17.9%	At 23.9%
P	3rd	3rd	3rd	2nd
Q	2nd	2nd	2nd	1st
R	1st	1st	1st	3rd

The highest cost of capital where the rankings agree to the ROI rankings is therefore 17.9%.

25 D Imputed interest is £1,280,000 – £480,000 = £800,000. With interest at 10%, capital must be £8m. ROI = £1,280,000/£8,000,000 = 16%.

If you got 6% you did RI/capital. If you got 10% you did interest/capital. If you got 22% you did profit + RI/capital.

26 C Current ROI is 400/2,000 = 20%

Project ROI = 30/200 = 15%, so reject as overall result would fall below 20%

Project RI = 30 – (0.16 × 200) = (2), so reject

Failing to evaluate the project separately eg, combining it with existing results would produce an ROI in excess of 16% and a positive RI which may have led you to say yes.

27 B Current profit = 0.2 × £1.2m = £240,000

Current plus K (highest ROI > 20%) ROI = (240 + 100)/(1,200 + 300) = 22.66%

Current plus K plus L (ROI > 22.66%) ROI = (240 + 100 + 210)/(1,200 + 300 + 700) = 25%

Current plus K, L, M (ROI > 25%) ROI = (240 + 100 + 210 + 130)/(1,200 + 300 + 700 + 500) = 25.2%, so do not add N as ROI < 25.2%

28 B To get a constant ROI both profits and capital should be constant. Reducing balance depreciation would increase profits over the life. Net book value would decrease the capital figure.

1   D   Performance standards in operation

Performance standards would be taken into account when estimating **material usage,** they would not have a direct effect on material price.

All of the other factors would be used to estimate standard material prices for a forthcoming period.

2   C   (1) only

Statement (1) is correct. **The use of standards is limited to situations where output can be measured.**

Statement (2) is not correct. Standards can include allowances for inefficiencies in operations, through the use of **attainable standards.**

Statement (3) is not correct. Standards and budgets are both used for **planning and control purposes.**

3   D   Actual prices are different from forecast prices

All of the other options given will give rise to a variance.

Forecast prices are merely a prediction of what prices might be in the future. Once these forecasts are incorporated into budgets or standards, then they become formalised plans that the organisation will aim to achieve. Differences between the actual results and the budgets or standards will cause variances.

4   C   £328 adverse

Material price variance

	£
8,200 kg did cost	6,888
But should have cost (× £0.80)	6,560
	328 (A)

If you calculated the variance to be £286 you based your calculations on the materials issued to production. However, the material inventory account is **maintained at standard cost,** therefore the material price variance is **calculated when the materials are purchased.** If you selected £328 favourable you calculated the size of the variance correctly but you misinterpreted it as favourable.   SAMPLE PAPER

5   B   £152 adverse

870 units did use	7,150 kg
But should have used (× 8 kg)	6,960 kg
Usage variance in kg	190 (A)

Usage variance in £ = (190 kg × standard price per kg £0.80)	£152 A

If you selected £152 favourable you calculated the size of the variance correctly but you misinterpreted it as favourable.

If you selected £159.60 adverse you evaluated the usage variance in kg at the actual price per kg, instead of the standard price per kg.

The result of £280 adverse bases the calculation of standard usage on the budgeted production of 850 units. This is not comparing like with like. The comparison should be based on a flexed budget for the actual production level.   SAMPLE PAPER

6   B   £1,130 favourable

	£
Budgeted direct labour cost for September =	£117,600
Budgeted direct labour hours = (3,350 + 150 units) × 4 =	14,000 hours
Standard direct labour rate =	£8.40/hour

	£
13,450 hours should have cost (× £8.40)	112,980
But did cost	111,850
Direct labour rate variance	1,130 (F)

The option of £710 favourable is the direct labour total variance.

If you selected £1,130 adverse you calculated the correct money value of the variance but you misinterpreted its direction.

The variance of £5,750 adverse is derived from a fixed budget comparison of the budgeted direct labour cost of 3,500 units with the actual direct labour cost of 3,350 units. A flexible budget comparison should be used.

7   B   £420.00 adverse

3,350 units should have taken (× 4)	13,400 hrs
But did take	13,450 hrs
Direct labour efficiency variance in hours	50 hrs (A)

Direct labour efficiency variance (in £) = (Direct labour efficiency variance in hours × standard rate per hour £8.40)	£420 (A)

If you selected £415.80 (A) you valued the labour efficiency in hours at the actual rate instead of the standard rate.

If you selected £420 (F) you calculated the correct money value of the variance but you misinterpreted its direction.

The option of £710 favourable is the direct labour total variance.

8   B   £672 adverse

Standard variable overhead cost per unit = £3,120/520 units = £6 per unit

	£
Standard variable overhead cost for 560 units (× £6)	3,360
Actual variable overhead cost	4,032
	672 adverse

If you selected £240 adverse you compared the standard cost for 560 units with the standard cost for 520 units. This indicates the **volume effect** of the change in output but it is not the variable production overhead total variance.

If you selected £672 favourable you calculated the correct money value of the variance but you misinterpreted its direction.

The variance of £912 adverse is the difference between the standard cost for 520 units and the actual cost for 560 units. This is not a valid comparison for **control purposes** because of the **different output volumes**.

9   A   £448 favourable

Standard variable production overhead cost per hour = £3,120/1,560 = £2 per hour

	£
2,240 hours of variable production overhead should cost (× £2)	4,480
But did cost	4,032
	448 (F)

If you selected £448 adverse you calculated the correct money value of the variance but you misinterpreted its direction.

£672 adverse is the variable production overhead total variance.

The variance of £912 adverse is the difference between the standard cost for 520 units and the actual cost for 560 units. This is not a valid comparison for **control purposes** because of the **different output volumes**.

10   B   £1,120 adverse

Standard time allowed for one unit	= 1,560 hours/520 units
	= 3 hours/unit
Standard variable production overhead cost per hour	= £3,120/1,560
	= £2/hour

560 units should take (× 3 hours)	1,680 hrs
But did take	2,240 hrs
Efficiency variance in hours	560 hrs (A)

Efficiency variance in £ = (Efficiency variance in hours × standard variable production overhead per hour £2)	£1,120 (A)

If you selected £1,008 adverse you valued the efficiency variance in hours at the actual variable production overhead rate per hour.

If you selected £1,120 favourable you calculated the correct money value of the variance but you misinterpreted its direction.

If you selected £1,360 adverse you based your calculation on the difference between the original budgeted hours for 520 units and the actual hours worked for 560 units. This is **not comparing like with like**. You should have flexed the allowance for comparison purposes.

11   A   £1,200 adverse

	£
Budgeted fixed overhead cost £10 × 1,000	10,000
Actual fixed overhead cost	11,200
Fixed overhead expenditure variance	1,200 (A)

If you calculated the variance to be £800 you flexed the budget cost allowance for fixed overhead. By definition, the budgeted expenditure on fixed overhead does not alter when the activity level changes.

12 D Sales price variance = £1,800 favourable

Sales volume variance = £900 adverse

Sales price variance

	£
Sales revenue from 900 units should have been (x £20)	18,000
But was (900 × £22)	19,800
Sales price variance	1,800 (F)

Sales volume variance

Budgeted sales volume	1,000 units
Actual sales volume	900 units
Sales volume variance in units	100 units (A)

Sales volume contribution variance in £ = (sales volume variance in units x standard contribution per unit £9)	£900 (A)

If you calculated a sales price variance of £2,000 favourable you simply calculated the extra sales revenue that would have been achieved if the budgeted sales volume had been sold at the higher price. Variances must be based on a flexed budget for the actual volume achieved.

If you calculated a sales volume variance of £2,000 adverse you calculated the reduction in budgeted **sales revenue** due to the reduction in sales volume. However, the sales volume variance measures the reduction in budgeted **contribution** due to the actual sales volume being lower than budgeted.

13 A All sales variances and all marginal cost variances

Budgeted contribution is different from actual contribution because of all of the sales and marginal cost variances which have arisen.

SAMPLE PAPER

14 A £424,810

	Favourable £	Adverse £	£
Budgeted contribution 83,000 × £8			664,000
Variances			
Sales volume		42,400	
Sales price	7,310		
Material total	7,720		
Labour total		6,450	
Variable overhead total	–	4,250	
	15,030	53,100	38,070 (A)
Actual contribution			625,930
Budgeted fixed overhead		210,000	
Fixed overhead expenditure variance		8,880 (F)	
			201,120
Actual profit			424,810

If you calculated the profit to be £435,650 you double-counted the material price variance, which would be included within the material total variance.

If you selected £483,190 you added the adverse variances to the budgeted contribution and deducted the favourable variances. However, an adverse variance will reduce the actual profit to a result below the budgeted profit and vice versa for favourable variances.

If you selected £634,810 you forgot to deduct the budgeted fixed overhead.

ICAEW

15 B 11,160 kg

Total standard cost of 11,280 kg	= £46,248
Standard cost per kg = £46,248/11,280	= £4.10 per kg
Usage variance in kg = £492/4.10	= 120 kg

11,280 kg were used. There was an adverse usage variance of 120 kg and so (11,280 – 120) kg

= 11,160 should have been used.

If you selected 10,788 kg you deducted the money value of the usage variance from the actual quantity used. You were correct to deduct the variance, but you should first have **converted it to a quantity of material**.

11,280 kg is the actual material used, which cannot be the same as standard because there is a usage variance.

If you selected 11,400 kg you added the usage variance to the actual usage, instead of subtracting it. The variance is adverse, therefore standard usage must be lower than actual usage.

16 D 18,700

Production should have taken	= X	hours
But did take	= 17,500	hours
Variance in hours	= X – 17,500	hours (F)
× standard rate per hour	= × £6.50	
Variance in £	= £7,800	(F)
∴6.5 (X – 17,500)	= 7,800	
X – 17,500	= 1,200	
X	= 18,700	

1,200 hours is the efficiency variance in terms of hours, and 17,500 is the actual number of hours worked.

If you selected 16,300 hours you treated the efficiency variance as adverse instead of favourable.

17 A £1.50

Materials price variance per kg purchased and used	= (£21,000/210,000)
	= £0.10 (A) per kg
Actual price per kg = £336,000/210,000	= £1.60
Standard price per kg	= £1.50

If you selected £1.70 you added the adverse variance per kg to the actual price instead of deducting it. If the variance is adverse then the standard price must be lower than the actual.

If you selected £1.80 you based your unit rate calculations on the standard materials usage instead of the actual materials purchased and used. The price variance is always based on actual quantities.

18 B Both statements are incorrect

Favourable variances may not always be good. For example, a favourable materials variance might be achieved by buying poorer quality material which means that the labour force have to spend much longer working on the material leading to an adverse labour variance.

Variance reporting is the reporting of differences between the actual results and the flexed budget not the original budget.

19   B   Uncontrollable

Uncontrollable variances are variances which have arisen by chance. They are random deviations.

Controllable variances result from a manager's actions and decisions.

Marginal cost is the cost of producing one more unit of production.

20   D   (1), (2) and (4) only

All of these apart from personnel would influence the decision to investigate a variance as they include cost/benefit considerations, whether the variance can be controlled and what the movement of the variance suggests is a trend.

21   B   Achieving a lower output volume than budgeted

Variations in output volume should not affect usage of materials per unit produced. The calculation of the usage variance is based on a flexed budget allowance for the actual volume achieved.

A high quality material might reduce wastage or scrap levels that in turn would improve the materials usage rate.

Lower quality control standards should lead to fewer items being rejected, a higher proportion of successfully-completed items, and so an improvement in materials usage.

A reduction in material wastage rates will also improve the materials usage rate.

22   A,F,G

If the standard material price was set too low then an adverse material price variance is likely to arise.

Early settlement discounts are a financial management matter and do not affect the actual price paid for material purchases.

Material of a higher quality is likely to have a higher price, leading to an adverse material price variance.

23   B   Working fewer hours than the flexed labour hours budget predicts

Variable overhead efficiency variance = (standard hours for actual output – actual hours) × standard variable overhead rate per hour.

Of the options available, only working fewer hours than standard will result in a favourable variance. Material usage and fixed overhead will have no impact on the efficiency variance. Since the variance is evaluated at the standard rate per hour it will not be affected by the actual variable overhead cost per hour.

24   C   Lower hourly rates than standard and lower than standard labour hours for the actual production

To be certain of a favourable labour total variance it would be necessary for both the labour rate variance and the labour efficiency variance to be favourable.

All of the options will result in a favourable labour rate variance.

If labour hours are lower than budgeted it is possible that the labour efficiency variance will be favourable, but not certain. The hours could be lower because production output was lower than budgeted, not because labour were working efficiently. The efficiency variance could still be adverse when the correct comparison is made with the flexed budget.

25 A £1,250 adverse

Flexed budget £14,000 × 1,250/1,000   = £17,500

Actual cost   = £18,750

Variance   = £1,250 adverse

If you calculated the variance to be £4,750 you compared the actual material cost for 1,250 units with the budgeted cost for 1,000 units. This is not a valid comparison for control purposes.

26 C 7.2% adverse

Flexed budget 12,000 units × £15.50   = £186,000

Actual cost   = £199,400

Variance   = £13,400 adverse

Percentage of flexed budget 13,400/186,000 × 100   = 7.2% adverse

If you calculated the variance as 2.1% of budget you were basing your calculations on the original budgeted labour cost for 12,600 units.

However, since the actual output was only 12,000 units the control comparison should be made of the actual cost with the flexible budget cost allowance for 12,000 units.

27 B £50,000

	£
Actual expenditure on overheads	108,000
Fixed overheads under budget	8,000
Budgeted expenditure on overheads	116,000
Less budgeted variable overhead expenditure	
= actual expenditure (£3 × 22,000)	66,000
Budgeted fixed overhead expenditure	50,000

If you selected £34,000 you adjusted for the fixed overheads under budget by subtracting them instead of adding them to the actual expenditure. £66,000 is the budgeted variable overhead expenditure for the actual production and £116,000 is the total budgeted overhead for the period.

28 D Absorption costing always uses the budgeted (or standard) production time, as flexed by the actual output in a period. This means that the **actual** output is multiplied by the **standard** machine hours per unit in order to establish a flexed budget of machine hours for the actual production. The value of overheads absorbed would therefore be the absorption rate multiplied by this flexed budget.

If you selected (planned output) × (standard machine hours per unit) then the result would be the budgeted level of absorbed overhead rather than the actual absorbed overhead.

If you selected (actual output) × (actual machine hours per unit) then the result would include any production efficiencies or inefficiencies in the actual machine hours and this would result in an incorrect calculation of absorbed overhead.

If you selected (planned output) × (actual machine hours per unit) then you have reversed the selections you should have made.   SAMPLE PAPER

29 A   The cost of material purchased was £1,500 / 2,500 per kg, or 60p per kg. The standard cost is 50p per kg, an adverse variance of 10p per kg. In February a total of 2,500 kg were purchased of which 2,300 kg were used and as there was no opening inventory 200 kg was left in closing inventory. If inventory were valued at actual cost then some of the adverse price variance would be carried forward in inventory. However, we are told that inventory is valued at standard cost and therefore the closing inventory is valued at 50p per kg. This means that the whole of the price variance (2,500 kg × 10p = £250) would be included in the February results. This variance is adverse as the price paid for the material was higher than the standard.

If you selected £230 adverse then you had ignored the fact that the inventory is valued at standard cost.

If you selected £230 favourable then you had ignored the fact that the inventory is valued at standard cost and also misinterpreted the additional cost of the material to be a favourable variance.

If you selected £250 favourable then you correctly calculated the variance but made the mistake of thinking that the additional cost of the material was a favourable variance. An additional cost will always be **adverse** whereas additional revenue will be **favourable**.

30 D   The first important consideration is to ignore the effect of the wage rise, because this did not arise because of the decision to procure the superior quality material. The adverse labour rate variance should therefore be discounted.

The favourable material usage variance arose because the superior material generated less waste. However, the superior material was more expensive leading to the adverse material price variance, and also could be converted by the workforce more efficiently, leading to the favourable labour efficiency variance.

The answer is therefore 8,000F + 4,800F – 10,800A = 2,000F. A favourable cost variance means that profits will rise.

If you selected a rise of £4,800 then you incorrectly ignored the labour efficiency and material price variances.

If you selected a fall of £1,600 then you incorrectly also included the adverse labour rate variance of £3,600.

If you selected a fall of £6,000 then you included the material price and usage variances but incorrectly ignored the favourable labour efficiency variance.   SAMPLE PAPER

31 D   The sales volume variance is defined as variance in sales volume × the budgeted unit contribution.

The volume variance is 100 units favourable.

The budgeted contribution was:

£16,000/10,000 = £1.60 per unit

The favourable sales volume variance is therefore £1.60 × 100 = £160

If you incorrectly calculated the sales volume variance as £180 then you used the actual contribution per unit rather than the budgeted contribution per unit.

100 × £10.20 = £1,020 uses the standard selling price rather than contribution and 100 × £10.40 uses the actual selling price.

32 D   The labour efficiency variance (L) is defined as the variance in labour hours (V) x the standard rate per hour (R), or

L = V × R

Or V = L/R

L = £10,000 (positive, as it is a favourable variance)

R = £2.00

Therefore V = £10,000/£2 = 5,000

The variance in labour hours is therefore 5,000 favourable meaning the actual hours taken were 5,000 lower than the standard. The actual hours were 130,000 therefore the standard hours were 130,000 + 5,000 = 135,000

130,000 – 5,000 = 125,000 incorrectly **deducts** the favourable hours variance from the actual hours. £10,000 / £4 = 2,500 incorrectly uses the actual rather than the standard rate of pay. 130,000 ± 2,500 = 127,500 and 132,500 hours.

33 A,E,I

Sales prices increased: Adverse

Successful advertising campaign: Favourable

Increased labour pay rates: No impact

If sales prices were increased then market theory would predict a reduction in sales volumes as potential purchasers switch to less expensive alternative products.

If an advertising campaign were successful then it would encourage potential purchasers to try the product and therefore an increase in sales volumes would be expected.

If labour pay rates increased then this would have no impact on sales volumes unless the increase in costs were passed on by an increase in the sales price, which is not the case here.

Management Information: Answer Bank

Chapter 10: Breakeven analysis and limiting factor analysis

1   C   Total fixed costs

Contribution required to break even is the same value as total fixed costs.

Unit selling price less unit variable cost is the unit contribution.

Unit contribution × number of units sold is the total contribution.

Total fixed costs/Contribution ratio provides the sales revenue at breakeven point.

SAMPLE PAPER

2   A   Total fixed costs/contribution per unit

    B   Contribution required to break even/contribution per unit

Breakeven point is the activity level at which there is neither a profit nor a loss. Alternatively, it is the activity level at which total contribution equals fixed costs.

3   B   3,000 units

Breakeven point = Fixed costs/Contribution per unit

$$= £30,000/(£15 - £5)$$

$$= 3,000 \text{ units}$$

If you selected 2,000 units you divided the fixed cost by the selling price, but remember that the selling price also has to cover the variable cost.

The option of 4,000 units is the margin of safety, and if you selected 6,000 units you seem to have divided the fixed cost by the variable cost per unit.

4   A   20%

Breakeven point	= Fixed costs/Contribution per unit
	$= £96,000/(£12 - £8)$
	$= 24,000$ units
Budgeted sales	$= 30,000$ units
Margin of safety	$= \underline{6,000 \text{ units}}$
Expressed as a % of budget	$= 6,000/30,000 × 100\% = 20\%$

If you selected 25% you calculated the correct margin of safety in units, but you then expressed this as a percentage of the breakeven point.

If you selected 73% you divided the fixed cost by the selling price to determine the breakeven point, but the selling price also has to cover the variable cost.

You should have been able to eliminate the option of 125%; the margin of safety expressed as a percentage must always be less than 100%.

5   A   2,000

Breakeven point	= Fixed costs/Contribution ratio
	= £76,800/0.40
	= £192,000
Actual sales	= £224,000
Margin of safety	= £224,000 − £192,000
	= £32,000
Margin of safety in units	= £32,000/£16
	= 2,000 units

If you selected 12,000 units you calculated the breakeven point in units, but forgot to take the next step to calculate the margin of safety.

14,000 is the actual sales in units and 32,000 is the margin of safety in terms of sales value.

6   C   £300,000

Total fixed costs	= £137,500 + £27,500
	= £165,000
Contribution ratio	= £275,000/£500,000
	= 0.55
Breakeven sales revenue	= Fixed costs/Contribution ratio
	= £165,000/0.55
	= £300,000

If you selected £250,000 you included only the fixed production costs in your breakeven calculation. However, all fixed costs must be covered by the contribution in order to breakeven.

If you selected £366,667 you misread the question and treated the £275,000 as variable cost rather than as the budgeted contribution.

7   B   £100,000

Margin of safety	= 20% × 5,000 units
	= 1,000 units
Breakeven sales	= Budget sales − Margin of safety
	= (5,000 − 1,000) units
	= 4,000 units
Breakeven sales volume	= Total fixed costs/Contribution per unit
4,000	= Total fixed costs/£25
Total fixed costs	= 4,000 × £25
	= £100,000

If you selected £25,000 or £125,000 you calculated the monthly profit and contribution respectively, rather than the fixed costs.

If you selected £150,000 you added the margin of safety to the budgeted sales to determine the breakeven sales volume. If the margin of safety is positive then the budgeted sales will always be higher than breakeven sales.

8 D 4,600 units

Sales units that will earn a required profit = (Fixed costs + Required profit)/Unit contribution

$$= (£11,125 + £11,875)/£5$$

$$= 4,600$$

If you selected 1,533 units you divided the target contribution by the selling price, but the variable costs must also be taken into account.

If you selected 2,225 units you calculated the breakeven point.

If you selected 2,375 units you divided the £11,875 target profit by the £5 contribution per unit. But the fixed costs must be covered before any profit can be earned.

9 D £196,000

Contribution ratio	= 50% – 8%
	= 42%
Sales required to earn target profit	= (Fixed costs + Required profit)/Contribution ratio
	= (£23,520 + £58,800)/0.42
	= £196,000

If you selected £56,000 you calculated the breakeven point and did not allow for the target profit.

If you selected £140,000 you divided the £58,800 target profit by the contribution ratio, but the fixed costs must be covered before any profit can be earned.

If you selected £164,640 you based your calculations on a contribution ratio of 50% and did not allow for the other expenses which are 8% of sales.

10 B 90,000

	£
Total cost of 150,000 units (× £41.50)	6,225,000
Total cost of 100,000 units (× £47.50)	4,750,000
Variable cost of 50,000 units	1,475,000
Variable cost per unit	£29.50

Substituting	£
Total cost of 100,000 units	4,750,000
Variable cost of 100,000 units (× £29.50)	2,950,000
Fixed costs	1,800,000

Breakeven point = £1,800,000/(£49.50 – £29.50) = 90,000 units

If you selected 36,364 you divided the fixed cost by the unit selling price, but the variable costs must also be taken into account.

If you selected 101,020 you assumed that the production overheads and the marketing and administration costs were wholly fixed. In fact the marketing costs are the only wholly fixed costs. You can test this by multiplying the unit rate by the output volume at each level of activity.

If you selected 225,000 you divided the fixed cost by the profit per unit instead of the contribution per unit.

11 A £330

Currently weekly contribution = 12% × £280,000 = £33,600

	£
Extra contribution from 5% increase in sales = 5% × £33,600	1,680
Loss on product Z each week 3,000 × (1.90 – 2.20 – 0.15)	(1,350)
Weekly increase in profit	330

If you selected £780 you forgot to allow for the variable cost of distributing the 3,000 units of Z.

If you selected £5,700 you made no allowances for the variable costs of either product Z or the extra sales of other products.

The option of £12,650 is based on a 5% increase in **revenue** from the other products; however extra variable costs will be incurred, therefore the gain will be a 5% increase in **contribution**.

12 C 7,132

Current profit	= Total contribution – Fixed costs
	= (8,000 × £8) – £24,400
	= £39,600
Required profit	= £39,600

If the new production methods are implemented the required contribution will be:

Required contribution	= Revised fixed costs + Required profit
	= (£24,400 × 1.30) + £39,600
	= £31,720 + £39,600
	= £71,320

$$\textbf{Required sales} = \frac{\text{Contribution required}}{\text{Contribution per unit (revised)}}$$

$$= £71,320/(£15 – £5)$$

$$= 7,132 \text{ units}$$

If you selected 3,960 units you did not add the revised fixed costs to the required contribution figure. The fixed costs must be covered before any profit can be earned.

If you selected 4,755 units you divided the required contribution by the selling price but this does not take account of the need to cover the variable costs.

If you selected 8,915 units you assumed that a £1 change in both the variable cost and the selling price would leave the contribution per unit unaltered.

13 B (1) and (3) only

Statement (1) is correct. The line which passes through the origin indicates the sales revenue at various levels of activity. At an activity level of 10,000 units, the sales revenue is £100,000 therefore the selling price is £10 per unit.

Statement (2) is incorrect. The sloping line which intercepts the vertical axis at £30,000 shows the total cost at various levels of activity. The **total cost** for 10,000 units is £80,000, from which we subtract the £30,000 fixed costs to derive the variable cost of 10,000 units, which is £50,000. Therefore the variable cost per unit is £5.

Statement (3) is correct. The fixed cost is the cost incurred at zero activity and is shown as a horizontal line at £30,000.

Statement (4) is incorrect. The profit for 10,000 units is the difference between the sales value (£100,000) and the total cost (£80,000) which amounts to £20,000.   SAMPLE PAPER

14 B The sales revenue line passes through the origin

C The total cost line cuts the vertical axis at the point which is equal to the period fixed costs

Since sales revenue is zero when activity is zero the sales revenue line must pass through the origin.

When activity is zero the only cost incurred is the fixed cost. Therefore the cost line cuts the vertical axis at the point which is equal to the period fixed costs.

Statement A is incorrect because the fixed costs are depicted by a straight line parallel to the **horizontal** axis.

Statement D is incorrect because the breakeven point is the point where the sales revenue line crosses the **total cost line.**

15 B Fixed costs in total are not changed by increases or decreases in production volume

C Variable costs per unit are not changed by increases or decreases in production volume

E Estimates of sales demand, prices and resources required for each product are known with certainty

Fixed costs in total are not changed by increases or decreases in production volume (so that the profit-maximising and contribution-maximising output levels are the same).

Variable costs per unit are not changed by increases or decreases in production volume and estimates of sales demand, prices and resources required for each product are known with certainty (so that contribution per unit of scarce resource is constant).

16 A Material only

	Quantity per unit		Quantity required	Quantity available
Material (£8/2)	4kg	(× 6,000)	24,000 kg	22,000 kg
Labour (£18/6)	3hrs	(× 6,000)	18,000 hrs	19,000 hrs

Sales demand is not a limiting factor because there is not sufficient material to satisfy the demand of 6,000 units.

There is sufficient labour to satisfy the demand of 6,000 units.

17 A B then A then T

This answer ranks the products by contribution per kg of material (the limiting factor).

	B	A	T	Total
Maximum sales (units)	1,000	1,200	1,500	N/A
Material kg needed	1,000	2,400	4,500	7,900
Labour hours needed	2,000	2,400	4,500	8,900

Thus, labour is not a limiting factor but material is a limiting factor.

The products must be ranked according to their contribution per kg of material.

	B	A	T
Contribution per unit (£)	£50	£60	£55
Kg of material per unit	1	2	3
Contribution per kg of material (£)	£50	£30	£18.33
Rank by contribution per kg of material	1	2	3

18 C Contribution: £600,000, Profit: Insufficient information to calculate

To maximise contribution, we must produce the product with the greatest contribution per £ spent on labour.

	X £ per unit	Y £ per unit	Z £ per unit
Contribution per unit	50	40	60
Labour cost per unit	30	10	5
Contribution per £ of labour	1.67	4	12
Ranking	3	2	1

Thus the company will make £50,000 / 5 = 10,000 units of Z.

This will produce 10,000 × £60 = £600,000 of contribution.

Remember that the fixed costs per unit are based on budgeted production quantities (not actual production) and as we do not know these quantities we cannot calculate budgeted monthly fixed costs. Therefore there is insufficient information to calculate the profit.

19 B £5,700

We begin by calculating the contribution per unit of limiting factor.

			Priority ranking
Scratch = £6/2	= £3 per labour hour		1
Purr = £7/3	= £2.33 per labour hour		3
Buzz = £8/3	= £2.66 per labour hour		2

		Hours		Contribution
Production priorities	1st Scratch			
	(700 units × 2 hours)	1,400	(700 × £6)	£4,200
	2nd Buzz			
	(400 units × 3 hours)	1,200	(400 × £8)	£3,200
		2,600		7,400
	Less fixed costs			(1,700)
	Maximum profit achievable			£5,700

If you selected £5,062 you allocated the available hours according to the contribution earned per unit of product. However, this does not take account of the **limiting factor**.

If you selected £6,100 you allocated all the available hours to Scratch, the product which earns the highest contribution per hour. However, the maximum demand for Scratch is 700 units. Once that demand has been met the remainder of the available hours must be allocated to Buzz, the next product in the priority ranking.

£13,000 is the profit earned from satisfying the maximum demand for each product, but there are insufficient labour hours available to manufacture this volume of output.

20 **B** **£660**

	Product M	Product Q
Contribution per labour hour	= (£85/6)	= (£110/8)
	= £14.17	= £13.75
Priority ranking	1	2
Optimum allocation of hours	6,000	9,000
	(1,000 units)	(1,125 units)

An additional 48 hours would be used to produce 6 units of Q, earning a contribution of (6 × £110) £660.

If you selected £680 you allocated the hours to product M but according to the ranking and maximum demand it is not possible to sell further units of M.

If you selected £180 you allocated the available hours correctly but you then deducted the cost of the labour from your calculated contribution. However the cost of the labour has already been deducted when deriving the contribution per unit.

21 **C** **£2,240**

Since product N does not feature in the optimum planned production this product must rank last in utilising the raw material (you could check this for yourself). The optimum production with the additional 1,000 kg would therefore be as follows:

	kg used		Contribution £
(1,000 – 720) units of M (× (£1.25/£0.50))	700	(280 × £4.50)	1,260
100 units of N (× (£1.50/£0.50))	300	(100 × £4.80)	480
	1,000		1,740

However, the contribution is after charging £0.50 per kg.

The maximum amount that should be paid is the contribution before the material cost

$$= £1,740 + (1,000 × £0.50) = £2,240$$

If you selected £1,740 you forgot to add back the £0.50 per kg already included for material.

If you selected £2,300 you assumed that the 1,000 kg would all be used on Product M (an additional 400 units). However, the maximum demand for Product M means only 280 units can be sold, with the remainder being used on Product N.

If you selected £1,800, you again incorrectly allocated all the material to Product M, and also forgot to add back the £0.50 per kg of material cost already included.

22 **A** **X: 130 units, Y: 840 units, Z: 100 units**

	X	Y	Z
Unit contribution	£82	£108	£100
Kg required per unit	2 kg	1 kg	3 kg
Contribution per kg	£41	£108	£33.33
Ranking	2	1	3

	kg used
Produce 100 units of Z for contract (× 3 kg)	300
Produce 130 units of Y for contract (× 1 kg)	130
	430
Produce remaining (840 – 130) units of Y (× 1 kg)	710
Use balance to produce 130 units of X (× 2 kg)	260
	1,400

If you decided not to produce any units of Z you took no account of the requirement to produce 100 units of Z.

If you decided not to produce any units of X you ranked the products on the basis of unit profit and took no account of the contract.

If you decided to produce only one unit of X you ranked the products on the basis of contribution per unit.

23 D   Alpha: Produce 4,000 units

Beta: Produce 2,000 units, Buy in 2,000 units

The units subcontracted should be those which add least to the costs of Green Ltd. The cheapest policy is to subcontract work which adds the least extra cost per machine hour saved.

	Alpha £	Beta £
Variable cost of internal manufacture	20	36
Variable cost of buying	29	40
Extra variable cost of buying	9	4
Machine hours saved by buying	3 hours	2 hours
Extra cost of buying, per hour saved	£3	£2

It is cheaper to buy Betas than to buy Alphas. Therefore the priority for making the components in-house will be to allocate the available hours to the manufacture of Alphas.

Component	Production Units	Hours per unit	Hours allocated
Alpha	4,000	3	12,000
Beta	2,000	2	4,000
			16,000

The remaining 2,000 units of Beta should be purchased from the sub-contractor.

SAMPLE PAPER

24 C   Aura: Produce 233 units, buy in 167 units

Venta: Produce 400 units

The units subcontracted should be those which add least to the costs of Blue plc. The cheapest policy is to subcontract work which adds the least extra cost per machine hour saved.

	Aura £	Venta £
Variable cost of internal manufacture	360	360
Variable cost of buying	390	400
Extra variable cost of buying	30	40
Machine hours saved by buying	30 hours	20 hours
Extra cost of buying, per hour saved	£1	£2

It is cheaper to buy Auras than to buy Ventas. Therefore the priority for making the components in-house will be to allocate the available hours to the manufacture of Ventas.

Component	Production Units	Hours per unit	Hours allocated
Venta	400	20	8,000
Aura	233	30	7,000
			15,000

The remaining 167 units of Aura should be purchased from the sub-contractor.

25 D This question relates to limiting factor analysis. The key to these questions is ranking the contribution per unit of the limiting factor, in this case Grunch. In this question the contribution per unit of Grunch will be calculated pre-fixed costs, as these will be constant whatever production schedule is chosen.

Product X: Contribution = £1.50 and £1.50/0.3 = £5 contribution per kg of Grunch

Product Y: Contribution = £1.60 and £1.60/0.40 = £4 contribution per kg of Grunch

Product Z: Contribution = £2.40 and £2.40/0.80 = £3 contribution per kg of Grunch

The ranking of the products is therefore X, Y, Z.

The production schedule that will maximise profit will therefore be:

4,000 units of X (maximum demand), utilising 4,000 × 0.3kg of Grunch, ie 1,200kg

3,000 units of Y (maximum demand), utilising 3,000 × 0.4kg of Grunch, ie 1,200kg

This is a total of 2,400kg and therefore 3,600kg of the 6,000kg will be available to manufacture Product Z. This will produce 3,600/0.8 units = 4,500 units.

Any other production schedule will not maximise profit.   SAMPLE PAPER

26 D The first step is to calculate the profit achieved in 20X7. Contribution is £120 per unit and 12,000 units were produced and sold generating £120 × 12,000 = £1,440,000. Fixed costs were £20 × 10,000 (per the budget) = £200,000 meaning the net profit was £1,240,000.

In 20X8 the unit selling price will be £200 × 1.05 = £210. Unit variable costs will be £80 × 1.1 = £88. The unit contribution is therefore (£210 – £88) = £122. In 20X8 fixed costs will be £200,000 × 1.1 = £220,000.

Profits in 20X8 are the same as 20X7, ie £1,240,000, meaning the contribution must be £1,240,000 + £220,000 = £1,460,000. The number of units sold to generate this contribution will be £1,460,000/£122 = 11,967.

If you calculated the number of units as 12,000 then you probably incorrectly calculated the fixed costs in 20X7 as £20 x 12,000 = £240,000 and the 20X7 profits as £1,200,000. This would mean that you calculated the 20X8 fixed costs as £240,000 × 1.1 = £264,000 and therefore the required contribution in 20X8 as £1,464,000. At a unit contribution of £122 this would mean 12,000 units.

If you calculated the number of units as 11,639 then you probably also incorrectly calculated the fixed costs in 20X7 as £20 × 12,000 = £240,000 and the 20X7 profits as £1,200,000. However, in 20X8 you correctly calculated the fixed costs as 10,000 × £20 × 1.1 = £220,000 and therefore the required contribution in 20X8 as £1,420,000. At a unit contribution of £122 this would mean 11,639 units.

Chapter 11: Investment appraisal techniques

1   A   PP is 1.56 years and ARR is 52.0%

Depreciation must be added back to the annual profit figures to derive the annual cash flows.

Annual depreciation   = £(46,000 – 4,000)/4 years

                       = £10,500

Adding £10,500 to each year's profit figure produces the following cash flows.

	Cash flow £	Cumulative cash flow £
Initial investment	(46,000)	(46,000)
Year 1	27,000	(19,000)
Year 2	34,000	15,000

Payback period   = 1 year + ((19,000/34,000) × 1 year)

                  = 1.56 years

If you selected a payback period of 2.44 years you based your calculations on the accounting profits after the deduction of depreciation. The calculation of the payback period should be based on **cash flows**.

Accounting rate of return (ARR)

Average profit   = £(16,500 + 23,500 + 13,500 – 1,500)/4

                    = £13,000

Average investment = £(46,000 + 4,000)/2

                    = £25,000

ARR   = £(13,000/25,000) × 100%

                    = 52.0%

If you selected an ARR of 56.5% you forgot to include the residual value of £4,000 in your calculation of the average investment.

2   B   DPP is 2.4 years and NPV is £2,323

Net present value

Year	Cash flow £	Discount factor 16%	Present value £
0	(5,000)	1.000	(5,000)
1	(2,000)	0.862	(1,724)
2	7,000	0.743	5,201
3	6,000	0.641	3,846
Net present value (NPV)			2,323

If you selected an NPV of £3,013 you treated the £5,000 cash flow as occurring in year 1 and discounted it. Cash flows occurring 'now' should not be discounted.

Discounted payback period

Year	Present value (PV) £	Cumulative PV £
0	(5,000)	(5,000)
1	(1,724)	(6,724)
2	5,201	(1,523)
3	3,846	2,323

DPP = 2 years + ((1,523/3,846) × 1 year)

= 2.4 years

If you selected 2.0 years you calculated the non-discounted payback period.

3   C   £4,561

Using cumulative present value tables:

We require the 15% factor for years 3 - 7.

Cumulative discount factor for years 1 - 7 at 15%	4.160
Less: cumulative discount factor for years 1 - 2 at 15%	1.626
Cumulative discount factor for years 3 - 7 at 15%	2.534

Present value = £1,800 × 2.534

= £4,561

If you selected £3,377 you made the common mistake of deriving the cumulative discount factor for years 4 to 7 instead of years 3 to 7.

4   D   £42,000

Year	Payment £	Discount factor 8%	Present value £
0	10,000	1	10,000
1	x	0.926	0.926x
2	x	0.857	0.857x
3	x	0.794	0.794x
4	x	0.735	0.735x
			3.312x

The present value of the four equal payments is £26,496.

Therefore each payment = x = £26,496 / 3.312 = £8,000

The total amount to be paid during the lease period is therefore

(£10,000 + (4 × £8,000)) = £10,000 + £32,000 = £42,000.

If you selected £32,480 you made the common mistake of discounting each year's payment by the factor for the year in which the payment is made. However, the payments are made at the beginning of each year. The convention used in discounted cash flow is treated as though it occurs at the end of the previous year. Hence a cash flow at the beginning of year 2 is discounted using the factor for year 1 and so on.

5   C   13.33%

The IRR can be calculated using the following formula.

If a = 10%

   B = 15%

   A = £4,000

   B = – £2,000

Then:

IRR = a% + [A / (A – B)] × (b – a)%

     = 10% + 3.33%

     = 13.33%

If you selected 20% you did not account correctly for the fact that the NPV was negative at a discount rate of 15%. You treated the £2,000 NPV as a positive figure in the calculation.

If you selected 11.67% you swapped A and B around in the formula, using A = £2,000 and B = £4,000.

If you selected 12.5% you have simply calculated the mid-point of the two rates instead of using the IRR formula.

6   A   The graph of the NPV against the discount rate has a negative slope

     D   An estimate of the IRR requires the calculation of the NPV at two different discount rates

As the discount rate increases, the NPV decreases. If the discount rate is viewed as the cost of capital, the NPV will fall as financing the project becomes more expensive.

The NPV falls as the discount rate increases and so a lower discount rate of s% will result in a higher NPV.

The interpolation and graphical methods both approximate as linear the behaviour of the IRR as discount rates increase and decrease. In fact the behaviour is curvilinear. Neither can therefore give exact answers.

By calculating the NPV at two different discount rates, the IRR can generally be estimated by linear interpolation.

7   D   (1), (2), (3) and (4)

NPVs are extensively used in practice to ascertain whether or not a project is a viable investment or not.

8   D   £7,500

Discount factors (DCF) of 24% are not shown on the tables therefore it is necessary to calculate the factors yourself.

Year	Cash flow		DCF	Present value
	£			£
0	(160,000)	1	1	(160,000)
1	31,700	× 1/1.24	0.806	25,565
2	179,000	× $1/(1.24)^2$	0.650	116,415
3	48,900	× $1/(1.24)^3$	0.524	25,647
NPV				£7,627

If you selected £38,500 you discounted the initial investment but since this occurs at the beginning of the project it should not be discounted.

If you selected £(84,000) you discounted each year's cash flow by the factor for cash flows in the following year.

9 B £9,500

NPV = −£400,000 + (£300,000)/1.15 + (£200,000) / (1.15 × 1.17)

= £9,500

If you selected £2,500 or £12,000 you discounted both years' cash flows at 17% and 15% respectively.

If you selected £32,000 you used a discount factor of (1/1.17) for the year 2 cash flow instead of (1/(1.17 × 1.15)).

The year 2 cash flow has to be discounted twice: one year at 17% and one year at 15%.

10 D Statement 1: False   ARR places equal value on all cash flows throughout a project's life. NPV places less value on later cash flows. Therefore, statement (1) is false.

Statement 2: True   The IRR is the rate that equates PV of inflows with the PV of the initial outflow(s). If the IRR is greater than the cost of capital, later cash flows have been discounted too much. Therefore, statement (2) is true.

11 D (1), (2) and (3)

The decision rule is to accept all investments with a positive NPV. Therefore (1) is correct.

NPV is the absolute measure and is therefore superior to IRR which is a relative measure (percentage). Therefore (2) is correct.

Finally, (3) is the correct definition of NPV.

12 C It quantifies the effect of the timing of cash flows through the investment

Although the payback period does take some account of the timing of cash flows, it does not quantify the effect of the timing of cash flows within the payback period. Furthermore the method ignores the cash flows that occur after the end of the payback period.

13 A It is based on objective accounting profits

B The calculation method of ARR is universally agreed

Neither of these factors are advantages of the ARR method of investment appraisal.

Accounting profits are not objective. They are subject to a number of different accounting policies.

The calculation method of ARR can be based either on the initial investment or on the average investment. The basis is not universally agreed and this can make it difficult for managers to interpret calculated ARRs.

14 C The NPV approach is superior if discount rates are expected to vary over the life of the project

Variable discount rates can be incorporated easily into NPV calculations, but not into IRR calculations.

The methods only give the same accept or reject decision when the cash flows are conventional. There may be several IRRs that decision makers must be aware of to avoid making the wrong decision.

NPV is technically superior to IRR and easier to calculate. It is unlikely that the NPV and ARR will be confused. However, the ARR can be confused with IRR because both measures are expressed in percentage terms.

15 C £183,000

We need to calculate the terminal value of the project.

Year	Cash flow £	10% factor	Present value £
0	(154,000)	1.000	(154,000)
2	4,000	0.826	3,304
			(150,696)

This is the present value of the cash flows without any revenue from the contract. The minimum acceptable contract price is the terminal value (TV) at the end of year 2.

TV × 10% discount factor for year two = PV

TV   = £150,696 / 0.826

             = £182,441

If you selected £151,000 you calculated the correct present value of the cash flows but did not allow for the fact that the contract revenue was to be received at the end of year two.

16 B Project I because it has the higher net present value

The NPV method is superior to all the other criteria for investment appraisal.

17 A True and True

Consider the following three projects.

Time	A £		B £		C £	
0	(200)		(200)		(200)	
1	100		50		40	
2	100		50		40	
3	100		50		40	
4	100		50		40	
Ranking under:						
Payback	(2 years)	1	(4 years)	2	(–)	3
NPV at 10%	(£117)	1	(- £41)	2	(–£73)	3
IRR	(+35%)	1	(0%)	2	(-8%)	3

18 A £111,700

Present value of replacement cost in five years' time = £750,000 × 0.621

= £465,750

Annual investment required $= \dfrac{£465,750}{1 + \text{discount factor for four years at 10\%}}$

= £465,750/(1 + 3.170)

= £111,691

If you selected £197,800 you did not take account of the fact that the first amount will be invested immediately and thus should not be discounted.

19   D   £13,690

Present value of investment to be made in one year	$= £50,000/1.12$
	$= £44,643$

Present value of perpetuity stream beginning in one year $= \dfrac{a}{r}$

	$= £7,000/0.12$
	$= £58,333$
NPV of investment	$= £58,333 - £44,643$
	$= £13,690$

If you selected £7,440 you made the common mistake of failing to appreciate that the $\dfrac{£a}{r}$ formula finds the present value of a perpetuity stream one year before the first cash flow.

20   B   25%

Net initial investment	$= £(305,000 - 61,000)$
	$= £244,000$

The IRR is the interest rate at which the NPV of the investment is zero.

PV of perpetuity	$= £61,000/r$
The IRR is where £61,000/r	$= £244,000$
IRR	$= £61,000/£244,000 = 25\%$

If you selected 20% you divided £61,000 by £305,000. This fails to take account of the fact that the first inflow is simultaneous with the initial investment.

If you selected 400% you calculated the £244,000 net investment correctly but your final calculation was 'upside-down'.

If you selected 500% you combined both of the errors above.

21   A   10%

The IRR is the discount rate that results in a zero NPV in the following calculation.

Year	Cash flow £	Discount factor	Present value £
0	(400,000)	1.000	(400,000)
2-6	116,300	?	400,000
NPV			0

Discount factor for year 2 to 6	$= 400,000/116,300$
	$= 3.439$

Using the annuity table the nearest factor to 3.439 for years 2 to 6 is at 10%

(Year 6 – Year 1 = 4.355 – 0.909 = 3.446)

If you selected 14% you used the annuity table to find the nearest factor to 3.439 for years 1 to 5 instead of years 2 to 6. However, if the investment is made at the **beginning** of 20X0, any receipt at the **end** of 20X0 would be deemed to be received at the end of year 1. Therefore the first receipt at the end of 20X1 is deemed to be received at the end of year 2.

22 C **10% and 20%**

Since there are only three cash flows the options can be tested by trial and error.

At 10%, (1,150 × 0.909) – (660 × 0.826) – 500 = 0.19

This is close to zero and probably eliminates the option of 13% but as a quick check:

At 13%, (1,150 × 0.885) – (660 × 0.783) – 500 = 0.97

This is not as close to zero therefore the option of 13% can be eliminated.

Since the cash flows are non-conventional there could be as many IRRs as there are sign changes, ie, up to two IRRs. Therefore a discount rate of 20% should also be checked.

At 20%, (1,150 × 0.833) – (660 × 0.694) – 500 = -0.09.

This is close to zero therefore the project has a second IRR of 20%.

If you selected 13% you used the NPVs provided to calculate the IRR. This produces a less accurate IRR than the trial and error process because it assumes that the NPV rises in linear fashion between the two NPVs provided. It also fails to take account of the non-conventional cash flows and the existence of two IRRs.

23 D **Zero, one or two**

In general, it is possible for a project to have up to as many IRRs as there are sign changes in the cash flows. Since the project's cash flows have two sign changes there can be **up to** two IRRs.

The NPV profile could take various forms depending on the relative magnitudes of the cash flows, as shown below.

24 B **6 years**

This is calculated as follows:

Year	Cashflow £	Cumulative cashflow £
0	(400,000)	(400,000)
1	70,000	(330,000)
2	70,000	(260,000)
3	70,000	(190,000)
4	70,000	(120,000)
5	70,000	(50,000)
6	50,000	0

This means the payback period is exactly 6 years.

The discounted payback period is calculated as follows:

Year	Cashflow £	DCF	Discounted cashflow £	Cumulative discounted cashflow £
0	(300,000)	1.000	(300,000)	(300,000)
1 – 5	70,000	3.791	265,370	(34,630)
6	50,000	0.564	28,200	(6,430)
7	50,000	0.513	25,650	19,220

This means the discounted payback period is 6 + [£6,430/£25,650] years = 6.25 years

26 A,E A project's IRR is the return at which the net present value (NPV) of the cash flows is zero. The IRR is therefore independent of a company's cost of capital. The revision to the cost of capital by the project analyst will therefore not impact on the IRR, hence there is **no change**.

A project's DPP is the period of time taken for the project's cumulative discounted cash flows to turn from the initial negative outflow to a cumulative positive position. The revision to the cost of capital from 10% to 12% will reduce each future discounted cash inflow, and therefore **increase** the time taken for the cumulative discounted cash flows to become positive.

                                                                                     SAMPLE PAPER

27 D   A project's IRR is defined as the return at which the net present value (NPV) of the cash flows is zero. This means that for a project with a normal pattern of cash flows the internal rate of return is the interest rate that equates the present value of expected **future cash inflows** to the **initial cost** of the investment outlay.

A project's cost of capital is the benchmark return that is used to evaluate the residual income of a project.

Zero is the present value of expected future cash inflows and the initial cash outflow discounted at a project's IRR.

The terminal (compounded) value of future cash receipts for a project will bear no resemblance to the present value of expected future cash inflows.

28 A   As the net present value of the project's cash flows is positive at the opportunity cost of capital, this means that the project is viable and its IRR must be higher than the cost of capital.

If the internal rate of return of a project were sometimes lower than the opportunity cost of capital then the net present value in those instances would be negative.

If the internal rate of return were always lower than the opportunity cost of capital then the net present value would always be negative.

If the internal rate of return of a project were sometimes higher than the opportunity cost of capital then this would imply that sometimes it would be lower.   SAMPLE PAPER

29 B The best way to attempt this question is to draw graphs of the net present value of each project at various discount rates. The IRR of each project tells us at what point the x-axis is crossed and the number of changes in sign of the cash flows (from positive to negative or vice versa) tells us how many changes in direction each graph will have. The starting sign (positive or negative) for the graph can be easily established at a discount factor of 0% by adding the cash flows up.

The graphs of net present values for Projects X, Y and Z must look like this:

The answer is 8% because at a discount factor of 8% the NPV of project X is positive (accepted), project Y is also positive (accepted) and project Z is also positive (accepted).

Examining the other discount factors shows that:

At a discount factor of 12% the NPV of project X is negative (rejected), project Y is positive (accepted) as is project Z.

At a discount factor of 6% the NPV of project X is positive (accepted), project Y is negative (rejected) and project Z is positive (accepted).

At a discount factor of 4% the NPV of project X is positive (accepted), project Y is negative (rejected) and project Z is also negative (rejected).

SAMPLE PAPER

30 B   The ARR in this question is defined as average annual profits divided by the average investment.

In Year 1 profits are –£2,000 less depreciation of (£60,000/10), ie –£8,000

In Year 2 profits are £13,000 less depreciation of £6,000, ie £7,000

In Year 3 profits are £20,000 less depreciation of £6,000, ie £14,000

In Year 4 to 6 profits are £25,000 less depreciation of £6,000, ie £19,000

In Year 7 to 10 profits are £30,000 less depreciation of £6,000, ie £24,000

The average profits are therefore:

(–8,000 + 7,000 + 14,000 + (19,000 × 3) + (24,000 × 4))/10 = £166,000/10 = £16,600

The investment in Year 1 is £60,000 and the investment in Year 10 is £nil. The average investment is therefore (£60,000)/2 = £30,000

The ARR is therefore £16,600/£30,000 = 55%

The average cash flow (rather than profit) = $(16,600 + \frac{60,000}{10}) = £22,600$

£22,600 ÷ £30,000 = 75%

£16,600 ÷ £60,000 = 28% ie incorrect using the initial investment

£22,600 ÷ £60,000 = 38%, ie incorrect using the initial investment and average cash flow

31 C   The cash flows for the project are:

T_0 -£200,000

T_1 +£20,000

T_2 +£25,000 and each year thereafter

The T_0 outflow is not discounted.

The T_1 inflow is discounted for one year at 8%, giving a NPV of £20,000/(1.08) = £18,519

Thereafter we have a perpetuity at a discount rate of 10% starting after one year. The perpetuity factor is 1/0.1 = 10, and therefore the NPV is £25,000 × 10/1.08 = £231,481.

The NPV of the project is therefore (–£200,000 + £18,519 + £231,481) = £50,000

B Incorrectly discounting the perpetuity back from T_1 at 10% (rather than 8%) gives

£25,000 × 10/1.1 = £227,273 + £18,519 – £200,000 =

£45,792 ie £45,800

Discounting the perpetuity as $\frac{£25,000 \times 10}{1.1 \times 1.08} = £210,438$

+ £18,519 - £200,000 = £28,957 ie £29,000

32 D   As the ten annual inflows start immediately then in Year 0 the net outflow is actually – £150,000 + £30,000 = –£120,000

The NPV of this initial outflow is –£120,000.

The NPV of the nine remaining annual cash inflows (years 1 to 9) of £30,000 each can be found from the discount tables by taking the annuity factor for years 1 to 9 at 10%. This is 5.759. Therefore the NPV of these cash inflows is £30,000 × 5.759 = £172,770.

The NPV of the outlay at the end of ten years is –£50,000 × 0.386 = –£19,300.

The project NPV is therefore (–£120,000 + £172,770 – £19,300) = £33,470 or £33,500 to the nearest £100.

If you incorrectly calculated the NPV as £15,100 (to the nearest £100) then you treated the ten annual inflows as being received in Years 1 to 10 rather than Years 0 to 9. This meant you calculated the NPV as –£150,000 + £30,000 × 6.145 – £19,300 = £15,050.

If you incorrectly calculated the NPV as £31,600 (to the nearest £100) then you probably completed every calculation correctly except the discounting of the final £50,000. You probably used a discount factor of 0.424 rather than 0.386 meaning the NPV became £31,570 (£31,600 to the nearest £100).   SAMPLE PAPER

33   D   Imagine there are no cash flows beyond year 5 ie, outflow equals inflows exactly. The NPV at 20% would be negative so A is ruled out. The IRR would be 0% so C is out. If cash flows occur beyond year 5 there is no reason why the NPV could not be positive, so B is out.

34   D   Both are normal projects so statement 1 is false. As they are normal projects there will be no conflict between the NPV and IRR methods so 2 is also false. However, the methods may rank the projects in a different order so 3 is true.

35   C   Rate at which both NPVs are equal is between the IRRs and 15% (at which Y's NPV is greater). Only C shows this.

36   D   Both the IRR and payback period do not involve the cost of capital in their calculation.

37   C   The IRR does not use the cost of capital in its calculation. If the cost of capital increases the present value of inflows decreases and the DPP gets longer.

38   B   The project is normal ie, outflow and inflows which exceed the outflow, therefore it will have a single IRR (statement 1 is true) and if the IRR is less than the cost of capital the NPV will be negative (think about the normal NPV graph) so statement 2 is false.

39   A   The graph would be U-shaped with a negative NPV between 10% and 25% and positive NPVs at less than 10% or more than 25%.

40   A   As cash flows arise at the end of the year an increase in year 3's cash flow would not change the 3 year payback period. Higher cash flows require a greater discount rate to get a 0 NPV for the IRR.

41   B   NPV = (900,000 × 0.909) + 400,000 × 0.826 + 600,000 × 0.751 = (37,100)

          If you got (41,000) you started the flows at t_0 not t_1. If you got positive NPVs you had your cash flow signs reversed.

42   B   1 January 20X3 is the same point in time as 31 December 20X2

          75,000 × 1.08 = 81,000 at 31 December 20X1

          85,000 × 1.08 = 91,800 at 31 December 20X2 plus 4,000 on that day = 95,800

          £82,133 is the present value of the £95,800 terminal value.

1 Sunshine Ltd

Calculate the total value of the closing inventory for each product under marginal costing:

	£	Workings*
Standard	14,000	1,000 × (6 + 6 + 2)
Easy opener	5,000	1,000 × (2 + 2 + 1)
Dome	11,000	1,000 × (5 + 4 + 2)

1 mark each item, maximum 3 marks

* Number of closing inventory units × variable cost per unit

Calculate the fixed overhead absorption rate per labour hour for April:

	£ per labour hour
Fixed overhead absorption rate	10

3 marks

WORKINGS

Labour hours	= (6/10 × 10,000) + (2/10 × 6,000) + (4/10 × 4,000)
	= 8,800 hours
Fixed overhead absorption rate	= Fixed overheads / Labour hours
	= £88,000 / 8,800 hours
	= £10 per hour

Calculate the total value of the closing inventory for May for each product under absorption costing.

	£	Workings*
Standard	33,000	19,500 + (6/10 × 15) × 1,500
Easy opener	4,500	3,000 + (2/10 × 15) × 500
Dome	8,000	5,000 + (4/10 × 15) × 500

0.5 mark each item, maximum 1.5 marks

* The closing inventory value under marginal costing excludes the fixed overhead per unit. The fixed overhead per unit therefore needs to be added onto the value under marginal to work out the value under absorption costing.

Closing inventory under absorption costing = Closing inventory under marginal costing + (number of units of closing inventory × overhead absorption rate per hour × number of labour hours per unit)

Assuming the same actual production data and fixed production overheads in June as for April, complete the table below which calculates Sunshine's gross profit for June under marginal costing and absorption costing.

	Marginal costing £	Workings	Absorption costing £	Do not score items marked *	Workings
Sales revenue					
Standard	414,000	(1,500 + 10,000 = 11,500) × 36	414,000*	1 mark	
Easy opener	65,000	(500 + 6,000 = 6,500) × 10	65,000*	1 mark	

Dome	112,500	(500 + 4,000 = 4,500) × 25	112,500*	**1 mark**	
Total sales revenue	591,500		591,500		
Total marginal cost of sales	(233,500)	11,500 × 13 + 6,500 × 6 + 4,500 × 10		**2 marks**	
Total absorption cost of sales			(339,500)	**2 marks**	Should add 88,000 and 18,000 to calculated marginal costing cost of sales**
Fixed production overheads	**(88,000)**				
Gross profit	270,000	Calculated from above	252,000	**1.5 mark each, max 3 marks**	

** To work out the absorption cost of sales from the marginal cost of sales, we need to add the <u>fixed overheads for the period</u> and the fixed overheads in the <u>closing inventory units</u>. Fixed overheads for the period = £88,000. Fixed overheads in the closing inventory units = (1,500 × £15 × 6/10) + (500 × £15 × 2/10) + (500 × £15 × 4/10) = £18,000

Assuming the same actual production data and costs in July as for April, the gross profit in July was:

C   Exactly the same under absorption and marginal costing   **2.5 marks**

2   Kingsman Ltd

Calculate the profit or loss for October using both absorption costing and marginal costing:

Enter costs as negative values

	Absorption £	£	Marginal £	£	Marks	Workings
Sales		25,500		25,500	1, 0.5	150 × 170
Variable production costs	14,880		14,880		0.5, 0.5 allow –ves	155 × (78 + 12 + 6)
Fixed production costs absorbed	2,790		0		1.5 allow –ve, 0.5 for 0 or -	155 × 18
Opening inventory	2,280		1,920		0.5, 0.5 allow –ves	20 × (78 + 12 + 6 + 18) and 20 × (78 + 12 + 6)
Closing inventory	(2,850)		(2,400)		1, 1 allow +ves	25 × (78 + 12 + 6 + 18) and 25 × (78 + 12 + 6)
Production cost of sales		(17,100)		(14,400)	0.5 each	Opg + prodn – clsg
Under/over absorption		(810)		0	2 for –810 or 1 for 810, 1 for 0 or -	Absorbed overhead = 155 units × 18 = 2,790 Actual overhead = 1,200/6 × 18 = 3,600 2,790 – 3,600 = 810
Variable selling, administration and distribution		(375)		(375)	1 and 0.5 for –ves, 0.5 and 0.5 for +ves	2.50 × 150

Fixed selling, administration and distribution	(2,625)		(2,625)	1.5 and 0.5 for –ves 1 and 0.5 for +ves	36,000/12 × 0.875
Fixed production costs	0		(3,600)	0.5 for 0 or -, 1 for –ve or 0.5 for +ve	1,200/6 × 18
Profit/loss	4,590		4,500		

If there is no inventory of the B786 at the end of the first six months of production, will the profits calculated under marginal costing be higher than, lower than or the same as those calculated under absorption costing?

| Same | **1 mark for Same** | No opening or closing inventory so same |

Calculate the % mark-up for the B786 using marginal costing and the planned selling price.

| 47% (or 48%) | | Price is 420/0.75 = 560 |
| | **2.5 marks** | Margin is (560 – (420 – 40)) / (420 – 40) |

3 Numan Ltd

Calculate the budgeted prime cost per Gazza for March:

| £296 | 2.5 marks | Direct materials + direct labour = 48 × 5 + 16 × 3.5 |

Calculate the actual absorption cost per Gazza for March:

| £580 (or £581) | 2.5 marks | 4.5 × 52 + 16 × 3.5 + 6 × 3.5 + 4.5 × 52 × 1.15 |

Calculate the selling price per Gazza in April:

| £888 | 2.5 marks | 592/0.666667 |

Calculate the actual absorption cost per Gazza in May:

| £469 (or £470) | 2.5 marks | (4.5 × 52 + 16 × 3 + 6 × 3) + (4.5 × 52 + 16 × 3) × 0.6 |

Calculate the actual marginal cost per Gazza in June:

| £282 | 3 marks | 5 × 48 × 0.9 + 3 × 16 + 3 × 6 |

Using a corrected marginal cost of £302 and a target mark-up on absorption cost of 22%, calculate the selling price for July:

| £437 (or £436) | 2 marks | (302 + 56) × 1.22 |

Calculate the difference in the selling price of Gazzas that results from switching from a fixed overhead absorption rate based on Gazza's labour hours to a blanket fixed overhead absorption rate based on all of Numan's products:

| £12 (or £11) | 3 marks | *441.64 - 453.84 = 12.2 |

*Fixed overhead rate based on labour hours = 3 × £82,650 / 3 × 1,450 = £57 per unit
Fixed overhead per unit + variable cost per unit = £57 + £305 = £362. Price per unit = £362 × 1.22 = £441.64
Blanket overhead rate = £1,239,500 / 18,500 = £67 per unit
Overhead per unit + variable cost per unit = £67 + £305 = £372. Price per unit = £372 × 1.22 = £453.84

Calculate the total under or over absorption of fixed overheads for all of Numan's products using the blanket rate in August:

| £13,875 | | 2 marks, 1 for 13,875 and 1 for under | 1,239,500 – 18,500 × 66.25 = 13,875 |
| | Under absorption | | |

4 Oaklea plc

Difference | £ 600 | **2 marks** | (400 – 380) × 30*

*Difference between opening inventory and closing inventory × fixed overhead cost per unit

Operating statement for May

	Favourable £	Adverse £	£	Marks	Workings
Budgeted profit			116,000	2	400(600 – 310)
Sales volume variance	0 or –	7,680		1.5	(400 × 0.94 – 400)(600 – 280)
Sales price variance	7,520	0 or –		1.5	(620 – 600)400 × 0.94
Cost variances					
Materials price	0 or –	800		1.5	(16,800/1,600 – 10)1,600
Materials usage	0 or –	960		1.5	(1,600 – 400 × 0.94 × 4)10
Labour rate	0 or –	4,060		1.5	(69,020/4,060 – 16)4,060
Labour efficiency	7232	0 or –		1.5	(4,060 – 400 × 0.94 × 12)16
Variable overhead expenditure	0 or –	1,015		1.5	(17,255/4,060 – 4)4,060
Variable overhead efficiency	1,808	0 or –		1.5	(400 × 0.94 × 12 – 4,060)4
Fixed overhead expenditure	0 or –	1,050		2	13,050 – 400 × 30
Total variances	16,560	15,565	995		
Actual profit			116,995	2	400 × 0.94 × 620 – 16,800 – 69,020 – 17,255 – 13,050

Alternative workings for variance calculations

Sales volume variance

Budgeted sales volume	400 units
Actual sales volume (400 × 94%)	376 units
Sales volume variance in units	24 units (A)
× Standard contribution £(600 – 40 – 192 – 48)	× £320
Sales volume variance	7,680 (A)

Sales price variance

	£
Sales revenue from 376 units should have been (× £600)	225,600
but was (376 × £620)	233,120
Sales price variance	7,520 (F)

Materials price variance

	£
1,600 kg should have cost (× £10)	16,000
but did cost	16,800
Material price variance	800 (A)

Materials usage variance

Units produced = 400 units × 94% = 376

376 units should have used (× 4 kg)	1,504 kg
but did use	1,600 kg
Usage variance in kgs	96 kg (A)
× Standard price per kilogram	× £10
Usage variance in £	£960 (A)

Labour rate variance

	£
4,060 hours of work should have cost (× £16)	64,960
but did cost	69,020
Labour rate variance	4,060 (A)

Labour efficiency variance

376 units should have taken (× 12 hours)	4,512 hrs
but did take	4,060 hrs
Efficiency variance in hours	452 hrs (F)
× Standard rate per hour	× £16
Efficiency variance in £	£7,232 (F)

Variable overhead expenditure variance

	£
4,060 hours of variable overhead should cost (× £4.00)	16,240
but did cost	17,255
Variable overhead expenditure variance	1,015 (A)

Variable overhead efficiency variance

376 units should take (× 12 hrs)	4,512 hrs
but did take	4,060 hrs
Variable overhead efficiency variance in hours	452 hrs (F)
× Standard rate per hour	× £4.00
Variable overhead efficiency variance in £	£1,808 (F)

Fixed overhead expenditure variance

	£
Budgeted fixed overhead (400 units × 12 hrs × £2.50)	12,000
Actual fixed overhead	13,050
Fixed overhead expenditure variance	1,050 (A)

5 VanHensen plc

Allocate and apportion the budgeted overheads to the four departments:

	Assembly £	Finishing £	Stores £	Maintenance £	Marks	Workings
Rent and rates	16,000	32,000	24,000	8,000	0.5 each	2:4:3:1
Plant depreciation	25,000	60,000	7,500	7,500	0.5 each	25:60:7.5:7.5
Light and heat	10,000	20,000	15,000	5,000	0.5 each	2:4:3:1
Canteen costs	17,000	34,000	17,000	17,000	0.5 each	1:2:1:1
Finishing costs	0 or –	32,000	0 or –	0 or –	2	Direct allocation

Reapportion the service department overheads (Stores and Maintenance) to the production departments (Assembly and Finishing):

	Assembly £	Finishing £	Stores £	Maintenance £	Marks	Workings
Total overhead	70,000	185,000	65,000	38,000		
Stores reapportionment	32,500	13,000	–65,000	19,500	1.5 marks for –65000 0.5 marks each for other 3 positive figs (3 total)	5:2:3
Revised total overheads (enter figures in all 4 boxes)	102,500	198,000	0	57,500	Only score 1 for a zero in stores column	
Maintenance reapportionment	16,912 (or 16,911)	40,588 (or 40,589)	0	–57,500	1 mark for correct answer in each of A and F (max 2 in total)	25:60
Revised total overheads (enter figures in all 4 boxes)	119,412 (or 119,411)	238,588 (or 238,589)	0	0	Only score 0.5 + 0.5 for a zero in S and M columns	

Calculate the budgeted overhead absorption rate per labour hour in Finishing:

| £12 | 1 mark | 243,000/20,250 |

Calculate the under or over absorption of overheads in Assembly:

| £7,008 | | 1 mark for £7,008 | (15,876 – 15,000) × 8 |
| Over absorption | | 1 mark for over |

6   Basket Ltd

Calculate the budgeted prime cost per Large Hamper for January:

| £54 | 2 marks | Direct materials + direct labour = 6 × 5 + 3 × 8 |

Calculate the actual absorption cost per Medium Hamper in January:

| £144 | 3 marks | 6 × 4 + 8 × 3 + 2 × 3 + £90* |

*Hours worked relating to the Medium Hamper = 2,400 hours / 3 = 800 hours

Fixed overhead cost per hour = £24,000 / 800 hours = £30 per hour

Fixed overhead cost per Medium Hamper = £30 × 3 = £90

Calculate the selling price per Large Hamper in January:

| £231 | 2 marks | 165 × 1.4 |

Calculate the fixed overhead absorption rate per labour hour in February for Large Hampers:

| £54 (or £53) | 3 marks |

Fixed overhead cost relating to Large Hampers = (£85,000 - £24,000)/ 2 × 110% = £33,550

Fixed overhead cost per hour = £33,550 / (800 hours × 78%) = £53.76 per hour

Calculate the absorption cost per Large Hamper in March:

£106 (or £105)		3 marks	$5 \times 6 \times 1.15 + 3 \times 8 \times 0.78 + 2 \times 3 \times 0.78 + 48$

Calculate the selling price per Small Hamper for March:

£105		2 marks	84/0.8

Calculate the decrease in the selling price per Large Hamper that results from switching to a fixed overhead rate absorption rate based on the labour hours for Large Hamper's from a blanket fixed overhead absorption rate based on all three hamper sizes:

£4 (or £3)		3 marks	$(88,000 \times 0.3/1,000 + 100)/0.80 = 158$
			$(88,000/(3 \times 1,000) + 100)/0.80 = 161.67$
			Difference = 3.67

Calculate the total under or over absorption of fixed overheads for all three hamper sizes using Basket's wide blanket absorption rate in April:

£26,000		2 marks, 1 for 26,000	$88,000 - (3 \times 1,000) \times 38$
	Over absorption	and 1 for over	= 26,000

7 Geartop plc

Calculate the total value of the cost of sales for each product for July using marginal costing:

	£	Workings
AVX12	62,100	$3,000 \times 0.9 \times (15 + 6 + 2)$
PUH78	56,250	$2,500 \times 0.9 \times (14 + 8 + 3)$
YTF65	55,080	$1,800 \times 0.9 \times (21 + 9 + 4)$

1 mark each item, maximum 3 marks

Calculate the fixed overhead absorption rate as a percentage of the labour cost for July:

	% of labour cost	Workings
Fixed overhead absorption rate	148 (or 147)	$80,000/(3,000 \times 6 + 2,500 \times 8 + 1,800 \times 9)$

3 marks (give 1 mark for an answer of 1.48 or 1.47)

Calculate the total value of the closing inventory for each product line for August using marginal costing.

	£	Workings
AVX12	5,200	$7,000 - 200 \times (6/12) \times 18$
PUH78	4,200	$6,000 - 150 \times (8/12) \times 18$
YTF65	3,650	$5,000 - 100 \times (9/12) \times 18$

0.5 mark each item, maximum 1.5 marks

Assuming fixed production overheads of £81,300 were incurred during September and that there was a total of £4,950 of fixed production overheads included in the absorption costing value of opening inventory, complete the table below which calculates Geartop's profit for September under marginal costing and absorption costing.

	Marginal costing £	Workings	Absorption costing £	Workings	Do not score items marked *
Sales revenue					
AVX12	144,000	45 × 3,200	144,000*		1 mark
PUH78	159,000	60 × 2,650	159,000*		1 mark
YTF65	133,000	70 × 1,900	133,000*		1 mark
Total sales revenue	436,000*		436,000*		
Total marginal cost of sales	(226,750)	313,000 – 81,300 – 4,950 ie, remove fixed overheads from absorption cost of sales			
Total absorption cost of sales			(313,000)	3,200 × 35 + 2,650 × 40 + 1,900 × 50	3 marks for MC, 2 marks for AC, max 5 marks (allow –ve values for these figs)
Fixed production overheads	(81,300)		n/a		
Gross profit	127,950	Marginal higher by the 4,950 fixed overhead in opening inventory	123,000		1 mark each, max 2 marks

Assuming the same actual production data and costs in October as for September, the gross profit in October was:

C   Exactly the same under absorption and marginal costing

No opening or closing inventory in October
Correct answer scores 2.5 marks

8 Borehole Ltd

Calculate the total value of the cost of sales for each pump for May using marginal costing:

	£	Workings
High load	46,350	(250 – 25) × (150 + 36 + 20)
Standard load	66,230	(400 – 30) × (125 + 36 + 18)
Low load	71,540	(500 – 10) × (100 + 30 + 16)

1 mark each item, maximum 3 marks

Calculate the fixed overhead absorption rate as a percentage of the labour cost for May:

	% of labour cost	Workings
Fixed overhead absorption rate	57 (or 58)	22,000/(250 × 36 + 400 × 36 + 500 × 30)

3 marks (give 1 mark for an answer of 0.57 or 0.58)

Calculate the total value of the closing inventory for each pump type for June using marginal costing.

	£	Workings
High load	4,168	4,600 – 20 × (36/10) × 6
Standard load	5,352	6,000 – 30 × (36/10) × 6
Low load	710	800 – 5 × (30/10) × 6

0.5 mark each item, maximum 1.5 marks

Assuming there was a total of £1,170 of fixed production overheads included in the absorption costing value of opening inventory, complete the table below which calculates Borehole's profit for July under both marginal costing and absorption costing.

	Marginal costing £	Workings	Absorption costing £	Workings	Do not score items marked *
Sales revenue					
High load	86,400	270 × 320	86,400*		1 mark
Standard load	98,900	230 × 430	98,900*		1 mark
Low load	117,975	195 × 605	117,975*		1 mark
Total sales revenue	303,275*		303,275*		
Total marginal cost of sales	(224,230)	256,400 – 31,000 – 1,170 ie, remove fixed overheads from absorption cost of sales			
Total absorption cost of sales			(256,400)	320 × 230 + 430 × 200 + 605 × 160	3 marks for MC, 2 marks for AC, max 5 marks (allow –ve values for these figs)
Fixed production overheads	(31,000)		n/a		
Gross profit	48,045	Marginal higher by the 1,170 fixed overhead in opening inventory	46,875		1 mark each, max 2 marks

Borehole's profit in August was:

B   Higher under absorption costing

No opening but closing inventory in August
Correct answer scores 2.5 marks

9 Hector plc

Allocate and apportion the overheads to the four departments:

	Service 1 £	Service 2 £	Canteen £	Administration £	Marks	Workings
Rent and rates	150,000	200,000	75,000	75,000	0.5 each (2 marks total)	3,000:4,000: 1,500:1,500
Fixtures depreciation	240,000	160,000	100,000	200,000	0.5 each (2 marks total)	120:80:50: 100
Electricity, gas and water	52,500	70,000	26,250	26,250	0.5 each (2 marks total)	3,000:4,000: 1,500:1,500
Supervisors' salaries	300,000	225,000	37,500	187,500	0.5 each (2 marks total)	40:30:5:25
Canteen costs	0	0	50,000	0	2 (for 50,000) and all three others either 0 or -	Direct allocation net of takings (60,000 – 10,000)

Reapportion the Canteen and Administration overheads to Service 1 and Service 2:

	Service 1 £	Service 2 £	Canteen £	Administration £	Marks	Workings
Total overhead	740,000	650,000	280,000	500,000		
First reapportionment	266,667 (or 266,666)	200,000	33,333 (or 33,334)	–500,000	2.5 marks for –500,000 0.5 marks each for other 3 positive figs (4 marks total)	Start with largest costs using employees 40:30:5
Revised total overheads (enter figures in all 4 boxes)	1,006,667 (or 1,006,666)	850,000	313,333 (or 313,334)	0	Only score 1 for a zero in Admin column	
Second reapportionment	179,047 (or 179,048)	134,286 (or 134,285)	–313,333 (or 313,334)	0	0.5 marks for correct answer in each of Service 1 and Service 2 (max 1 in total)	Employees 40:30
Revised total overheads (enter figures in all 4 boxes)	1,185,714 (or 1,185,715 or 1,185,713)	984,286 (or 984,285)	0	0	Only score 0.5 + 0.5 for a zero in canteen and admin columns (max 1 in total)	

Calculate the budgeted overhead absorption rate as a percentage of labour cost in Service 2:

33% (or 34%) 1 mark 980/2,940 × 100

Calculate the under or over absorption of overheads in Service 1:

£82,560

Over absorption 1 mark for £82,560 (5,344 – 5,000) ×
1 mark for over 1,200,000/5,000

10 Oakbeam Ltd

Allocate and apportion the overheads to the four departments:

	Cabinets £	Worktops £	Warehousing £	Administration £	Marks	Workings
Rent and rates	8,800	7,200	40,000	4,000	0.5 each (2 marks in total)	£60,000 allocated 2,200:1,800: 10,000:1,000
Machinery depreciation	24,000	18,000	18,000	0	0.5 each (2 marks in total)	£60,000 allocated 400:300:300:0
Building utility costs	13,200	10,800	60,000	6,000	0.5 each (2 marks in total)	£90,000 allocated 2,200:1,800: 10,000:1,000
Managers' salaries	31,200	16,800	24,000	48,000	0.5 each (2 marks in total)	£120,000 allocated 65:35:50:100
Warehousing department costs	0	0	175,000	0	1	Direct allocation
Administration department costs	0	0	0	50,000	1	Direct allocation

Reapportion the Warehousing and Administration department overheads to the Cabinets and Worktops departments:

	Cabinets £	Worktops £	Warehousing £	Administration £	Marks	Workings
Total overhead	170,000	70,000	300,000	80,000		
Administration reapportionment	37,333 (or 37,334)	16,000	26,667 (or 26,666)	−80,000	1.5 marks for −80,000 (and 0.5 marks for 80,000) 0.5 marks each for other 3 positive figs (3 total)	£80,000 allocated 70:30:50 ignoring Admin itself
Revised total overheads (enter figures in all 4 boxes)	207,333 (or 207,334)	86,000	326,667 (or 326,666)	0	Only score 1 for a zero in Admin column	
Warehousing reapportionment	186,667 (or 186,666)	140,000 (or 140,001 or 139,999)	−326,667 (or 326,666)	0	1 mark for each correct answer (max 2 in total)	£326,667 allocated: 400:300
Revised total overheads (enter figures in all 4 boxes)	394,000 (or 393,999 or 394,001)	226,000 (or 226,001 or 225,999)	0	0	Only score 0.5 + 0.5 for a zero in Warehousing and Admin columns	

Calculate the budgeted overhead absorption rate as a percentage of labour cost in the Cabinets department:

| 533% | 1 mark | 400,000/(75,000) |
| | (0.5 mark for 5.33 or 534 or 5.34) | |

Calculate the under or over absorption of overheads in the Worktops department:

| −8,175 | 1 mark for −8,175 (allow 8,175) | (33,365 − 35,000) × 5 |
| Under absorption | 1 mark for under | |

11 Jitinder plc

Calculate the profit or loss for February using both absorption costing and marginal costing:

Enter costs as negative values.

	Absorption			Marginal	Marks	Workings
	£	£	£	£		
Sales		132,000		132,000	1, 0.5 (max 1.5)	440 × 300
Variable production costs	46,200		46,200		0.5, 0.5 allow −ves (max 1)	420 × (4 × 15 + 2.5 × 16 + 10)
Fixed production costs absorbed	16,800		0		1.5 allow −ve, 0.5 for 0 or dash (max 2)	420 × 192,000/4,800
Opening inventory	8,250		6,050		0.5, 0.5 allow −ves (max 1)	55 × (4 × 15 + 2.5 × 16 + 10 + 192,000/4,800) and 55 × (4 × 15 + 2.5 × 16 + 10)
Closing inventory	(5,250)		(3,850)		1, 1 allow +ves (max 2)	35 × (4 × 15 + 2.5 × 16 + 10 + 192,000/4,800) and (35 × 4 × 15 + 2.5 × 16 + 10)
Production cost of sales		(66,000)		(48,400)	0.5 each (max 1)	Opg + prodn − clsg
Under/over absorption		426		0	2 for 426, 1 for −426, 1 for 0 or dash (max 3)	16,374 − 420 × (192,000/4,800)
Variable selling, administration and distribution		(3,080)		(3,080)	1, 0.5 for −ves or 0.5, 0.5 for +ves (max 1.5)	7 × 440
Fixed selling, administration and distribution		(10,080)		(10,080)	1.5, 0.5 for −ves or 1, 0.5 for +ves (max 2)	27,000/3 × 1.12
Fixed production costs		0		(16,374)	0.5 for 0 or dash, 1 for −ve and 0.5 for +ve (max 1.5)	
Profit/loss		53,266		54,066	No marks for totals (Table max 16.5)	

ICAEW

If Jitinder were to switch to using Activity Based Costing (ABC), would the total cost per Salis be higher or lower than the cost calculated using traditional absorption costing?

Lower	1 mark for lower	Traditional underallocates overheads to low volume products ie Gromett

Calculate the difference in the price of a Salis from applying either a 25% mark-up or 25% margin.

£7	2.5 marks (0.5 mark for £6)	80 / 0.75 = 106.67 80 × 1.25 = 100

12 Flag Ltd

Calculate Flag's profit or loss for the quarter September to November under both marginal costing and absorption costing:

Enter costs as negative values.

	Absorption £	Absorption £	Marginal £	Marginal £	Marks	Workings
Sales		147,525		147,525	1, 0.5 (1.5 max)	4,215 × 35
Variable production costs	46,200		46,200		0.5, 0.5 allow –ves (1 max)	4,200 × (3.5 + 6.5 + 1)
Fixed production costs absorbed	16,800		0		1.5 allow –ve, 0.5 for 0 or dash (2 max)	4,200 × 4
Opening inventory	1,725		1,265		0.5, 0.5 allow –ves (1 max)	115 × (3.5 + 6.5 + 1 + 4) and 115 × (3.5 + 6.5 + 1)
Closing inventory	(1,500)		(1,100)		1, 1 allow +ves (2 max)	100 × (3.5 + 6.5 + 1 + 4) and 100 × (3.5 + 6.5 + 1)
Production cost of sales		(63,225)		(46,365)	0.5 each for –ve (1 max)	Opening + Production – Closing
Under/over absorption		(800)		0	2 for –740 or 1 for 740, 1 for 0 or dash (3 max)	(4,200 – 4,400) × 4
Variable sales, administration and distribution costs		(12,645)		(12,645)	1, 0.5 where –ves or 0.5, 0.5 where +ves (1.5 max)	4,215 × 3
Fixed sales, administration and distribution costs		(12,480)		(12,480)	1.5, 0.5 where –ves or 1, 0.5 where +ves (2 max)	12,000 × 1.04
Fixed production costs		0		(17,600)	0.5 for 0 or dash, 1 for –ve or 0.5 for +ve (1.5 max)	4,400 × 4
Profit/loss		58,375		58,435	(No marks for totals) Total 16.5 marks	

If there is a high inventory of the Substandard at the end of the first year it is manufactured, but no inventory at the end of the second year, will the profits calculated under absorption costing for the second year be higher or lower than those calculated under marginal costing?

Lower	1 mark for Lower	There is opening inventory but no closing inventory so profits must be reduced by overhead being released from inventory

Calculate the % margin for the Substandard using marginal costing and the planned selling price.

51%	2.5 marks (0.5 mark for 52%)	$(9 \times 1.6 - (9 - 2))/(9 \times 1.6)$

13   Hexabeast plc

Complete the table below to generate the operating statement for August:

Make **one** entry (adverse or favourable) for each variance **and** enter a zero or dash in the other column.

Enter the net total of adverse and favourable variances as either a positive number (favourable total) or negative number (adverse total) in the final column.

Operating statement for August

	Favourable £	Adverse £	£	Marks	Workings
Budgeted contribution			111,600	2	$1,200 \times (199.50 - 24 - 66 - 16.50)$
Sales volume variance	8,370	0		1.5	$(1,290 - 1,200) \times (199.50 - 24 - 66 - 16.50)$
Sales price variance	0	12,900		1.5 allow –ve	$10 \times 1,290$
Variable cost variances					
Materials price	0	1,161		2 allow –ve	$(29,025/((2 - 0.2) \times 1,290) - 12) \times (2 - 0.2) \times 1,290$
Materials usage	3,096	0		1.5	$0.2 \times 1,290 \times 12$
Labour rate	0	2,376		2 allow –ve	$22 \times 0.03 \times 3,600$
Labour efficiency	5,940	0		1.5	$(3,600 - 1,290 \times 3) \times 22$
Variable overhead rate	0	1,800		1.5 allow –ve	$(21,600/3,600 - 5.5) \times 3,600$
Variable overhead efficiency	1,485	0		1.5	$(3,600 - 1,290 \times 3) \times 5.5$
Total variable cost variances	18,891	18,237	654		
Fixed overhead budgeted			(100,000)	1.5	$300,000/3$
Fixed overhead expenditure variance			1,235	1.5	$98,765 - 100,000$
Actual profit			13,489	2	$1,290 \times 189.50 - 29,025 - 3,600 \times 22 \times 1.03 - 98,765 - 21,600$

Alternative workings for variance calculations

Sales volume variance

Budgeted sales volume	1,200 units
Actual sales volume	1,290 units
Sales volume variance in units	90 units (F)
× Standard contribution £(199.50 – 24 – 66 – 16.50)	× £93
Sales volume variance	8,370 (F)

Sales price variance

	£
Sales revenue from 1,290 units should have been (× £199.50)	257,355
but was (1,290 × £189.50)	244,455
Sales price variance	12,900 (A)

Materials price variance

Kg used = 1,290 units × (2 kgs – 0.2 kgs) = 2,322 kgs

	£
2,322 kgs should have cost (× £12)	27,864
but did cost	29,025
Material price variance	1,161 (A)

Materials usage variance

1,290 units should have used (× 2 kgs)	2,580 kgs
but did use (× 1.8 kgs)	2,322 kgs
Usage variance in kgs	258 kgs (F)
× Standard price per kilogram	× £12
Usage variance in £	£3,096 (F)

Labour rate variance

	£
3,600 hours of work should have cost (× £22)	79,200
but did cost (× £22 × 1.03)	81,576
Labour rate variance	2,376 (A)

Labour efficiency variance

1,290 units should have taken (× 3 hours)	3,870 hrs
but did take	3,600 hrs
Efficiency variance in hours	270 hrs (F)
× Standard rate per hour	× £22
Efficiency variance in £	£5,940 (F)

Variable overhead expenditure variance

	£
3,600 hours of variable overhead should cost (× £5.50)	19,800
but did cost	21,600
Variable overhead expenditure variance	1,800 (A)

Variable overhead efficiency variance

1,290 units should take (× 3 hrs)	3,870 hrs
but did take	3,600 hrs
Variable overhead efficiency variance in hours	270 hrs (F)
× Standard rate per hour	× £5.50
Variable overhead efficiency variance in £	£1,485 (F)

Fixed overhead expenditure variance

	£
Budgeted fixed overhead (£300,000 / 3)	100,000
Actual fixed overhead	98,765
Fixed overhead expenditure variance	1,235 (F)

14 Yarn & Co

Complete the operating statement table below for the month of November:

Make **one** entry (adverse or favourable) for each variance **and** enter a zero or dash in the other column.

Enter the net total of adverse and favourable variances as either a positive number (favourable total) or negative number (adverse total) in the final column.

	Favourable £	Adverse £	£	Marks	Workings
Budgeted contribution			30,000	1.5	1,200 × (105 – 40 – 24 – 16)
Sales volume variance	3,000	–		1.5	(1.1 × 1,200 – 1,200) × (105 – 40 – 24 – 16)
Sales price variance	–	6,600		1.5 allow –ve	–5 × 1,200 × 1.1
Variable cost variances					
Skilled labour rate	–	3,000		2 allow –ve	(2,200 adv – fav eff var below of 800) = –3,000
Skilled labour efficiency	800	–		2 allow –ve	(1,200 × 1.1 × 4 – 5,200) × 10
Materials price	–	3,280		2 allow –ve	(2,200 adv – fav usage var below of 1,080) = –3,280
Materials usage	1,080	–		2	(1,200 × 1.1 × 4 – 5,100) × 6
Variable overhead rate	–	2,600		2 allow –ve	(23,400/5,200 – 4) × 5,200
Variable overhead efficiency	320	–		1.5	(5,200 – 1,200 × 1.1 × 4) × 4
Total variances	5,200	15,480	–10,280		
Budgeted fixed overheads			–6,000	1 allow +ve	72,000/12
Fixed overhead expenditure variance			500	1 allow –ve	5,500 – 6,000
Actual profit			14,220	2	1,200 × 1.1 × (105 – 5) – (1,200 × 1.1 × 40 + 2,200) – (1,200 × 1.1 × 24 + 2,200) – 5,500 – 23,400

Alternative workings for variance calculations

Sales volume variance

Budgeted sales volume	1,200 units
Actual sales volume (1,200 × 1.1)	1,320 units
Sales volume variance in units	120 units (F)
× Standard contribution £(105 – 40 – 24 – 16)	× £25
Sales volume variance	3,000 (F)

Sales price variance

	£
Sales revenue from 1,320 units should have been (× £105)	138,600
but was (1,320 × £100)	132,000
Sales price variance	6,600 (A)

Labour variances

The information in the question allows us to calculate the labour efficiency variance:

Labour efficiency variance

1,320 units should have taken (× 4 hours)	5,280 hrs
but did take	5,200 hrs
Efficiency variance in hours	80 hrs (F)
× Standard rate per hour	× £10
Efficiency variance in £	£800 (F)

We are given the total variance in the question and now we know the efficiency variance. We can calculate the rate variance because efficiency + rate = total variance.

Total variance = £800 (F) + price = £2,200 (A)
Rate variance = £2,200 (A) + £800 = £3,000 (A)

Material variances

The information in the question allows us to calculate the materials usage variance:

Materials usage variance

1,320 units should have used (× 4 m)	5,280 m
but did use	5,100 m
Usage variance in m	180 m (F)
× Standard price per m	× £6
Usage variance in £	£1,080 (F)

We are given the total variance in the question and now we know the usage variance. We can calculate the price variance because usage + price = total variance.

Total variance = £1,080 (F) + price = £2,200 (A)
Price variance = £2,200 (A) + £1,080 = £3,280 (A)

Variable overhead expenditure variance

	£
5,200 hours of variable overhead should cost (× £4.00)	20,800
but did cost	23,400
Variable overhead expenditure variance	2,600 (A)

Variable overhead efficiency variance

1,320 units should take (× 4 hrs)	5,280 hrs
but did take	5,200 hrs
Variable overhead efficiency variance in hours	80 hrs (F)
× Standard rate per hour	× £4.00
Variable overhead efficiency variance in £	£320 (F)

Fixed overhead expenditure variance

	£
Budgeted fixed overhead (£72,000 / 12)	6,000
Actual fixed overhead	5,500
Fixed overhead expenditure variance	500 (F)

15   Johnson & Redmond plc

Calculate the budgeted prime cost per Large carton for 20X1:

| £20 | 2 marks | $2 \times 8 + 2 \times 2$ |

Calculate the actual absorption cost per unit of output for Medium cartons in 20X1:

| £37 | 3 marks | $8 \times 2 + 2 \times 1.5 + 4 \times 2 + ((336{,}000 - 216{,}000)/2/12{,}000) \times 2$ |

Calculate the selling price Large cartons in 20X1:

| £55 | 2 marks | 44×1.25 |

Calculate the fixed overhead absorption rate per labour hour for Large cartons in 20X2:

| £25 (or £26) | 3 marks | $1.05 \times (216{,}000)/(10{,}000 \times 0.9)$ |

Calculate the budgeted absorption cost per Medium carton for 20X3:

| £52 (or £53) | 3 marks | $2 \times 8 \times 0.9 + 1.5 \times 2 \times 0.95 + 4 \times 2 \times 0.9 + 28$ |

Using the 20X3 data for Small cartons and the target margin, calculate the selling price for 20X4:

| £47 (or £48) | 2 marks | $40/0.85$ |

Calculate the decrease in the selling price of a Medium carton that results from switching from a fixed overhead rate absorption rate based on the specific carton's labour hours to a single blanket fixed overhead absorption rate based on all three carton sizes:

£1 (or £2)	3 marks	$((350{,}000 \times 0.35)/5{,}000 + 50)/0.85 = 87.65$
		$(350{,}000/(3 \times 5{,}000) + 50)/0.85 = 86.27$
		Difference = 1.38

Calculate the total under or over absorption of fixed overheads for all three carton sizes using the company wide blanket absorption rate in 20X4:

£12,500	under	2 marks:	$350{,}000 - (3 \times 5{,}000) \times 22.5 = 12{,}500$
		1 for 12,500	
		1 for under	

Appendix:
Discount rate tables

DISCOUNT TABLES

Interest rate p.a. r	Number of years n	Present value of £1 receivable at the end of n years $\dfrac{1}{(1+r)^n}$	Present value of £1 receivable at the end of each of n years $\dfrac{1}{r}\left[1-\dfrac{1}{(1+r)^n}\right]$
1%	1	0.990	0.990
	2	0.980	1.970
	3	0.971	2.941
	4	0.961	3.902
	5	0.951	4.853
	6	0.942	5.795
	7	0.933	6.728
	8	0.923	7.652
	9	0.914	8.566
	10	0.905	9.471
5%	1	0.952	0.952
	2	0.907	1.859
	3	0.864	2.723
	4	0.823	3.546
	5	0.784	4.329
	6	0.746	5.076
	7	0.711	5.786
	8	0.677	6.463
	9	0.645	7.108
	10	0.614	7.722
10%	1	0.909	0.909
	2	0.826	1.736
	3	0.751	2.487
	4	0.683	3.170
	5	0.621	3.791
	6	0.564	4.355
	7	0.513	4.868
	8	0.467	5.335
	9	0.424	5.759
	10	0.386	6.145
15%	1	0.870	0.870
	2	0.756	1.626
	3	0.658	2.283
	4	0.572	2.855
	5	0.497	3.352
	6	0.432	3.784
	7	0.376	4.160
	8	0.327	4.487
	9	0.284	4.772
	10	0.247	5.019
20%	1	0.833	0.833
	2	0.694	1.528
	3	0.579	2.106
	4	0.482	2.589
	5	0.402	2.991
	6	0.335	3.326
	7	0.279	3.605
	8	0.233	3.837
	9	0.194	4.031
	10	0.162	4.192

Mock exam
guidance notes

Management Information: Mock exam guidance notes

MANAGEMENT INFORMATION

Suggested structure for mock exam in 2016

Exam standard

The mock exam should be set at the level of difficulty reflected in the three sample papers which are available on the ICAEW website.

Exam format

The mock should consist of one scenario-based question worth 20% of the marks and 32 objective test questions worth 80% of the marks with equal marks per objective test question.

Style of exam questions

The scenario-based question will be drawn from one of the two syllabus areas below, covering the subject topics as indicated:

- Syllabus area 1 (costing and pricing):

    - Allocation, apportionment and absorption of overheads; activity based costing, absorption v marginal profits/losses; mark-up and margin (learning outcomes 1b, c and e)

- Syllabus area 3 (performance management):

    - Calculation of variances; reconciling absorption and marginal costing profits/losses (learning outcomes 3e and f).

Each objective test question should conform to the style used in the sample paper ie

- Multiple Choice Question (MCQ) (1 from 4), or
- Multi-Part Multiple Choice Question (MPMCQ), or
- Multiple Response Question (MRQ) (more than 1 from 4 or more)

Exam coverage and balance

A mock exam should have roughly the syllabus coverage and balance set out in the table below.

The objective test questions should be chosen after the scenario-based question to ensure an appropriate balance of topics.

Syllabus area	Weighting (%)	Number of Questions
1 Costing and pricing	25	1 × scenario-based question and
5 Ethics		2 × objective test questions
		(At least 1 × OTQ should be written style and 1 × OTQ on ethics)
		OR
		10 × objective test questions
		(6 × calculation and 4 × written)
2 Budgeting and forecasting	25	10 × objective test questions
		(6 × calculation, 4 × written style)

Syllabus area	Weighting (%)	Number of Questions
3 Performance management	25	1 × scenario-based question and
		2 × objective test questions
		(At least 1 × OTQ should be written style and 1 × OTQ on ethics)
		OR
		10 × objective test questions (6 × calculation and 4 × written)
4 Management decision-making	25	10 × objective test questions
		(7 × calculation, 3 × written style)
Total	**100**	**33**

A good mock exam might contain the following balance of questions:

1 scenario-based question (calculating variances, syllabus area 3) and 32 objective test questions as follows:

Q number	Syllabus ref	Example
1	1a	Use of cost information
2	1b	Classify costs
3	1c	Calculate unit costs
4	1c	Calculate unit costs
5	1d	Select the method of costing
6	1d	Select the method of costing
7	1e	Calculate selling price
8	1e	Calculate selling price
9	1f	Calculate transfer price
10	5a	Ethics
11	2a	Apply forecasting techniques
12	2a	Apply forecasting techniques
13	2b	Prepare budgets
14	2b	Prepare budgets
15	2c	Budgeting approaches
16	2c	Budgeting approaches
17	2d	Preparing a cash budget
18	2e	Calculate the cash cycle
19	2f	Working capital
20	2g	Surpluses and deficits in cash budgets
21	3a	Features of effective performance measures
22	3b	Select appropriate performance measures
23	4a	Break even
24	4a	Break even

Q number	Syllabus ref	Example
25	4b	Key factor analysis
26	4b	Key factor analysis
27	4c	Calculate NPV, IRR, Payback, ARR
28	4c	Calculate NPV, IRR, Payback, ARR
29	4c	Calculate NPV, IRR, Payback, ARR
30	4c	Calculate NPV, IRR, Payback, ARR
31	4c	Calculate NPV, IRR, Payback, ARR
32	4d	Advantages and disadvantages of investment appraisal techniques

REVIEW FORM – MANAGEMENT INFORMATION: Question Bank

Your ratings, comments and suggestions would be appreciated on the following areas of this Question Bank

	Very useful	Useful	Not useful
Number of questions in each section	☐	☐	☐
Standard of answers	☐	☐	☐
Amount of guidance on exam technique	☐	☐	☐
Quality of marking guides	☐	☐	☐

	Excellent	Good	Adequate	Poor
Overall opinion of this Question Bank	☐	☐	☐	☐

Please return completed form to:

The Learning Team
Learning and Professional Department
ICAEW
Metropolitan House
321 Avebury Boulevard
Milton Keynes
MK9 2FZ
E learning@icaew.com

For space to add further comments please see overleaf.

REVIEW FORM (continued)

TELL US WHAT YOU THINK

Please note any further comments and suggestions/errors below.